A SURVEY OF 20TH-CENTURY REVIVAL MOVEMENTS IN NORTH AMERICA

Richard M. Riss

A *Survey of*

20TH-CENTURY REVIVAL MOVEMENTS IN NORTH AMERICA

HENDRICKSON
PUBLISHERS
PEABODY, MASSACHUSETTS 01961-3473

Dedicated to Ian S. Rennie

Scholar, Teacher, Mentor, Friend

Copyright © 1988.
Hendrickson Publishers, Inc.
P.O. Box 3473
Peabody, Massachusetts 01961-3473
All rights reserved.
Printed in the United States of America

ISBN 0-913573-72-8

Excerpts from Stanley M. Frodsham, *With Signs Following*, © 1946,
Gospel Publishing House. Used with permission.

TABLE OF CONTENTS

80557

INTRODUCTION

TWENTIETH-CENTURY REVIVALS

IN THE TWENTIETH CENTURY there have been at least three major re-awakenings of Christian faith in North America. The first of these took place during the first decade of this century. It was part of a worldwide awakening that originated with the well-known 1904 Welsh revival.[1] By 1905 this revival had already reached global proportions, and eventually, one of its effects was to spawn the Pentecostal move-ment.[2] Originating with the 1906 Azusa Street revival in Los Angeles, Pentecostalism eventually became one of the most potent and nu-merically significant Christian movements of the twentieth century.[3]

The second important awakening of this century occurred shortly after the close of the Second World War. Probably not as well-known or noteworthy from a statistical standpoint as the first awakening, the mid-twentieth-century revival nevertheless catapulted such evange-lists as Billy Graham and Oral Roberts into worldwide fame, as crowds clamored to learn more about God and about the life of faith. Al-though this awakening began among Pentecostals with the Healing and Latter Rain movements in 1947 and 1948, the following few years brought large numbers of non-Pentecostal Christians into the experi-ence of revival as well, bringing about many mass conversions and reawakenings of faith.[4]

The third major awakening took place in the late 1960s and early 1970s, when the Charismatic renewal made significant inroads into the mainline denominations,[5] untold numbers of young adults be-came involved in the "Jesus movement,"[6] and Evangelicalism began making appreciable strides within the mainstream of American life.[7]

The Uniqueness of the Twentieth Century

Because there are many senses in which the twentieth century was unique, it will be helpful in what follows to put the revivals of that period into historical perspective. From the fourth century onward, Western culture as a whole held to a Christian consensus that regarded natural disasters, such as earthquakes or floods, as judgments from God.[8] Such calamities were considered a call to all people everywhere to repent from evil and to turn to faith in God.[9] Then, for the first time, a predominant number of people began to see natural disasters as accidental or irrelevant to God's purposes.

This was only part of a much broader change in viewpoint that no longer saw Providence in all that happened, whether significant or insignificant.[10] God was no longer perceived as sovereign over history. For the first time it had become meaningless to talk of teleological explanations for natural phenomena; most people considered themselves too sophisticated to attempt to assign purpose to historical events. It came to be taken for granted that there was no guiding hand of history. With the exception of certain dissenting elements within society, previous generations had not usually thought in this way.

Closely related to this implicit rejection of all references to God's active role in guiding history was the assumption that miracles could not occur. This was also a recent innovation in the history of Western thought,[11] and its prevalence during most of the twentieth century should be taken into account in any consideration of revivals of this period. If a society assumes that miracles cannot take place and that the hand of God is not evident in the events of history, then those within it who experience revivals will probably be restricted either to those who dissent from the prevailing world view or to those who are willing to change their minds about such matters. When a society begins to hold to an antisupernaturalistic understanding of reality in general, then most of its people will not take seriously any reports of miraculous outpourings of the Holy Spirit or of any forms of divine intervention. Indeed, interpretations according to which God could intervene in history were repugnant to the world view that began to predominate in the early twentieth century, and vast numbers of people therefore did not have the slightest interest in becoming involved in revival. It is interesting to note, however, that of those who did become involved, a large number were subsequently converted to faith in Christ, despite either an initial lack of interest in revivals or hostility toward them. It is therefore not surprising that, although there were important revivals during the twentieth century, they were limited in scope and did not have the wider societal impact that characterized many of the earlier awakenings of history in which entire localities, and in some cases even entire nations, were completely transformed.[12]

The intelligentsia of the early twentieth century repudiated the idea of taking the Christian Scriptures at face value as a naive "return to precritical methodology." Therefore, those who accepted the accounts of miraculous phenomena in the Bible became displaced from the mainstream of society, losing positions of power in every arena, even within their own denominations and seminaries.

The stigma that came to be associated with simple faith in the Bible rendered upward mobility nearly impossible for people who held to it. Professional people who retained such a belief system became laughingstocks and could continue in their professions only under extreme duress. If those who believed the Bible, the "Fundamentalists," found themselves anathematized at the beginning of the twentieth century, how much more ostracized were those who believed that the miracles described in the Bible could conceivably take place even in their own generation. These "Holiness" and "Pentecostal" groups were indeed "disinherited"; but their beliefs did not arise because they lived in poverty and ignorance. Rather, these conditions were a direct result of a rejection by Western culture of what it had begun to consider at that time to be outmoded categories of thought.

Yet, miracles such as those found in the Scriptures had been taking place throughout all of history during times of revival. A full understanding of twentieth-century awakenings is not possible without some appreciation of the characteristics of earlier Christian revivals. It will therefore be helpful, first, to outline some of the characteristics of these revivals and, second, to provide a brief overview of some of the important awakenings of the past.

CHARACTERISTICS OF REVIVALS

Positive Distinctives

During times of revival, people usually develop a sudden intense enthusiasm for Christianity. People have often become so preoccupied with the things of God that they have had little desire to talk about anything else.[13] Word of a revival spreads very quickly, and people come from miles away, flocking to fill any and all available facilities far beyond capacity.[14] Because of an unusually vivid sense of love, joy, peace, and the presence of God, people don't want to leave, and they often remain for incredibly long periods of time, sometimes day and night. Many people describe the experience as heaven upon earth, and time seems to pass exceedingly quickly.[15]

Much of the preaching, teaching, counseling, and music during a revival seems to have an unusual ability to penetrate the hearts of the hearers.[16] There is usually a deep thirst for the word of God, and people hang upon every word that is preached.[17] The Bible takes on new and immediate relevance, and there are phenomenal increases in the sales of New Testaments and Bibles, hymnbooks, and Christian literature.[18] Evangelists usually receive far more calls to preach than they can ever answer, and they are often harried mercilessly.[19]

Within the context of an awakening, people are almost invariably orthodox theologically with respect to the great basics of the Christian faith. Great emphasis is placed on the Bible and its teachings. Stress is usually laid upon the suffering, cross, blood, death, and resurrection of Jesus Christ.[20]

Under these circumstances, the church receives an infusion of new life. Multitudes become new believers, while those who are already Christian enter more deeply into the fulness of faith.[21] Backsliders are reclaimed, and many skeptics and curiosity seekers become believers.[22] There are even conversions of ministers and members of the clergy, who may claim that they knew nothing of the power of God until they encountered him in the midst of these circumstances.[23]

In a revival, people receive an immediate revelation of God's glory and of their own sinfulness and inadequacy before him. Many become deeply distressed over their own wickedness, and an awesome fear of God and his judgment comes upon them. They recognize that they are worthy of nothing but death and divine retribution, and many of them cry out in anguish, begging God for forgiveness for their waywardness and seeking to know what they must do to be saved. As people recognize that there is forgiveness from God available through Christ's shed blood, they find redemption and are given a pronounced assurance of forgiveness and of salvation. Even the skeptical and stubborn will grieve over their sins until they find assurance.[24] Individuals are freed from bondage to sinful habits, bad attitudes, and emotional disturbances.[25] Old prejudices are radically changed, broken homes are mended, and there is widespread reconciliation. People usually receive a fresh sense of the unity of believers in all times and places.

Prior to the twentieth century, an awakening typically brought lasting results to every community touched by it, bringing about an end to cursing, blasphemy, drunkenness, and uncleanness. There was usually a cessation of fighting, clamor, and bitterness among the inhabitants, and in place of these things, joy and peace would often become predominant. In the twentieth century, it was only rarely that an entire locality would be affected by revival in this way;[26] however, entire churches and schools have experienced transformations of this type.

In all revivals, those involved feel refreshed; there is a new lilt in everyone's steps. This feeling of freedom in the Spirit ordinarily gives rise to heartfelt praise to God. There is enthusiastic singing, and in some cases there have been accounts of heavenly choirs accompanying such praise. Some people have heard harmony and melody of unparalleled beauty.[27] During revivals there are often manifestations of spiritual gifts. In some cases, children have brought exhortations with an eloquence and depth of knowledge and understanding far beyond their years. In almost all cases, people report that they have experienced a very clear sense of the presence of God. Divine visitations of this type tend to be contagious. If phenomena of this type break out in one place, they have a tendency to spread rapidly, just as sparks can quickly spread fire in many directions. Very often, when those who visit the scenes of such awakenings go home, their reports of what they have witnessed will spark similar events in their home environments.

Awakenings usually emerge against a backdrop of very serious spiritual and moral decline or during a time of intense spiritual dryness.[28] In response to these conditions, many usually come together for intense prayer. Very often people make serious agreements with one another to pray together regularly for a fresh outpouring of God's Spirit. This engenders an exhilarating sense of expectancy that God will move in a miraculous manner. Then suddenly the power of God falls, for there is usually a specific point in time at the outset of an awakening at which God's presence is immediately recognized by the people.[29]

Important awakenings seem to emerge simultaneously in many different locations.[30] Initially there is very little organization, and advertising is largely by word of mouth. Nevertheless, people will flock from large distances, causing enormous crowds. The location of a revival's outbreak may be of great surprise to those who have been praying for a sovereign move of God's Spirit.[31] Women and lay people have found a greater place for leadership during times of revival than at other periods in the history of the church.[32]

Usually such a powerful anointing of God's Spirit occurs that, despite themselves, many people fall uninjured to the ground, overcome by God's power.[33] Physical healings and other miracles sometimes take place.[34] In addition, many people conclude that these great demonstrations of God's power are an indication that Christ's second coming is imminent and that he is pouring out his Spirit one last time in preparation for his immediate return.

A spirit of sacrifice is often prevalent during an awakening. People spend whole nights in prayer, and there can be a tremendous zeal for the saving of the lost and, therefore, for missions. People gather together to share their experiences and to help one another along as they attempt to live lives of faith. Superficial profession of faith, baptism, and church membership pale in significance, and a great emphasis is placed upon spiritual life. Institutional forms seem inadequate to people in revival, and new denominations are often birthed.

Difficulties

Human frailty is an inevitable ingredient in any reawakening of this kind. Some will attempt to mold a revival to their own tastes or to take control of it. Because there are so many young, inexperienced converts involved, there will be many excesses. There will be temptations to spiritual pride, and many people will begin to mistake their own imaginations for impressions from God. There will thus be some who violate biblical truth. Various groups and individuals will become convinced that they alone are instrumental in the accomplishment of God's purposes.

Because of excesses and the violations of biblical truth, many critical reports, both true and false, will circulate. There will be reports that revival leaders are deceiving everyone, bribing people to make fabricated claims. Some of these criticisms will have a foundation in fact, and for that reason, many people will stand aloof, fearing to enter into something that may not be genuinely born of God's Spirit.

For these reasons, all genuine awakenings are accompanied with a great deal of controversy. Many innocent people experience intense opposition and persecution; every revival has been criticized extensively, bringing reproach on all aspects of it. For this reason, an awakening usually crests and then decreases. After a revival crests, stumbling blocks become commonplace. Some participants begin to feel animosity toward the leaders of the awakening, disapproving of many of the things that they formerly approved and grasping at reports of evil, both true and false, in order to justify their changes in attitude. Many previously convinced that there had been a visitation of God become afraid or ashamed to acknowledge their former conviction of faith.

Effects

Nevertheless, in the wake of a significant reawakening, a new flood of hymns and scriptures set to music gains widespread circulation and use. Because of the profound impression that a revival has upon many of those who experience it, its effects are long lasting. Great ministries are spawned that then thrive well past the time of the awakening.[35]

Prior to the twentieth century, revival usually had a tremendous impact upon society, bringing about the advancement of important humanitarian causes and resulting in significant social reforms.[36] Because of the more limited scope of the twentieth-century revivals, such effects were less pronounced. A much smaller proportion of the population was involved in such movements in the twentieth century due to the shifts in world view that had taken place in Western culture as a whole.

REVIVALS PRIOR TO THE TWENTIETH CENTURY

There is certainly nothing uniquely American about revivals. Nor are they solely a twentieth-century phenomenon. Most of the hallmarks of revival discussed above are evident, at least to some degree, in all of the great awakenings of the past, including the revivals under Josiah in 2 Kings 22 and 23, and under Ezra in Nehemiah 8.

Pre-Reformation Revivals

In the Christian era, the first major revivals began with the day of Pentecost as recorded in the second chapter of Acts. About twelve years later there was a subsequent revival beginning in Antioch in which Gentiles began coming to faith in Christ (Acts 11:19–26). The entire book of Acts contains accounts of revivals, particularly during Paul's three missionary journeys in AD 45–48 (Acts 13:1–14:28), AD 51–54 (Acts 15:36–18:22), and AD 54–58 (Acts 18:23–21:19). It is likely that after the Apostle John returned from Patmos to Ephesus in AD 96, there was revival in Asia Minor until his death two years later during the first year of the reign of Emperor Trajan.[37]

In the second century, according to Irenaeus, the city of Lyons, Gaul (present day France), was the scene of a local revival at some time subsequent to AD 178. In it many people were delivered of demons and came to Christ and many others were healed of sicknesses through the laying on of hands. Irenaeus also reported that prophetic gifts were in operation at this time and that people were raised from the dead.[38]

Revival phenomena were also prevalent in the monastic movement of the fourth and fifth centuries, as is evident in two important biographies of this period, The Life of Anthony by Athanasius and The Life of St. Martin by Sulpitius Severus. Monasticism was an attempt to avoid the compromises that the church had made during the fourth century when Christianity first became the preferred and finally the state religion of the Roman Empire and much of Roman pagan culture became incorporated into Christian faith and worship.

In the year AD 601, Gregory the Great, bishop of Rome, found it necessary to write to Augustine of Canterbury exhorting him not to be puffed up with pride that great miracles were taking place during the course of his missionary endeavors in Britain.[39] This is a good indication that revival had taken place during the course of his ministry.

One of the most remarkable awakenings of the past appears to have taken place in Europe between AD 1220 and AD 1231. Three of the figures associated with revival phenomena at this time were St. Dominic (AD 1170–1221), founder of the Dominican Order, St. Francis of Assisi (AD 1182–1226), founder of the Franciscan Order, and Anthony of Padua (AD 1195–1231), a member of the Franciscan order, who a year before his death devoted himself to preaching. Two of Anthony's favorite topics in preaching were repentance and contempt for the things of this world. According to historian Mary E. Rogers, his extraordinary gifts as a preacher included, in addition to a clear voice and a compelling manner, prophetic powers and miracles. At his Lenten series in Padua in 1231, there were 30,000 in attendance at one time, and there were massive reconciliations and restitutions to such an extent that the number of clergy was insufficient for the needs of the people.[40]

Between 1494 and 1498 there was a significant revival in Florence, Italy, under the ministry of Girolamo Savonarola (1452–1498). Due to this revival, in 1496 the Florentines made a great bonfire of cosmetics, false hair, pornographic books, and gambling equipment. Savonarola appears to have had prophetic gifts. He called for repentance on the part of the leaders of the city and pled the cause of the poor and oppressed.[41] He accurately predicted the demise of Lorenzo the Magnificent.[42] He warned of a great judgment to come on the city, after which a golden age would arrive for Florence. This prophecy was fulfilled when Charles VIII, king of France, invaded Italy and the Medici rulers of Florence fled.[43] On two occasions Savonarola persuaded the king not to sack the city, and Charles VIII finally left without doing any deliberate damage. After Savonarola denounced the corruption of Pope Alexander VI's court, he was excommunicated, tried for heresy, and executed.[44]

The Reformation

Perhaps one of the greatest awakenings of all time is known as the Protestant Reformation. During the Reformation (1517–ca. 1590), considerable emphasis was placed on the Bible, the principal doctrines of the Christian faith, and on the reformation of many of the corrupt practices of the medieval Roman Catholic Church. Luther's complete confidence in God's protection over him as he continued to advocate the principles of the Reformation encouraged many others to take a stand despite fears of reprisal from the Roman Catholic authorities.[45]

There was widespread revival throughout all of Europe during the time of the Protestant Reformation. While Martin Luther and Philip Melanchthon were among the important leaders of the Reformation in Germany, Ulrich Zwingli soon became prominent in the Swiss Reformation; Jacques Lefèvre became known as a leader in French circles; and William Tyndale among the British, although he had left Britain before pursuing his work on an English translation of the New Testament.

Some groups were persecuted not only by Roman Catholics, but also by other reformers. The Zwickau Prophets, for example, who re-

jected infant baptism, denied the need for a professional ministry
or organized religion, and maintained that all godly people were
under the direct guidance of the Holy Spirit, were expelled from Wit-
tenberg in 1522. Considered radical, the Zwickau Prophets believed
in the imminent return of Christ and in special revelation through
visions and dreams, which, when taken to extremes, gave them a bad
reputation among the reformers.

The Anabaptists also experienced persecution from other Protestants during the Reformation. In Zurich, Switzerland, during the time
of Zwingli, members of the new Anabaptist movement were persecuted
because of their belief that only those who were old enough to understand the meaning of faith and repentance should be baptized.

The Puritan Era

After the time of the Reformation, there were many significant local
revivals, particularly in Scotland and in Ireland. For example, under
the ministry of John Welch (whose father-in-law John Knox had been
an important figure in Scotland during the time of the Reformation),
there was a considerable depth of revival in Ayr, Scotland, between
1590 and 1606. One of the secrets of the power of Welch's ministry
was that, from its beginning until the time of his death, he considered his time poorly spent if he had not been in continual prayer
seven or eight hours every day.[46] In 1596, under the preaching of
Robert Bruce, there was a revival at a meeting of the Scottish General Assembly. Fewer than thirty years later in 1625 was the "Stewarton
Sickness" in the west of Scotland, a revival which lasted five years
under the ministry of David Dickson of Irvine.[47] Between 1625 and
1626, according to James S. Reid, there were awakenings at Six-
mile-water, Temple-Patrick, and elsewhere in Northern Ireland under
the ministries of John Welch's son Josiah Welch, Robert Blair, and several others.[48] A year later in Scotland, under Robert Bruce of Kin-
naird, there were revivals at Edinburgh and Inverness.[49]

Perhaps one of the most well-known early seventeenth-century revivals took place on June 21, 1630, under John Livingstone ("Livingstone of Shotts") at Kirk of Shotts in Scotland. John Gillies quoted
Robert Fleming's *Fulfilling of the Scriptures* concerning this event:

> there was so convincing an appearance of God, and downpouring of the
> Spirit, even in an extraordinary way, that did follow the ordinances, espe-
> cially that sermon on Monday, June 21, with a strange unusual motion on

the hearers. . . . Many of the most eminent Christians in that country could date either their conversion, or some remarkable confirmation in their case, from that day.[50]

Gillies also reported showers of revival in Scotland between 1650 and 1661[51] and in London in 1665 during the time of the plague.[52]

On the other side of the Atlantic, Solomon Stoddard, the grandfather of Jonathan Edwards, reported that there were revivals in Northampton, Massachusetts, in 1679, 1683, 1696, 1712, and 1718.[53] Particularly between 1704 and 1705, there were also reports of an awakening in Taunton, Massachusetts, under Danforth's ministry.[54] In New Jersey there were awakenings in the 1720s under Theodore Frelinghuysen's ministry[55] and from 1730 until 1733 under John William Tennent in Freehold.[56]

The Great Awakening

These revivals were all precursors to the Great Awakening in America that began in 1734 under the ministry of Jonathan Edwards in Northampton, Massachusetts, and brought into prominence the itinerant ministries of such men as George Whitefield and John Wesley. Wesley's ministry was centered primarily in Britain, where this great outpouring of God's Spirit was known as the Evangelical Awakening. While some historians consider the Great Awakening to have lasted forty or more years, its most powerful period was between 1739 and 1743.[57] One of the high points of the awakening was on February 18, 1742, when revival broke out in Cambuslang, Scotland, under the ministries of William McCulloch and George Whitefield. The Cambuslang reawakening seems to have touched off the fires of revival throughout all of Scotland.[58] The Great Awakening also affected Indians in North America in 1745–1746 under the ministry of David Brainerd, whose stirring biography was written by Jonathan Edwards.[59]

Another important awakening occurred in England from 1761 through 1763 and in New England between 1763 and 1764. While most historians consider these to be later phases of the continuing Great Awakening, it would probably be more accurate to recognize that while local revivals were taking place in many places, the larger awakenings of the eighteenth century occurred from 1739 to 1743 and again from 1761 to 1764 and were therefore approximately twenty years apart.[60]

Another awakening arose among Methodists in Virginia in 1775 and 1776. One eyewitness described it as the greatest revival of religion he had ever seen, and another called it "as great as perhaps ever was known, in country places, in so short a time."[61]

The Second Great Awakening

The Second Great Awakening, known in Britain as the Second Evangelical Awakening, was chronicled by J. Edwin Orr in his work, *The Eager Feet*. It began with the ministry of Charles Simeon at Holy Trinity Church in Cambridge, England, where he was ordained in 1783 and remained until his death in 1836. In the United States, the prelude to the second awakening was in 1787 at Hampden-Sydney College in Virginia under its president, John Blair Smith. According to Wesley M. Gewehr, this revival became the center of a "great interdenominational awakening which marked the final triumph of evangelical Christianity in Virginia."[62] There was also revival in Brunswick County, Virginia, that year among Methodists under Francis Asbury.[63]

In the mid-1790s the Great Yorkshire revival among Methodists in northern England helped to triple Methodist membership from 70,000 in Wesley's day (1791) to almost a quarter of a million people within a generation.[64] During the 1790s there were also many local revivals in New England. Edward D. Griffin, president of Williams College, wrote that from 1792 onward he

saw a continued succession of heavenly sprinklings at New Salem, Farmington, Middlebury, and New Hartford (all in Connecticut), until, in 1799, I could stand at my door in New Hartford, Litchfield county, and number fifty or sixty contiguous congregations laid down in one field of divine wonders, and as many more in different parts of New England.[65]

In the years 1798 and 1800, there were remarkable revivals in Moulin, Scotland, under the ministry of Alexander Stewart.[66] Other revival leaders in Scotland shortly after this time included Thomas Chalmers and Robert and James Haldane.

It was in the year 1800, however, that one of the greatest revivals of all time began on the American frontier. This move of God ushered in the awakening that, according to a later historian, Winthrop S. Hudson, swept "back and forth across the country for almost two generations after 1800."[67] A four-day sacramental meeting was held in June at Red River, Kentucky, where Presbyterian minister James McGready, assisted by two of his colleagues, William Hodges and John Bankin, addressed about 500 people. Also present were William and John McGee. During the first two days of these meetings, the congregation was moved to tears on several occasions. On the third day, a Sunday, William Hodges's sermon caused one woman to scream loudly, and before long, others were dropping to the floor, crying out, "what shall I do to be saved?" The official meeting came to a close and the three ministers left, but no one in the congregation moved. The McGee brothers had remained behind. Without warning, William McGee sank down to the floor, and John was trembling. He made one final appeal to the people to "let the Lord Omnipotent reign in their hearts and submit to Him."[68] A woman shouted for mercy and John went to her side. Several people said to him, "You know these people. Presbyterians are much for order. They will not bear this confusion. Go back and be quiet." As a Methodist who perhaps did not wish to bring offense, he retreated and almost fell under the power of God. However, he returned, and "losing sight of the fear of man," he went through the place "shouting and exhorting with all possible ecstasy and energy." The floor was shortly "covered by the slain." According to McGready, the most notorious infidels were pricked to the heart, crying out, "what shall we do to be saved?"[69]

News of these events spread like wildfire, and the following month, when McGready held another sacramental service at Gasper River, people came from distances as great as 50 and 100 miles. At the end of John McGee's exhortation that Sunday, "the power of God seemed to shake the whole assembly."[70] This was the first of many camp meetings, the most famous of which was at Cane Ridge in Bourbon County, Kentucky. The attendance at the Cane Ridge meetings was variously estimated to be between ten and twenty-five thousand.[71] This was at a time when Lexington, the largest settlement in Kentucky, had only 1,795 inhabitants.

Although the western frontier was known for many excesses during the second awakening, the East Coast became the scene of widespread revival during this time as well. Yale College experienced a revival during the presidency of Timothy Dwight, the grandson of Jonathan Edwards. After Dwight's 1796 baccalaureate sermon on "The Nature and Danger of Infidel Philosophy," there was a reawakening of faith among many of the students. By 1802 there had been widespread revival, and one-third of the students turned from the infidelity that formerly reigned throughout the entire student body due to influence of the French Enlightenment.

In the South the second awakening spread from Kentucky to Tennessee, North and South Carolina, western Virginia, and Georgia. At the University of Georgia in 1800–1801, for example, "they swooned away and lay for hours in the straw prepared for those 'smitten of the Lord', . . . or they shouted and talked in unknown tongues."[72]

The second awakening brought unprecedented growth to many of the denominations in the United States. Methodism received its initial impetus in the U.S. during this time, growing from only 15,000 members in 1784 to slightly less than one million in 1830. The Baptists doubled in number from 1802 until 1812, and the Presbyterians grew from 18,000 in 1807 to almost 250,000 in 1835. That this growth was not due to immigration is evident in view of the British interference with European migrations into North America during the Napoleonic wars until 1815.

Nineteenth-Century Revivals

During the first few decades of the nineteenth century, revival was continuing simultaneously in Scotland and in the United States. The island of Skye in the Hebrides of Scotland was the scene of powerful revivals in 1812 and in 1814,[73] while the island of Arran, also in Scotland, was shaken by revival from 1812 until 1813 under the powerful ministry of Neil McBride.[74] A few years later, from 1816 to 1817, Breadalbane, Scotland, had an awakening under the ministry of John McDonald of Urquhart. Then the well-publicized awakenings on the island of Lewis took place in 1824 and 1835.[75] Perhaps the most powerful revival of this period in Scotland, however, began on July 23, 1839, at Kilsyth, Scotland, where William Chalmers Burns touched off a reawakening by retelling the story of the Kirk of Shotts.[76]

Meanwhile, America was also experiencing many aftershocks of the second awakening, particularly in 1815–1818,[77] and in central and western New York State from 1820 until 1825.[78] There was revival in Connecticut and Massachusetts under Asahel Nettleton's ministry in 1821,[79] and in Oneida County, New York, from 1825 until 1827 under Charles G. Finney,[80] whose efforts were similarly blessed in Rochester, New York, from 1830 until 1831[81] and in New York City in 1832.[82] By that time, however, an outpouring of the Holy Spirit was once again being experienced throughout all of America.[83]

By the 1840s, there were reawakenings of world renown throughout Europe, particularly in Heemstede, Netherlands, under Nicholaas Beets in 1840 and in Mötlingen, Germany, under Johann Christoph Blumhardt in 1844.[84] Jacob Knapp also brought revival to the U.S. in cities like Baltimore, New Haven, Hartford, and Boston.[85]

There was an extremely powerful, worldwide outpouring of the Holy Spirit from 1857 until about 1860 that began with a prayer revival on Fulton Street in New York City. This awakening began inauspiciously with a prayer meeting attended by six people at the Dutch North Church at Fulton and William Streets on September 23, 1857. The meeting had been arranged by Jeremiah C. Lanphier, a merchant with no experience as an evangelist. The second meeting, which took place the following week, was attended by twenty people; the third meeting had double this number. Lanphier decided to hold the meetings daily in a larger room, and on the very week that they were to begin this schedule, the nation was hit with one of the worst financial panics in its history. As a result of this, people flocked to the Fulton Street meeting by the thousands.[86]

By November 5, 1857, news reached New York of a revival in Hamilton, Ontario, Canada, in which more than 300 people were converted within a few days. News of other local revivals throughout North America began to surface throughout November. By January of 1858, twenty prayer meetings patterned after the Fulton Street meetings sprang up in New York City, and newspapers began covering "The Progress of the Revival" on a daily basis.[87]

In August of 1858, two Presbyterian ministers from Ireland went to New York City to ask the people at the Fulton Street prayer meetings to intercede on behalf of their synod of five hundred churches and congregations. These prayers were answered, and within a year there was widespread revival in Ulster, Ireland.[88] Soon, the fires of revival began to spread worldwide.[89]

In April of 1860, at a conference of the Dutch Reformed Church in Worcester, South Africa, Dr. James Adamson gave an account of "the rise and progress of the revival which had recently visited America, and of the circumstances which fostered its growth and spread."[90] As a result, "the village of Worcester was powerfully affected by the rising tide of blessing, and, for a time at least, strange scenes were witnessed, which an outsider, unacquainted with the workings of the Spirit of God, would have called undiluted fanaticism."[91]

In nearby Montagu, similar events were taking place. One of the eyewitnesses reported:

> On Sunday evening (22nd July) a prayer-meeting was conducted by Revs. Shand and de Smidt, when the spiritual fervour was so great that people complained that the meeting ended an hour too soon. A year ago prayer-meetings were unknown: now they are held daily, and sometimes as frequently as three times a day, and even among children. Some have doubted whether this be the work of God's Spirit; but we have witnessed cases in which a man has come under strong conviction of sin, and on that account has suffered indescribable anguish, from which nothing was able

to deliver him but prayer and simple faith in the expiatory sufferings of our Lord Jesus Christ.[92]

As revival continued to circle the globe, its progress in the U.S. was hindered by the Civil War, although in 1865, America did experience another awakening.[93]

During the late nineteenth century, there were local revivals in South Wales in 1871,[94] and in Scotland and Ireland beginning November 23, 1873, under the ministry of Dwight L. Moody. These revivals continued until 1875, when Moody returned to America with the celebrated singer and song leader with whom he had collaborated, Ira D. Sankey. They brought awakenings to Brooklyn, Philadelphia, New York City, Chicago, and Boston.[95]

The late nineteenth century was a period of great evangelistic activity, resulting in many powerful outpourings of the Holy Spirit. Much of this activity was associated with the Holiness movement, the subject of the next chapter.

1

THE BACKGROUND OF
TWENTIETH-CENTURY REVIVALS

IT IS IMPOSSIBLE TO UNDERSTAND the revivals of the early twentieth century apart from their background in the Holiness movement, which provided the milieu both for the rise of Pentecostalism and for the other revival activity of that era.

It is true that many of the great revivalists of the late nineteenth century either were not a part of the Holiness movement or were only partially involved in it. Nevertheless, one of the great emphases of the Holiness movement was the need for revival, and because of this, by the outset of the twentieth century North America was ripe for an awakening.

The Holiness movement can be dated from about the mid-nineteenth century in America. Its central emphasis was on the Methodist teaching of "entire sanctification" or "Christian perfection," advocated by John Wesley. His *Plain Account of Christian Perfection* taught that an instantaneous experience subsequent to conversion enables a person to live a sanctified life, without conscious or deliberate sin. Many Holiness leaders, such as A. J. Gordon and A. B. Simpson, were also involved in the parallel Healing movement that developed in the latter half of the nineteenth century.

Crucial for the beginning of the Healing movement was Ethan O. Allen, who was healed of tuberculosis by the prayer of faith at a Methodist class leaders' meeting in 1846.[1] After receiving entire sanctification, he said, "Brethren, if you will pray for me, I believe that this mighty power that has come upon me will heal my lung."[2] Although the class leaders were reluctant to comply with this request since it was not part of their normal practice, they did so based on their knowledge of Mark 16:17, 18. To their amazement, Allen was healed "instantly and perfectly."[3]

After his healing, Allen took it upon himself to visit poorhouses, where he prayed for the sick and continued a ministry of healing throughout the eastern United States for fifty years. One of Allen's first assistants was Mrs. Elizabeth Mix, a black woman from Wolcott-ville, Connecticut, who had been healed of tuberculosis under his ministry.[4] She and her husband, Edward, travelled with Allen until they began their own independent faith healing ministry.[5]

THE HOLINESS MOVEMENT

Phoebe Palmer

Although Allen associated the doctrine of Christian perfection with that of divine healing as early as 1846,[6] the Holiness movement had earlier origins, including the work of Phoebe Palmer, the wife of a prominent physician in New York City. Her "Tuesday Meetings for the Promotion of Holiness" began as early as 1835 under the auspices of Sarah Worrall Lankford, Phoebe's sister. These meetings played an important part in promulgating the doctrine and experience of entire sanctification.[7] While the Wesleyan doctrine of Christian perfection was held by many people in the late 1830s, notably Charles G. Finney and Asa Mahan, it was Phoebe Palmer who began using the vocabulary that is usually associated with the beginnings of the Holiness-Pentecostal movement.

Palmer began to popularize the use of the phrase "baptism of the Holy Ghost," which she felt was synonymous with the experience of "entire sanctification,"[8] in 1857. At a Millbrook, Canada, Methodist camp meeting in June of that year, she asked the people in the audience whether everyone might not at that time receive a baptism of the Holy Ghost similar to that received by the believers at Pentecost. She stated that such a baptism was every believer's privilege and duty. She testified that the meeting ended with many receiving "the baptism of fire" and others "in expectation of receiving a Pentecostal Baptism."[9]

As a result of the revival of 1857–1858, Phoebe Palmer's teachings spread far and wide. Holiness doctrines were also disseminated far beyond the confines of Methodism with the publication of *The Higher*

Christian Life by W. E. Boardman,[10] a Presbyterian who at this time launched the "higher life" movement, the objective of which was to make the doctrine of Christian perfection interdenominational.[11] A similar development occurred among Baptists with the inauguration of a noteworthy "higher life" movement in 1858 by a group of Baptist ministers who had experienced the second work of grace.[12] In the following year, there was an all-day union meeting in Baltimore at which prominent pastors of nearly every denomination joined in urging a distinct experience of the baptism of the Holy Spirit subsequent to conversion.[13] Of course, it was not until the twentieth century that this Spirit baptism was considered to be related to speaking in tongues.

Charles Cullis

In some Holiness circles a strong emphasis came to be laid upon divine healing. To a large degree, this was due to the efforts of Charles Cullis, a Boston physician. On April 20, 1862, he was confronted by a stranger seeking a place of care for an indigent consumptive who had been refused admittance by Massachusetts General Hospital. It was common practice at that time for such institutions to turn away people who were deemed incurable. Unable to advise the stranger of any home for people with incurable diseases, Cullis began to think about the possibility of assisting such patients himself.[14] Four months later he received the experience of sanctification.[15] An Episcopalian, he had been exposed to this doctrine at Phoebe Palmer's Tuesday Meetings for the Promotion of Holiness in New York City.[16] Then, in January of 1864, Cullis shared his idea of a home for consumptives with Captain R. Kelso Carter, who encouraged him and gave him a donation toward the project.[17] Cullis purchased a home in May, and it was officially dedicated on September 27.[18] Influenced by reports of the ministry of Dorothea Trudel, who began taking sick people into her home in Switzerland in 1851 and who prayed successfully for their healing, Cullis began to pray for healing for his patients in 1870. The idea of rest homes for the sick and homeless became quite popular in Holiness circles, and there were over twenty-five "faith homes" in the U.S. by 1887.[19]

The National Camp Meeting Association

By the time Cullis opened his home for consumptives, spirituality was at a low ebb in America, primarily as a result of the Civil War.

The "Pastoral Address" of the Methodist bishops to the 1864 General Conference, for example, decried a loss of spirituality in the church and called for revival.[20] Then, in April of 1865, Methodist Episcopal papers were reporting spiritual awakenings throughout the church. In Indiana, there were 11,494 converts within a period of six weeks.[21] The revivals were localized, however, and seemed only to cause a greater thirst among people for an outpouring of the Holy Spirit. This was the primary impetus for a meeting held in Philadelphia on June 13, 1867, where a group of Methodist Episcopal ministers voted to hold a camp meeting at Vineland, New Jersey, on July 17–26.[22] Naming themselves "The National Camp Meeting Association for the Promotion of Christian Holiness," this group issued a call to people of all denominations to "make common supplication for the descent of the Spirit upon ourselves, the church, the nation, and the world."[23]

The opening of this camp meeting is often considered the beginning of the modern Holiness movement in the United States, since within forty years it resulted in the formation of over a hundred Holiness denominations throughout the world.[24] Ten years after the meeting, J. E. Searles wrote:

Space will only allow us to say, this First National Camp Meeting for the promotion of holiness was wonderful in its character and results; exceeding by far all the highest anticipations of its originators.

Never perhaps since the day of Pentecost was [sic] there more signal manifestations of the Spirit and power of God to purify human hearts and save sinners.[25]

Much more recently, historian Melvin E. Dieter wrote:

Crowded trains stopped at the Cape May Railroad station; long lines of buggies thronged the roads which led to the forty-acre park on the edge of town which served as the camp site. Overnight, the town's population swelled to almost double its 10,000 regular inhabitants as hundreds of tents sprang up around the speaker's stand on the camp ground. . . . The enthusiastic pastor of the Spring Garden Methodist Episcopal Church of Philadelphia [John S. Inskip] wrote to his sister that it "had only one disadvantage—it made every other service seem tame by comparison."[26]

From the time of this meeting until 1883, a total of fifty-two "national camps" were held.[27] The second was in the summer of 1868 near Manheim, Pennsylvania, where, after Dr. G. W. Woodruff began to pray aloud, the following events transpired:

All at once, as sudden as if a flash of lightning from the heavens had fallen upon the people, one simultaneous burst of agony and then of glory was heard in all parts of the congregation; and for nearly an hour, the scene beggared all description. . . . Those seated far back in the audience declared that the sensation was as if a strong wind had moved from the stand over the congregation. Several intelligent people, in different parts of the congregation, spoke of the same phenomenon. . . . Sinners stood awestricken, and others fled affrighted from the congregation.[28]

In the following year, Charles Cullis founded *Times of Refreshing*, a periodical which became an important organ of the Holiness movement and which regularly reported Holiness conferences.[29] Cullis also became a focal point of the Healing movement when, in January of 1870, Lucy Drake was dramatically healed under his ministry. Almost totally immobilized by a brain tumor and given little chance of surviving surgery, she was miraculously healed in answer to prayer.[30] William E. Boardman was so impressed by this that he persuaded Miss Drake to accompany his ministerial team during the following year in the West. Everywhere they went, she shared the dynamic testimony of her healing.[31]

Beginning at approximately the same time, John S. Inskip, president of the National Holiness Association, began conducting "holiness revivals" in the South.[32] National Camp Meetings were also being held in the North, at Hamilton, Massachusetts; Oakington, Maryland; Urbana, Ohio; and Des Plaines, Illinois, where "it seemed a heaven on earth."[33] Individual churches were also scenes of conventions, and at Inskip's church, there was a meeting in the fall of 1870 at which he stopped to pray for the baptism of the Holy Spirit to come upon the congregation and, "in an instant, very many in the audience began to weep." They all fell upon their knees, "some rejoicing, others in an agony of prayer for their friends."[34] In the following year, Inskip took a party to Sacramento, Santa Clara, and San Francisco, where a witness reported that he saw many prominent leaders of the California conference "stricken to the ground by the power of God," and lying for hours, "filled with the glory."[35]

THE HEALING MOVEMENT

John Inskip and Charles Cullis

Later the same year, Inskip became ill while ministering in Boston. Cullis had the opportunity to lay hands on him and pray, and he was healed. Inskip wrote of this:

> There seemed to come down upon all an awful sense of the presence and power of God . . . the sensation experienced was simply wonderful. . . . I have either been healed, or converted over again.[36]

Inskip's healing was astonishing to his associate and traveling companion, William McDonald, who reported that it was so complete that they travelled over 20,000 miles and conducted almost 600 services during the following year.[37]

Partly because of Inskip's status as president of the National Holiness Association, the healing ministry of Charles Cullis became widely known after this. He began holding yearly faith conventions in 1874, first in Framingham, Massachusetts, and later at Old Orchard Beach in Maine.[38] One of the countless people healed under his ministry was Smith H. Platt, an itinerating Methodist minister who in 1875 was instantly healed of knee and leg problems after Cullis prayed over him. Platt felt a sensation like electricity run through his body. From that time onward, he had no further need for his cane and became a devoted supporter of Cullis's work.[39]

Cullis was able to persuade Hannah Whitall Smith and Robert Pearsall Smith to conduct his 1876 faith convention.[40] The Smiths had been active leaders in the "higher life" movement in Britain which led to the founding of the Keswick Convention a year or two previously. Cullis published Hannah Whitall Smith's best-selling book, *The Christian's Secret of a Happy Life,* in 1875.[41]

A. J. Gordon

While Cullis was known as a pioneer in the ministry of divine healing, many followed in his footsteps. A. J. Gordon, for example, began including healing in his ministry after he observed an opium addict delivered and a missionary's cancerous jaw healed instantaneously through the prayers of concerned believers during Dwight L. Moody's revival meetings in Boston in 1877.[42] These meetings revitalized the life of Clarendon Street Church, which Gordon pastored, and brought reformed drunkards and all kinds of commoners into the ranks of this affluent church.[43]

Carrie Judd Montgomery

The power of God to heal physical illnesses was also taught by Carrie Judd, who later married George Montgomery. She had been an invalid since 1876, when she had suffered a severe fall on an icy sidewalk in Buffalo. On February 26, 1879, she was instantaneously healed as a result of a letter she received from Mrs. Edward Mix. This healing became a sensation in all of Buffalo and was reported in the local daily newspapers. From there, the story was circulated worldwide, and Miss Judd was flooded with requests for prayer for healing. This launched her into a healing ministry.[44]

A. B. Simpson

Another important evangelist of the Holiness movement who taught healing was A. B. Simpson. While still pastor of the fashionable 13th Street Presbyterian Church in New York City, he became convinced of the validity of divine healing as a result of Cullis's ministry. In 1881 Simpson attended a meeting held by Cullis at the Old Orchard convention center, where there were many miraculous healings.[45] Among the people Simpson met there was the veteran healing evangelist Ethan O. Allen,[46] who later became active in Simpson's ministry. Simpson left the Presbyterian denomination to form an independent work which later developed into the Christian and Missionary Alliance. R. Kelso Carter, who had been healed under Cullis's ministry in 1879, also became active in Simpson's ministry in 1881 and joined him in writing and publishing a hymnal which included the well-known song, "Standing on the Promises."[47]

Maria B. Woodworth-Etter and John Alexander Dowie

One of the most outstanding evangelists of this era was Maria B. Woodworth, who later married Samuel P. Etter. Her ministry began in 1879, when she was thirty-five years old.[48] However, it was not until 1885 that she began to preach divine healing.[49] Historian Wayne E. Warner has written concerning the revivals that took place under her ministry at this time that "the amazing Woodworth revivals between 1885–1889 would easily fill a book."[50]

Another healing minister of this era, John Alexander Dowie arrived in America in 1888.[51] He had come from Australia, although he was originally from Edinburgh. Dowie led the founding of the American Divine Healing Association in 1890.[52] He supported Woodworth's ministry until 1890, at which time he began to worry about the "trances" that he thought people experienced when they were slain in the Spirit at her meetings. Yet, those who fell under the power of God at Mrs. Woodworth's meetings usually, if not always, came to Christ as a result of the experience. She described one of her meetings at Oakland, California, in fall, 1889, as follows:

> The power of God was over all the congregation; and around in the city of Oakland. The Holy Ghost would fall on the people while we were preach-

ing. The multitude would be held still, like as though death was in their midst. Many of the most intelligent and best dressed men would fall back in their seats, with their hands held up to God, being held under the mighty power of God. Men and women fell, all over the tent, like trees in a storm; some would have visions of God. Most all of them came out shouting the praises of God.[53]

In one case, a man sixty-three years of age visited one of these meetings with some of his friends. Mrs. Woodworth wrote of this:

As he looked over the congregation he made some light remark to his friends about the display of the power of God, and started boldly up towards the pulpit to investigate, but before he reached the pulpit he was struck to the floor by the power of God and lay there over two hours. While [he was] in this condition God gave him a vision of hell and heaven, and told him to make his choice of the two places. He called upon the Lord to save him and said he would choose Christ and heaven.[54]

Dowie attributed such phenomena to the devil and warned people against Mrs. Woodworth's teachings.[55] It is possible that he had been upset because people had left his meetings in California in order to attend Woodworth's Oakland meetings. She told the people that she would "leave him in the hands of God," and that they would see him "go down in disgrace," and that she "would be living when he was dead."[56] Unfortunately, Dowie was left half paralyzed by a stroke in 1905 and did die in 1907, seventeen years before Woodworth-Etter's death.

On January 27, 1890, Maria B. Woodworth predicted that an earthquake and a tidal wave would strike the San Francisco-Oakland area and destroy three cities in four minutes.[57] She was quoted by the Oakland *Evening Tribune* as having set a date for this event, April 14, 1890.[58] In February, however, she told a *Tribune* reporter that she had been misquoted and said, "I cannot tell when the destruction will come, and have never set a day or a limit of time for it."[59] However, because no earthquake occurred at the time specified by the *Evening Tribune*, people began to fear that Woodworth was a false prophet, and her ministry was eclipsed to some degree for a number of years. Nevertheless, there was a major earthquake in San Francisco on April 18, 1906, killing thousands of people. During a campaign in Oakland in 1916, she reminisced about her ministry there twenty-six years previously:

I remembered how the Lord had shown me at that time the great earthquake that was coming on San Francisco, Oakland and adjoining towns, and that I would live to work over the ruins. Now, after all these years, I saw that prophecy fulfilled.[60]

In 1893 John Alexander Dowie began his work in Chicago, where he set up a wooden hut at the World's Fair and rang a dinner bell to get the people to the meetings. Among those healed at this time was Ethel Post, a girl of thirteen whose mouth had been so full of a bloody, spongy cancer that she could not close it. Dr. Lilian Yeomans wrote:

> The malignant growth withered away and fell out of the girl's mouth and throat, and she was completely and permanently healed. When I alluded to her case in a meeting quite recently, a lady stood and said Miss Post is alive and well and actively engaged in some branch of commercial art. She used to sell her photographs, "Before and After the Lord's Healing Touch," for the benefit of the Lord's work.[61]

Of course, many healings were taking place under the ministry of Maria B. Woodworth at this time as well. On April 16, 1893, for example, she began a series of meetings in St. Louis, where a girl of fourteen was healed of a spinal disease she had contracted two years previously, and a man was healed instantly of catarrh of the stomach, which he had suffered for five years.[62]

PRECURSORS TO PENTECOSTALISM

Churches of God

Between 1893 and 1900, twenty-three new denominations arose out of the Holiness movement in America.[63] Many had headquarters in the southeastern U.S. and used variations of the name "Church of God." Historian Vinson Synan has observed that Churches of God forming before 1894 generally continued to belong to the Holiness persuasion and never identified themselves with the Pentecostal movement after 1906, while those beginning after 1894 generally became Pentecostal later.[64] Perhaps this was partly due to the fact that the General Conference of the Methodist Episcopal Church, South, disavowed the Holiness movement in 1894.[65] As a result, a "war of extermination" began which helped to bring about the establishment of scores of new Holiness churches and denominations throughout the U.S.[66] Thus, in 1895, for example, Phineas Bresee and Dr. J. P. Widney in Los Angeles organized the first congregation of the "Church of the Nazarene," which was destined to become the nation's largest Holiness church after merging with other groups in 1914.[67] That same year Charles H. Mason and C. P. Jones came into contact with the Holiness doctrine of entire sanctification. When they began to preach it, they were ejected from the Baptist Association and later founded the Church of God in Christ, which became the largest black Pentecostal denomination.[68]

The Church of God of Cleveland, Tennessee, originated during a revival in 1896, when more than 100 people spoke in tongues at the Schearer Schoolhouse in Cherokee, North Carolina, not far away. This group was known at one point as the Holiness Church at Camp Creek, North Carolina, but changed its name to the Church of God in 1906. A. J. Tomlinson became a member in 1903 and acted as its general overseer for 20 years.[69]

Charles Fox Parham

In 1898, Charles Parham founded Bethel Healing Home in Topeka, Kansas, one of the many "faith homes" of the Holiness movement that came into operation during the late nineteenth century. Then, in early 1900, Parham established contacts with several evangelists who conducted services for him at Bethel. As a result, Parham decided to visit various places of ministry during that year, including Dowie's Zion, Malone's work in Cleveland, A. B. Simpson's in Nyack, the "Eye-Opener" in Chicago, and Sandford's "Holy Ghost and Us" in Shiloah, Maine, as well as many others. He then opened a Bible School, Bethel College, at Topeka, on October 15, in a mansion known as Stone's Folly.

In late December, Parham had to go to Kansas City, but he instructed each of the students to study the Bible individually to see if there were some special witness to the fact that a person had been baptized in the Holy Spirit. When he returned, he asked them the results of their study, and the students answered that the gift of tongues was the indication of baptism of the Holy Spirit in the book of Acts. Then, on January 1, 1901, one student, Agnes N. Ozman, received the gift of the Holy Ghost and spoke in tongues. She wrote:

> Like some others, I thought that I had received the baptism of the Holy Ghost at the time of consecration, but when I learned that the Holy Ghost was yet to be poured out in greater fulness, my heart became hungry for the promised Comforter. . . .
>
> On watch night we had a blessed service, praying that God's blessing might rest upon us as the New Year came in. During the first day of 1901 the presence of the Lord was with us in a marked way stilling our hearts to wait upon Him for greater things. The spirit of prayer was upon us in the evening. It was nearly seven o'clock on this first of January that it came into my heart to ask Bro. Parham to lay his hands upon me that I might

receive the gift of the Holy Spirit. It was as his hands were laid upon my head that the Holy Spirit fell upon me and I began to speak in tongues, glorifying God.[70]

On the following day, a Bohemian understood in his language what Agnes Ozman said when she spoke in tongues.[71] Then, on January 3, after three days of prayer, several other students began speaking in tongues. Miss Lillian Thistlethwaite wrote of this:

> An upper room was set apart for tarrying before the Lord. And here we spent every spare moment in audible or silent prayer, in song or in just waiting upon Him. . . . His presence was very real and the heart-searchings definite. . . .

> Then a great joy came into my soul and I began to say, "I praise Thee," and my tongue began to get thick and great floods of laughter came into my heart. . . . My mouth was filled with a rush of words I didn't understand. . . . Then I realized I was not alone for all around me I heard great rejoicing while others spoke in tongues and magnified God. . . . Then as with a simultaneous move we began to sing together each one singing in his own new language in perfect harmony.[72]

Many refer to these events as the beginning of the Pentecostal movement in America, since the gift of tongues was first taught as the evidence for the baptism of the Holy Spirit at this time, and since Parham's student, William J. Seymour, later took this teaching from Houston to Los Angeles, where the Azusa Street revival began under his ministry. In any case, Pentecostalism grew out of the milieu of the Holiness movement, with its emphases upon living the higher Christian life, a second work of grace, healing, and the need for revival in the church.

OTHER NINETEENTH-CENTURY REVIVALS

Important Evangelists

Of course, the Holiness movement was certainly not the sole province of revivals during the latter part of the nineteenth century. In fact, many of the greatest revivalists of that time were not part of the Holiness movement, including such giants as Henry Ward Beecher, pastor of the Plymouth Church of Brooklyn (Congregational) from 1847 to 1887; Phillips Brooks, rector of Trinity Church in Boston from 1869 until 1881; T. DeWitt Talmage of Brooklyn; Russell Conwell of Philadelphia; Dwight L. Moody of Boston and Chicago; the Presbyterian evangelist J. Wilbur Chapman; Henry Ostrom; Samuel Porter

Jones of Georgia; Benjamin Fay Mills; Rodney "Gipsy" Smith of England; Billy Sunday of Chicago; Reuben A. Torrey, who was the first superintendent of Moody Bible Institute; Milan B. Williams; Burke Culpepper; William E. Biederwolf; Warren A. Candler; F. B. Smith; and French Oliver.[73] The two most widely known were Dwight L. Moody and Billy Sunday. Sunday's ministry became more prominent in the early twentieth century, but the zenith of Moody's ministry in the U.S. was from 1875 until his death in 1899. He became widely recognized in America as a result of a two-year evangelistic tour in Britain, which brought him a worldwide reputation.

Dwight L. Moody

Moody and his song leader, Ira D. Sankey, arrived at Liverpool on June 17, 1873, only to learn that the three people who had pledged to support them had all died. Moody said, "God seems to have closed the doors. We will not open any ourselves. If He opens the door we will go in; otherwise we will return to America."[74] However, Moody found an unopened letter from the YMCA in York, England, inviting him to speak there, and opportunities continued in England and Scotland for two years. His ministry in Edinburgh that fall was described as follows:

> He has graciously answered . . . prayer, and His own presence is now wonderfully manifested among them. God is so affecting the hearts of men that the Free Church Assembly Hall, the largest public building in Edinburgh, is crowded every evening with meetings for prayer, and both that building and the Established Church Assembly Hall overflow whenever the gospel is preached. But the numbers that attend are not the most remarkable feature. It is the presence and power of the Holy Ghost, the solemn awe, the prayerful, believing, expectant spirit, the anxious inquiry of unsaved souls, and the longing of believers to grow more like Christ—their hungering and thirsting after holiness.[75]

This aptly describes Moody's ministry from that time onward, and before he returned to the U.S., the total attendance at his meetings in London during a four-month period was more than two and one-half million.[76]

When Moody and Sankey returned to the U.S., their ministry sparked national revival. Lyman H. Atwater wrote of this in 1876 in the *Presbyterian Quarterly and Princeton Review*:

> Of the great revivals of 1875–6 which formed the glorious close of the last, and beginning of the new century, the chiefest glory indeed of our

Centennial year, it is less necessary to speak, as they are familiar to all. Although the most conspicuous agents in them have been the lay evangelists, Moody and Sankey, through their labors in the two largest cities of the country, yet the great work through the land has, from the sheer impossibility of their presence in two places at the same moment, been carried forward chiefly under the lead of the pastors, seconded by the officers and membership of the churches. This is as it ever should, and, indeed, must, be in all healthy church progress—all increase with the increase of God. The work of these evangelists in New York and Philadelphia did not interfere with, it only assisted, genuine work of this sort in particular congregations, while it more largely than ordinary agencies reached the unevangelized.[77]

Moody's ministry continued to precipitate revival phenomena throughout the remainder of the nineteenth century. His death in 1899 brought about the end of an important era of revivals in North America. Billy Sunday, the professional baseball player who became one of the world's greatest evangelists, took up Moody's work and played an important part in the great revival of 1905 in North America.

2

THE WORLDWIDE AWAKENING
OF 1904–1906

T HE 1905–1906 AWAKENING IN North America was part of a worldwide outpouring of the Holy Spirit beginning in Wales the previous year. Apart from the fact that it helped to set the stage for
the Pentecostal revival that broke forth in 1906 from Azusa Street
in Los Angeles, its importance outside of Wales was minor compared
to such revivals as the Great Awakening of the eighteenth century.
It has therefore been ignored by many historians, but it deserves treat-
ment in any history of recent revivals.

THE WELSH REVIVAL

The Welsh revival of 1904–1905 was a very powerful visitation of God's
Spirit that arose simultaneously in many parts of Wales. One of its
earliest manifestations was at the chapel of Joseph Jenkins at New
Quay, Cardiganshire. One Sunday morning in February or March of
1904, at a prayer meeting for young people, Jenkins asked for testimonies of spiritual experience. Several people attempted to speak
on other topics, but he tried to redirect them to the subject. Finally,
a young girl, Florrie Evans, a recent convert, rose and spoke with
a tremor in her voice, saying, "if no one else will, then I must say
that I love the Lord Jesus with all my heart."[1] Journalist W. T. Stead
wrote:

The pathos and the passion of the avowal acted like an electric shock upon the congregation. One after another rose and made the full surrender, and the news spread like wildfire from place to place, that the Revival had broken out, and that souls were being ingathered to the Lord.[2]

Evan Roberts

The main focus of the revival later became Evan Roberts, a young theological student who eventually abandoned his studies at Newcastle Emlyn to give himself fully to the work of the revival. For a period of ten or eleven years prior to this time, he had prayed for revival. "I could sit up all night to read or talk about revivals. It was the Spirit that moved me to think about a revival."[3] In the spring of 1904, he underwent a series of unusual spiritual experiences, which he described in an interview with W. T. Stead, the British editor of *Review of Reviews*:

> For a long, long time I was much troubled in my soul and my heart by thinking over the failure of Christianity. . . . But one night, after I had been in great distress praying about this, I went to sleep, and at one o'clock in the morning suddenly I was waked up out of my sleep, and I found myself with unspeakable joy and awe in the very presence of the Almighty God. And for the space of four hours I was privileged to speak face to face with Him as a man speaks face to face with a friend. At five o'clock it seemed to me as if I again returned to earth. . . .
>
> . . . And it was not only that morning, but every morning for three or four months. . . . I felt it, and it seemed to change all my nature, and I saw things in a different light, and I knew that God was going to work in the land, and not this land only, but in all the world.[4]

Toward the commencement of his studies at Newcastle Emlyn, Roberts attended meetings held by W. W. Lewis and Seth Joshua of the Calvinistic Methodist Forward Movement, on Thursday, September 22, 1904, at nearby Blaenannerch. The day began with a 7:00 a.m. meeting of open discussion led by Lewis. Before they broke for breakfast, Joshua offered a prayer, during which he asked the Lord to do many things for them, one being that he would "bend us."[5] Roberts was particularly struck by this. " 'This is what you need,' said the Spirit to me. And as I went out I prayed, O Lord, bend me."[6]

When the 9:00 a.m. meeting began, Roberts was in considerable distress about his own spiritual state. Several people prayed in turn; then Roberts began to pray:

> For about two minutes it was terrible. I cried out "Bend me! Bend me! Bend us!" . . . It was God's commending His love which bent me, while I saw

nothing in it to commend. After I was bent, what a wave of peace flooded my bosom. . . . Then the fearful bending of the judgment day came to my mind, and I was filled with compassion for those who must bend at the judgment, and I wept. Following that the salvation of the human soul was solemnly impressed upon me. I felt ablaze with a desire to go through the length and breadth of Wales to tell of the Saviour; and had it been possible, I was willing to pay God for doing so.[7]

David Matthews wrote:

Suddenly new life had been infused into the campaign. All through that night and the following day, indeed for several successive days, the services continued without any signs of weariness. Evan Roberts was to all appearances a new man after this experience.[8]

It was probably after these events that Roberts was again awakened at one o'clock every morning for four hours of communion with God. He evidently experienced many visions during these times of refreshing. In one case, he had a vision of the moon, which appeared with greater brilliance than ever before. Eifion Jones wrote that

In a matter of moments the moon seemed to reflect the divine presence and there appeared an arm outstretched towards the world, claiming something for itself before being withdrawn. At another time, the arm and hand were indistinct, but the piece of paper which it held had the figures "100,000" written on it. After that, whenever he prayed, he had no peace until he had asked God specifically for that number of souls.[9]

Roberts began sharing with others at school his vision of 100,000 people to be won for Christ. One of the people who knew him at this time, Evan Phillips, said that Roberts "was like a particle of radium in our midst."[10] On October 10, Roberts wrote to his brother Dan at their home in Loughor, sharing this vision:

The wheels of the gospel chariot are to turn swiftly before long, and it is a privilege to give a hand in the work. . . . You must put yourself entirely at the Holy Spirit's disposal.[11]

As October passed, Roberts became more and more anxious about his home church in Loughor, especially the young people. Finally, on Sunday, October 30, as he was sitting in the evening service at Newcastle Emlyn, the Lord dealt with him about returning home. During his interview with W. T. Stead, Roberts said:

I could not fix my mind upon the service, for always before my eyes I saw, as in a vision, the schoolroom in Loughor, where I live. And there, sitting in rows before me, I saw my old companions and all the young people, and I saw myself addressing them. I shook my head impatiently, and strove to drive away this vision, but it always came back. . . . Then at last I could resist no longer, and I said, "Well, Lord, if it is Thy will, I will go." Then instantly the vision vanished, and the whole chapel became filled with light so dazzling that I could faintly see the minister in the pulpit, and between him and me the glory as of the light of the sun in Heaven.[12]

The following morning, he sent a note to his friend Florrie Evans of New Quay, advising her of his determination to return to Loughor immediately in order to hold meetings and asking the prayers of his friends.[13] Roberts told her a little about his experiences during the previous evening's service and said that he had consulted with his tutor, Mr. Phillips, who encouraged him to go.[14] He then returned to Moriah Chapel at Loughor and told his minister, Daniel Jones, what had happened. Jones told Roberts that he was welcome to see what he could do, but that "the ground was stony and the task would be hard."[15] Roberts referred to the succeeding events as follows:

> I asked the young people to come together, for I wanted to talk to them. They came and I stood up to talk to them, and behold, it was even as I had seen in the church at Newcastle Emlyn. . . . At first they did not seem inclined to listen; but I went on, and at last the power of the Spirit came down. . . .[16]

Eventually, all seventeen participants at the meeting found their way to Christ. Among them were Roberts's brother and three sisters, all of whom had come to the Lord that night.[17]

The following evening, Roberts spoke to a larger audience at Pisgah, a chapel of his home congregation of Moriah. Here, several who had come to the Lord the previous evening testified about the joy of their new experience. The meeting lasted three hours and was characterized by confession, prayer, and personal testimony. The next day, Roberts wrote that "the meeting last night was left entirely to the Spirit's direction. Reflecting on it I realized that the Spirit was teaching *obedience*."[18]

A larger audience awaited Roberts the next evening at Libanus Chapel, Gorseinon. They listened with careful attention as he provided details about his visions and spoke of the Spirit's revelation of the imminent, widespread revival. As previously arranged, many followed him back to Moriah, where he outlined a four-point plan for personal blessing:

> 1. If there is past sin or sins hitherto unconfessed, we cannot receive the Spirit. . . . 2. If there is anything doubtful in our lives, it *must* be removed. . . . 3. An entire giving up of ourselves to the Spirit. We *must speak* and *do* all He requires of us. 4. Public confession of Christ.[19]

On Thursday morning, November 3, Roberts had a vision of a candle burning, behind which was a rising sun in all of its glory. The light of the candle, he was shown, represented the revival as it was at that time, while the rising sun signified what was yet to come. That evening, Roberts spoke on Matthew 7:7 and said that "these things must be believed, if the work is to succeed. We must believe that God is willing and able to answer our prayers."[20]

By Friday evening, his activities had begun to attract public attention, and the congregation was larger than ever. He wrote, "we could have gone on all night . . . I believe there is to be a blessed revival in the near future."[21]

The Outbreak of Revival

On Saturday night, Roberts spoke to the crowded Libanus Chapel near Gorseinon at a meeting that lasted five hours. Although it had been announced as a meeting for young people, many parents attended, amazed at the radical changes in the youth. The following evening, Roberts called upon the people to concentrate on praying for the Holy Spirit. He described what happened as follows:

> I led in the prayer, then from seat to seat . . . I felt the place being filled, and before the prayer had gone half-way through the Church, I heard some brother weeping. . . . The prayer went on, the influence intensifying, the place being filled more and more.[22]

This Sunday evening meeting proved to be a turning point. There was a second round of prayer, each praying in turn for the Holy Spirit to come "more powerfully." Two women were filled with the Holy Spirit and, unable to contain themselves, began shouting loudly. Everyone gathered around Roberts, who smiled reassuringly, although overcome with awe himself. People started shouting, "No more, Lord Jesus, or I die!" Others cried for mercy, wept, sang, and praised God. This, together with "the sight of many who had fainted or lay prostrate on the ground in an agony of conviction," was, according to historian Eifion Evans, "as unbelievable as it was unprecedented."[23]

This unusual meeting became the talk of the town, and Moriah Chapel was filled to capacity on Monday evening, November 7. Overflowing with power, the service did not end until 3:00 a.m. Representatives of the Congregational Church from Bryn-teg then asked Roberts to take their meeting on Wednesday, and he gladly accepted their invitation.

The Spread of the Revival

By Tuesday, revival spirit was no longer confined to Evan Roberts's meetings. Thomas Francis, minister of Libanus Chapel in Gorseinon (where Roberts had spoken a few days earlier), wrote of his meeting:

> There was grave silence, with each child present in communion with God, asking Him to send the Holy Spirit for Jesus Christ's sake. God answered their prayer and He descended on sons and daughters of all ages alike. We had never seen such weeping and singing and praying before.[24]

On the same day, R. B. Jones began a series of ten meetings at the Baptist church in Rhos (Rhosllanerchrugog) in North Wales. At the climax on the last day, the meeting lasted twelve hours after the congregation had given way to general jubilation, praise, prayer, and testimony.[25]

A weekly periodical of the Keswick movement published in London, *The Life of Faith*, carried an article on November 9 by Mrs. Jessie Penn-Lewis, who observed that a "cloud as a man's hand" had arisen over Wales, portending revival. On the same day, Roberts preached at the Bryn-teg Congregational Chapel at a meeting that continued for about eight hours amidst scenes of wild jubilation. By the next day, *The Western Mail*, an English language newspaper in Cardiff, had received word of Roberts's meetings and reported:

> A remarkable religious revival is now taking place in Loughor. . . . Such excitement has prevailed that the road on which the chapel is situated has been lined with people from end to end. . . . Shopkeepers are closing early in order to get a place in the chapel, and tin and steel workers throng the place in working clothes.[26]

People travelled from considerable distances to attend the meeting on Thursday, November 10. A journalist from *The Western Mail* wrote that everything during the service was "left to the spontaneous impulse of the moment" and that Roberts "walked up and down the aisles, open Bible in hand, exhorting one, encouraging another, and kneeling with a third to implore a blessing from the Throne of Grace."[27] He continued:

> A young woman rose to give out a hymn, which was sung with deep earnestness. While it was being sung several people dropped down in their seats as if they had been struck, and commenced crying for pardon. . . . Finally, . . . at 4:25 o'clock the gathering dispersed. But even at this hour the people did not make their way home. When I left to walk back to Llanelly I left dozens of them about the road still discussing what is now the chief subject in their lives.[28]

By this time, Roberts realized that he would not be returning to school and wrote to his friend, Sidney Evans, asking for his belongings and stating his intention not to return. "What a blessed time! I am perfectly content and blissfully happy with enough work from morning till night."[29]

The Friday night meeting, November 11, brought an intensity of conviction; many found themselves on their knees, unable to speak, overcome with a sense of guilt. "Some of these fell in a heap and others cried out pitifully and loudly in their desire for mercy."[30] Eifion Evans wrote that "people lost all sense of time, and forgot their need for food, and were seemingly kept from physical exhaustion at their daily work."[31]

On Saturday, two young women held an open air meeting in Gorseinon, attracting a large crowd. Others met at a gipsy encampment at Kingsbridge Common, where there were many conversions. There were prayer meetings in many area homes for most of the day. Eifion Evans wrote:

> Eternal issues were discussed freely and unashamedly, and, above all, a sense of the presence and holiness of God pervaded every area of human experience, at home, at work, in shops and public houses. Eternity seemed inescapably near and real.[32]

That evening, meetings were held both at Moriah Chapel and at Pisgah, with Evan Roberts preaching at one chapel and Sidney Evans, who had just returned from Newcastle Emlyn, at the other. The meetinghouses were overcrowded hours before the services were due to begin, and the meetings ended at approximately 5:00 a.m.[33]

Roberts had received an invitation to fill another pulpit for the next day in Aberdare, where people had read with interest articles about him in *The Western Mail*. He accepted by telegram and set out the next morning for Bryn Seion, Aberdare, near Trecynon, with several young women who had recently been converted. Arthur Goodrich wrote of their arrival:

> Sunday morning at church time no preacher appeared, and it was not until the congregation had waited drearily, spasmodically singing hymns, for a long time, that a young man, with a springy step and an entire lack of gloomy solemnity, came in with five young women, and, to their surprise, made his way to the front.
>
> For a half hour he talked to them in his characteristic way, saying more or less conventional things in a way that somehow gripped their hearts and made them sit straight and then lean forward, so as not to lose either a word or a particle of that enthusiastic spirit.

Then some of the girls who had come with him sang, and the coldness of the people was half melted as they joined in and sang with Welsh voices and Welsh fervour.[34]

According to Eifion Evans, they had a cool reception at first, but, "undaunted, the revivalist and his team of five ladies from Gorseinon persevered, and their faith was rewarded. Scenes such as those witnessed at Loughor [Moriah, Pisgah, and Libanus Chapels] were repeated, bringing to the minds of some memories of the 1859 revival."[35] David Matthews supplied the following description:

It soon broke when one of the proudest members of that assembly fell on her knees in agonizing prayer and unrestrainedly confessed her sins. . . . Others followed rapidly and with such spontaneity as to cause bewilderment. . . .

That service, commenced so inauspiciously, continued without a break all day! There was no dinner hour nor Sunday school. All the worshippers apparently were oblivious to every physical discomfort. . . . When evening came, the other churches had received the news. The neighborhood seemed to have assembled in this one place, striving to enter the one comparatively small building where "the revival" was. The crush was terrible.[36]

From here, Roberts went to Pontcymmer, in the Garw coal-mining valley, about half-way to his hometown. He had been invited by the united religious bodies of the area, and many people came from far and wide, some out of pure curiosity. People were already referring to Roberts as "the John Wesley of Wales."[37] At five o'clock the next morning, he stopped at the entrance to the mines, waiting for the night shift to come up from below. When they appeared, he shook hands with all of them, inviting those who were not too tired to join in the prayer meeting, which was still in progress. Most came. "Stirring scenes were witnessed, strong men of rough exterior sobbing almost hysterically, and bearing testimony in quivering, broken accents."[38]

On Wednesday, November 16, Roberts went back to Trecynon to hold meetings at Ebenezer Congregational Chapel. David Matthews wrote of the meeting there:

Confronting and surrounding me was a mass of people, with faces aglow with a divine radiance, certainly not of this earth. . . . In another part of the building, scores were engaged simultaneously in prayer, some were wringing their hands as if in mortal agony, while others who had received "the blessing" were joyous in their new-found experience.[39]

Matthews recorded that when Roberts looked at him, his "innermost soul seemed to be laid bare."[40] Then the meeting was interrupted by a skeptic, who thundered, "I want to ask a question." Roberts remained calm, not even looking in the speaker's direction. Then, in a challenging tone, he repeated, "I want to ask a question." Roberts began praying silently, and soon somebody started a song that had become popular during the revival. Then, above the singing, the challenge came once again: "If you do not answer me, I will come to the pulpit to ask my question." Nobody heeded his interruption, so the man began to carry out his threat. According to Matthews:

> As in the case of Saul of Tarsus, on the Damascus Road, the Holy Spirit overpowered this man—he would have collapsed on the stairs had not the people upheld him—constraining him to cry out for mercy and pardon. What a scene followed! When the people realized the full import of what had happened, the shout went up, "He has been saved! He has been saved!"[41]

Evan Roberts was not alone in helping to spread revival in Wales. Seth Joshua, for example, experienced a tremendous divine visitation among the people at a meeting at Ammanford on November 20.[42] As a result, Bibles were sold out, taverns emptied, and at least one ordained minister, Nantlais Williams, converted to Christ.[43]

In North Wales, the fires of revival continued to burn brightly, especially in Rhos, where the most remarkable meeting took place on November 20, during afternoon prayer, when "scores of people took part in prayer simultaneously, large numbers were completely overcome, and the entire congregation was in tears."[44]

Huge crowds continued to pour into Roberts's meetings, although he attempted to remain as unobtrusive as possible in order to allow the Holy Spirit freedom. Many felt that this policy was one of the secrets of the phenomenal success of his meetings. People were free to express themselves in psalms, hymns, and exclamations of joy.

The heartfelt singing during the Welsh revival was one of its hallmarks. Arthur Goodrich wrote that "no oratorio society, no group of trained professional singers that it has been my good fortune to hear, sing as well as almost any one of the Welsh congregations I heard sing at the Roberts meetings."[45]

When David Matthews visited a meeting led by Roberts on November 23, he was struck by the anointing upon the singing.

> Such marvellous singing, quite extemporaneous, could only be created by a supernatural power, and that power the divine Holy Spirit. No choir, no conductor, no organ—just spontaneous, unctionized soul-singing!
>
> An irresistible attraction, resembling a tremendous magnetic force, drew us inside the vestry.[46]

Evan Roberts soon began to suffer from the constant responsibilities thrust upon him as a result of the revival. The demand upon his time was so great that it became necessary for someone else to take over responsibility for arranging Roberts's itinerary and seeing to all the details of his travel.[47] Matthews wrote:

> The minister, T. Mardy Davies, undertook to become the organizing secretary of the work, arranging services throughout the country as the overwhelming demands came in. . . . Throngs followed [Roberts] day and night, making life almost unendurable.[48]

By the end of November, Reuben A. Torrey, the great evangelist, wrote to Roberts, expressing hope to meet him some day.[49] Letters came from Ireland, Scotland, England, Norway, France, Spain, and Africa requesting prayer.[50] Roberts was confident that the prayers of these correspondents would be answered, ushering in a worldwide revival, and this confidence proved to be justified. Famed journalists, religious leaders, curiosity seekers, and others began visiting Wales to see for themselves what eyewitnesses and local journalists had reported, and their hopes were not disappointed.

Eyewitness Impressions

Some of the most remarkable events took place in the mining towns of South Wales. By the end of November, the revival was "sweeping like a wave" over most of the mining valleys of Glamorgan. At Porth, for example, a week before Roberts's first visit, R. B. Jones had seen much blessing and prayer among the miners.[51] Employers reported that the quality of their work improved considerably. "Waste is less, men go to their daily toil with a new spirit of gladness in their labor."[52] There was much less drinking, idleness, and gambling. G. Campbell Morgan wrote of the miners:

> The horses are terribly puzzled. A manager said to me,"The haulers are some of the very lowest. They have driven their horses by obscenity and kicks. Now they can hardly persuade the horses to start working, because there is no obscenity and no kicks."[53]

Stead visited three meetings held by Roberts at Maerdy in the Rhondda valley.[54] He wrote:

> Never in the history of Revivals has there been any Revival more spontaneous than this. It has burst out here, there, and everywhere, without leaders, or organization, or direction. Hence, if Mr. Evan Roberts is spoken of as the centre, it is only because it happens to be [that he is] one of

the few conspicuous figures in a movement which he neither organized nor controls.[55]

Stead felt that this lack of human leadership was one of the most unusual characteristics of these meetings:

The most extraordinary thing about the meetings which I attended was the extent to which they were absolutely without any human direction or leadership. "We must obey the Spirit," is the watchword of Evan Roberts, and he is as obedient as the humblest of his followers. . . .

You can watch what they call the influence of the power of the Spirit playing over the crowded congregation as an eddying wind plays over the surface of a pond.[56]

Arthur Goodrich was also amazed at Roberts's humility:

He strides along, stopping now and then to speak to people in the many groups that are walking down the middle of the road. . . . Up every hilly side street they come, and they do not hold themselves aloof from him as if he were different and greater than they. . . .

I feel the unassuming simplicity, the boyish ingenuousness, the commanding sincerity, and see how at one he is with the people, catching a hand here and grasping an arm or shoulder there in open-hearted friendliness, carrying his enthusiasm, his confidence, his dominating, cheerful spirit into their hearts.[57]

G. Campbell Morgan, the great Congregationalist Bible teacher and preacher who pastored Westminster Chapel in London, visited some of Roberts's meetings at Clydach Vale on Tuesday, December 20. The following Sunday, Christmas evening, he delivered an address at Westminster Chapel on the Welsh revival, which was later printed and distributed worldwide.[58] He spoke of it as "Pentecost continued," referring to the second chapter of Acts, and said, "we had better keep our hands off this work."[59] He wrote:

In connection with the Welsh revival there is no preaching, no order, no hymnbooks, no choirs, no organs, no collections, and, finally, no advertising. . . . There were the organs, but silent; the ministers, but among the rest of the people, rejoicing and prophesying with the rest, only there was no preaching. . . . No choir did I say? It was all choir. And hymns! I stood and listened in wonder and amazement as that congregation on that night sang hymn after hymn, long hymns, sung through without hymnbooks. . . . No advertising. The whole thing advertises itself. . . .

If you and I could stand above Wales, looking at it, you would see fire breaking out here, and there, and yonder, and somewhere else, without any collusion or prearrangement. . . . It is a visitation in which [God] is making men conscious of Himself, without any human agency. . . .

. . . I am inclined to think God is saying to us, Your organizations are right, providing you do not live in them and end in them. But here, apart from all of them, setting them almost ruthlessly on one side, Pentecostal power and fire are being manifested.[60]

The Waning of the Revival

On January 31, 1905, a Congregational minister, Peter Price, launched virulent opposition to Evan Roberts with the publication of his letters in the correspondence columns of *The Western Mail*. A protracted and heated public debate arose as a result, although Roberts took no part in it himself.[61] According to Price, there were two revivals in progress; one true and the other false. The one at his own church at Dowlais was genuine, while the Roberts movement was "a sham . . . a mockery, a blasphemous travesty of the real thing."[62]

Although public sympathy lay with Roberts, such criticisms, coupled with months of activity with very little sleep, began to take their toll, and he removed himself from public ministry for rest and renewal for a total of seven days beginning February 22 at Neath.[63] This time of silence was a shock to the entire world, but Roberts very wisely did not succumb to the pressure to continue his work unabated.[64] Afterwards, he continued his exhausting schedule for a little over a year. Then, in April of 1906, Mrs. Jessie Penn-Lewis and her husband convinced the harried evangelist to take complete rest at their home in Great Glen, Leicestershire.[65]

The road to recovery proved to be long and arduous. Although people constantly attempted to visit him, the Penn-Lewises very wisely refused almost all requests. David Matthews wrote:

Mr. Evan Roberts maintained and defended his host and hostess. If there were any faults or mistakes, he frankly accepted all responsibility for them. All his decisions were made unaided and uninfluenced.[66]

From this time onward, Roberts kept himself out of the public eye. Many years later, he said:

My work is devoted to prayer. By preaching I would reach the limited few but by and through prayer I can reach the whole of mankind for God. But I am afraid people do not understand what all this means and what it involves.[67]

Of some of the results of the Welsh revival, David Matthews wrote:

Lists of [criminal] convictions dwindled to nothing. Judges had, instead of the usual long lists of cases awaiting trial, blank sheets of paper, without a single name.

To celebrate the auspicious occasion, pairs of snow-white gloves were ceremoniously handed to them, to be preserved scrupulously as a witness to future generations of the reality and blessedness of real revival. This ancient custom, so rarely performed or witnessed, had persisted within the British Isles since the birth of the legal code. For that generation to have had the honor of gazing upon such a ceremony was a privilege that would be coveted by the people of any civilized country.[68]

Roberts moved to Cardiff in 1930 and died there in 1951. While still living with the Penn-Lewis family, he co-authored a book with Jessie Penn-Lewis entitled *War on the Saints*, a study of the demonic forces that seek to thwart the work of the Holy Spirit during worldwide revival.[69] They wrote:

At Revival dawn the ignorant are teachable, but through their "spiritual experiences," later on they become unteachable. Pre-Revival simplicity gives place to Satanic "infallibility," or an unteachable spirit. Dogged, stubborn obstinacy in a believer after a Revival is not from the source of the man himself, but from evil spirits deceiving his mind, holding his spirit in their grip, and making him unbending and unreasonable.[70]

The book indicates that the Welsh revival was marred by various types of fanaticism after its initial phase. It is written as a manual for Christians who wish to engage in serious spiritual warfare against the power of the enemy, who seeks to destroy the work of God during periods of revival. Despite the difficulties that arose in the wake of the Welsh revival, there were certain lasting effects. J. B. Jones, writing of the aftereffects of the revival, said that in 1930 the "atmosphere" of the revival still lingered in Wales.[71]

THE 1905–1906 AWAKENING IN NORTH AMERICA

Origins

During its initial stages, the Welsh revival had worldwide impact, and North America was no exception. Because the North American revival actually originated with events in Wales, no American location can be identified as the center from which the revival spread. As people received news of what was happening in Wales, the awakening soon became manifest in many locations.

One of the first places to feel its effects was Wilkes-Barre, Pennsylvania, where many Welsh people had settled. News arrived by word of mouth from across the Atlantic, resulting in a sudden revival in December of 1904, which soon spread to other Welsh-speaking settlers elsewhere in Pennsylvania.[72]

The Spread of the Revival

In 1905, particularly during the first few months of the year, there was an explosion of revival in many parts of the United States and Canada. In January there were reports of unusual revivals at Taylor University in Upland, Indiana;[73] at Baptist Temple in Brooklyn, New York, pastored by Dr. Cortland Myers;[74] among Methodists in Michigan;[75] among a cross-section of people in Gloversville, Fulton County, New York, under the ministry of Chester Ralston; [76] in Denver under J. Wilbur Chapman, W. E. Biederwolf, Henry Ostrom, and seven other leading evangelists;[77] and in Schenectady, New York, where many different denominations were involved.[78]

The situation in Schenectady probably typified, in many respects, what was beginning to happen around the country. The previous year, the Ministerial Association in Schenectady had heard reports of the Welsh revival and had united all evangelical denominations for meetings for prayer and evangelistic rallies. Participating churches included the Dutch Reformed, Baptist, Congregationalist, Lutheran, Methodist, and Presbyterian. By January 22, according to J. Edwin Orr, "all the evangelical churches in town had been moved, with packed congregations in each, and the movement continued for months on end."[79] The secular newspapers carried daily columns to keep people updated on the progress of the revival.

There were reports of revival in Danville, Kentucky;[80] Nebraska;[81] North and South Carolina; and Georgia in February.[82] At Asbury College in Wilmore, Kentucky, classes became arenas for prayer, confession, reconciliation, restitution, dedication, and conversion, as normal class activities were suspended.[83] The regular chapel service was suspended for spontaneous intercession, and the revival spread throughout the entire town.[84] Simultaneously, a prayer meeting among a few students in a dormitory room was the scene of a divine visitation, where "suddenly the Holy Spirit fell upon them, transforming their dutiful travail into a tryst with God upon the threshold of rapture."[85] One of the students present, E. Stanley Jones, soon committed himself to missions, later becoming one of the best known missionaries of the twentieth century.[86]

During March, there was revival in Providence, Rhode Island; Norfolk, Virginia; Louisville, Kentucky; Ypsilanti, Michigan; and, among Methodists, in Indiana, Illinois, Iowa, Minnesota, and North and South Dakota.[87] Thousands came to faith in Christ in meetings throughout Louisville. Henry Clay Morrison observed:

> The whole city is breathing a spiritual atmosphere. . . . Everywhere in shop and store, in the mill and on the street, salvation is the one topic of conversation.[88]

In the spring of 1905 there were also reports of revival at Dr. A. B. Simpson's Gospel Tabernacle in New York[89] and at Yale University, where one of the faculty members, Henry B. Wright, wrote a letter on March 25 to John R. Mott, exclaiming that "the Spirit of God is with us here in power . . . I have never known a time when there were so many inquiries."[90] Revivals were also taking place at this time among Baptists in New England;[91] Methodists in Grand Rapids, Michigan;[92] Baptists and Methodists in Houston, Texas;[93] and students and faculty at many colleges in Virginia, including Randolph-Macon and Emory and Henry.[94] The New England revival was probably typical, characterized by an "intense sensation of the presence of God" in the congregations.

Methodists in Philadelphia reported that June on a "revival of social righteousness" that had arisen as a result of the awakening when a regime of corruption was overthrown in the city government. The mayor, John Weaver, told a delegation of businessmen at City Hall that "the hand of the Lord is in it."[95]

By this time, Presbyterians were enjoying a nationwide revival having "four unusual characteristics: the unexpected interest of non-Christians, the desire of all classes to hear the Word of God, the ease and joy of interdenominational cooperation, and the abounding joy in participants as well as conviction and repentance among hearers."[96] There were similar reports from Baptists.[97]

The Effects of the Revival

The revival probably reached its high point by mid-1905, but its effects were felt for a long time to come. There were continued reports of local revivals for the next eight or nine months, and a reawakening of social conscience concurrent with the revival lasted far beyond this time, eliciting a comment from Washington Gladden that there was a moral revolution taking place.[98]

One of the effects of the awakening in Canada was the conversion of Dr. Oswald J. Smith, the world famous missions advocate. Smith and his brother, Ernest Gilmour Smith, attended meetings held by Dr. Reuben A. Torrey in Toronto in early 1906. Both professed faith in Christ and later entered the Christian ministry.[99]

At approximately the same time, a revival broke forth at Nyack Missionary Training Institute, which was founded by A. B. Simpson:

> For three weeks preachers, teachers and students were lying upon their faces. . . . Awful confessions were made. . . . It began at twelve o'clock noon and went on until the next morning. God had struck with mighty conviction. Some tried to get away because they didn't want to confess, but they had to come back and go through with it. I declare unto you that, when the confessions were over, the mighty presence of God filled the place. We walked on tiptoe, the atmosphere was so holy. We were afraid to hear the sound of our own heels in that school. . . . If you ever heard thunder rolls of intercession, they went forth from that school. You could have heard the body of students a mile away. They prayed as one man, and everybody as loudly as possible, but you knew that God was behind those prayers. I believe that these prayers found their answer in the Pentecostal revival . . . for it was just about three months before the Spirit was poured out in Los Angeles.[100]

As is evident from the above quotation, the Evangelical revival of 1904–1906 was a prelude to the Pentecostal revival, the subject of the next chapter.

3

THE EARLY PENTECOSTAL REVIVAL

I N THE WAKE OF THE Welsh revival, and a vital element of the worldwide awakening of 1904–1906, the early Pentecostal revival came
as one of the greatest revivals of the modern period, perhaps almost as important in its effects as the Protestant Reformation of the
sixteenth century.[1] Originating within the milieu of the Holiness
movement of the late nineteenth century, it brought into existence
hundreds of ecclesiastical bodies and denominations worldwide,
many of which quickly became some of the fastest growing religious
organizations in the world.[2]

ORIGINS

The Pentecostal revival started at Azusa Street in Los Angeles in a
dilapidated building that once served as a Methodist church.[3] Con-
tinuous meetings were held here every day for a period of three years
beginning in mid-April, 1906.[4] The Azusa Street meetings quickly became known throughout the world as the focal point of the Pentecostal outpouring of God's Spirit that began to sweep multitudes into
the experience of baptism in the Holy Ghost, the outward manifestation of which was speaking in unknown tongues.[5]

William J. Seymour

William J. Seymour, a black Holiness preacher who was blind in one
eye, was known as the leader and first proponent of the Azusa Street
revival, with its distinctive theological emphasis.[6] He had been a

disciple of Charles Parham and had attended his Bible School in Houston, Texas, in 1905.[7] There had been several local revivals associated with Parham's ministry.[8] A few years previously, Parham had founded another Bible school, Bethel College, in Topeka, Kansas, where there had been a local revival during the beginning of 1901 which had also been marked with the Pentecostal distinctive of baptism in the Holy Spirit with tongues following.[9] There had been further local revivals under Parham's ministry in El Dorado Springs, Missouri, and Galena, Kansas, in 1903. These were followed by revivals in Joplin, Missouri, in 1904 and in various parts of Kansas and Texas in the next year.[10] While these revivals were fairly localized, the meetings at Azusa Street quickly gained national and international attention.[11]

Cottage Prayer Meetings

The Pentecostal revival in Los Angeles originated in cottage prayer meetings led by William J. Seymour in the home of Richard and Ruth Asberry at 214 North Bonnie Brae Street.[12] It was in this house that the Spirit of God fell on April 9, 1906, after many months of concerted prayer.[13] Because enormous crowds were soon drawn to these meetings, it was necessary to secure a building at 312 Azusa Street, which came into use within a week of the outpouring of the Spirit.[14] One of the early eyewitnesses of these meetings reported:

> The news spread far and wide that Los Angeles was being visited with a "rushing mighty wind, from heaven." The how and why of it is to be found in the very opposite of those conditions that are usually thought necessary for a big revival. No instruments of music are used. None are needed. No choir. Bands of angels have been heard by some in the Spirit and there is heavenly singing that is inspired by the Holy Ghost. No collections are taken. No bills have been posted to advertise the meetings. No church organization is back of it. All who are in touch with God realize as soon as they enter the meeting that the Holy Ghost is the leader. One brother states that even before his train entered the city he felt the power of the revival. Travelers from afar wend their way to the headquarters at Azusa Street. . . .

> As soon as it is announced that the altar is open for seekers for pardon, sanctification, the Baptism in the Holy Ghost, and healing for the body, people rise and flock to the altar. There is no crying. What kind of preaching is it that brings that? The simple declaring of the Word of God. There is such power in the preaching of the Word in the Spirit that people are shaken on the benches. Coming to the altar many fall prostrate under the

power of God and often come out speaking in tongues. Sometimes the power falls on people and they are wrought upon by the Spirit during the giving of testimonies, or the preaching, and they receive the Holy Spirit. . . . No instrument that God can use is rejected on account of color or dress or lack of education.[15]

EVENTS PRECEDING THE REVIVAL

For about a year prior to this outpouring of the Spirit, the city of Los Angeles had been in earnest preparation and prayer for revival. Frank Bartleman, a young Holiness preacher who had arrived on December 22, 1904, distributed tracts in Los Angeles and spent time preaching on the streets and in the Holiness missions.[16] He wrote, "I only rested when I slept, and then I was often praying. I was greatly burdened for souls."[17]

The Influence of the Welsh Revival

The great revival in Wales proved to be a tremendous incentive for praying for similar results in Los Angeles. On April 8, 1905, F. B. Meyer, the great Keswick convention speaker who helped launch the first campaigns of Dwight L. Moody in England in 1873, arrived in Los Angeles to preach. He described the great revival in progress in Wales, which he had just visited. He had met Evan Roberts, who had been used of God in remarkable ways within the context of the Welsh revival. Frank Bartleman wrote of F. B. Meyer's visit in glowing terms:

> My soul was stirred to its depths, having read of this revival shortly before. I then and there promised God He should have full right of way with me, if He could use me.[18]

Local revivals began to arise in various parts of the Los Angeles area as a result of the reports from Wales. As early as May 1, a powerful revival came to the Lake Avenue Methodist Episcopal Church in Pasadena. Bartleman wrote:

> We had been praying for a sweeping revival for Pasadena. God was answering our prayers. I found a wonderful work of the Spirit going on at Lake Avenue. The altar was full of seeking souls. . . . One night nearly every unsaved soul in the house got saved. It was a clean sweep for God. Conviction was mightily upon the people. In two weeks time two hundred souls knelt at the altar, seeking the Lord. . . . We then began to pray for an outpouring of the Spirit for Los Angeles and the whole of Southern California.[19]

At about the same time, S. B. Shaw's book, *The Great Revival in Wales*, was gaining widespread circulation. This book contained accounts of the Welsh revival by G. Campbell Morgan and others, with numerous excerpts from the London *Times* and several denominational periodicals.[20] When Frank Bartleman came upon this small volume and read it on May 12, it had a great impact upon him.[21] Then, on June 17, Joseph Smale, pastor of the First Baptist Church in Los Angeles, returned from Wales, where "he had been in touch with the revival and Evan Roberts, and was on fire to have the same visitation and blessing come to his own church in Los Angeles."[22] Smale began prayer meetings in his church that led to a fifteen-week revival.[23]

Bartleman corresponded with Evan Roberts in Wales asking him to pray for revival in Los Angeles, and he received answers in June, August, and November confirming that prayers were being offered on behalf of the saints in Los Angeles.[24] Of course, people were praying fervently in many quarters of Los Angeles as well. After the outpouring of the Spirit the following year, a leading Methodist layman said:

> The scenes transpiring here are what Los Angeles churches have been praying for for years. I have been a Methodist for twenty-five years. I was a leader of a prayer band for the First Methodist Church. We prayed that Pentecost might come to the city of Los Angeles. We wanted it to start in the First Methodist Church but God did not start it there. I bless God that it did not start in any church in this city, but in a barn, so that we might all come and take part in it.[25]

In a similar statement, Mrs. Florence L. Crawford, who later founded the Apostolic Faith work in Portland, Oregon, said:

> I was a Methodist and felt sure that the Spirit should be poured out upon us. Some of my friends were Baptist, Christian and Missionary Alliance and others. We all said, "Surely God will pour out His Spirit on our particular group." But God had chosen the time, the place and the people upon whom He would send His blessing and power.[26]

In September of 1905, Joseph Smale was asked to resign as pastor of First Baptist Church of Los Angeles, where meetings had been running daily for fifteen weeks. He and others then organized the "New Testament Church" that began meeting at Burbank Hall.[27] Among those who left with Smale to become part of the New Testament Church was Jennie Evans Moore, who lived in her own home at 217 North Bonnie Brae Street and who was later to marry William J. Seymour.[28]

Important Holiness Influences

It was probably also at about this time that a small group led by Mrs. Julia W. Hutchins at Second Baptist Church in Los Angeles was forced to leave for accepting and propagating Holiness teachings.[29] This group organized as a small black Holiness mission, which elected Mrs. Hutchins to act as pastor of the group.[30] They found accommodation at the home of Richard and Ruth Asberry, Baptists who lived at 214 North Bonnie Brae Street.[31] One of the members of Mrs. Hutchins's flock was Neeley Terry, who had gone to Houston that fall to work among black Holiness missions there.[32] The leader of one of these missions in Houston was a black woman associated with Charles Parham, Lucy Farrow.[33]

Lucy Farrow had received the baptism in the Holy Spirit and had spoken in tongues under the ministry of Charles Parham in Kansas.[34] This may have been during the last series of meetings that Parham held in Kansas before going to Galveston and Houston; this would have been in Columbus, Kansas, from September 6 until October 16, 1905.[35] Much of the time, Lucy Farrow took care of Charles Parham's children while he conducted the meetings.[36] Meanwhile, Lucy Farrow's Holiness mission in Houston was led on a temporary basis by William J. Seymour.[37]

In December of 1905, Parham moved to Houston from Galveston and began a Bible school at 503 Rusk Street.[38] One of the regular attendants was William J. Seymour.[39] According to Parham's wife, Sarah, Lucy Farrow also attended the Bible school in Houston.[40] It was as a visitor at the services associated with this school that Neeley Terry received the baptism in the Holy Spirit and spoke in tongues.[41]

Seymour's Arrival in Los Angeles

While these things were happening in Houston, the group in Los Angeles led by Mrs. Julia W. Hutchins moved its meeting place from North Bonnie Brae Street to a store-front mission on Ninth and Santa Fe Avenues.[42] This work was growing and the group began looking for an associate pastor.[43] When Terry returned from Houston in March of 1906, she recommended that William J. Seymour be engaged for this purpose.[44] He was invited to the mission to preach, and he arrived in March.[45] Although Seymour had not yet spoken in tongues himself, he was convinced of Parham's view that speaking in tongues was the initial evidence of baptism in the Holy Ghost. Therefore, in his first sermon, he preached on this, using Acts 2:4 as his text. Mrs. Hutchins, as a Holiness minister, believed that she had already been baptized in the Holy Spirit, yet she had never spoken in tongues. Believing Seymour's doctrines to be seriously erroneous, she padlocked the door to the mission, barring him from preaching at the following service, even though most of the members had enthusiastically accepted his message.[46]

Seymour felt compelled to continue his work at all costs, and began preaching in the home of Edward Lee and his wife, who were black adherents of one of the Holiness missions in Los Angeles.[47] Lee was the janitor of a bank on Seventh and Spring Avenues and had been seeking the baptism of the Holy Spirit for some time.[48] While Seymour was staying at his home, Lee had a vision in which he saw the apostles Peter and John and heard them speak in tongues. After the vision ended, Lee was trembling.[49]

While Seymour was staying with the Lees, the group that had been turned out of the mission on Santa Fe Avenue by Mrs. Hutchins began once again to meet at the Asberry home at 214 North Bonnie Brae Street.[50] Frank Bartleman attended some of these meetings and had met William Seymour shortly before this time, probably at Lee's house.[51] Seymour also attended the meetings on Bonnie Brae Street, and at one of these meetings, he laid his hands upon Lee that he might receive the Spirit. Although Lee did not speak in tongues at this time, he was slain in the Spirit under the power of God. This caused considerable alarm to his wife, who thought he had fallen into a trance. She called an immediate end to the proceedings.[52]

In late March or early April, Lucy Farrow and J. A. Warren came from Houston in response to Seymour's requests of Parham for help in Los Angeles.[53] Lucy Farrow had already been quite successful in leading other people into the experience of tongues with the laying on of her hands.[54]

THE OUTBREAK OF THE REVIVAL

Bonnie Brae Street

On Monday, April 9, Edward Lee asked Lucy Farrow to lay hands on him for the baptism of the Holy Spirit. She fulfilled this request, and Lee burst forth in tongues. These things took place about an hour and a half before the meeting was to commence at the Asberry home. They walked to the meeting, where Seymour was in charge. After several had prayed and a few had given testimonies, Seymour began preaching from the second chapter of Acts and began recounting what had happened earlier that evening. As Lee began to give his testimony, he lifted his hands in the air and suddenly began speaking in tongues. The others at the meeting fell down to their knees. Seated at the piano, Jennie Evans Moore also fell to her knees.[55] An eight-year-old black boy was the first to be baptized in the Spirit and speak in tongues,[56] followed by Jennie Moore[57] and five others.[58] Carl Brumback described the event:

> As though hit by a bolt of lightning, the entire company was knocked from their chairs to the floor. Seven began to speak in divers kinds of tongues and to magnify God. The shouts were so fervent—and so loud!—that a crowd gathered outside, wondering "What meaneth This?" Soon it was noised over the city that God was pouring out His Spirit. White people joined the colored saints, and also joined the ranks of those filled with the Holy Ghost, Lydia Anderson being one of the first white recipients.[59]

As a result of these events, Richard and Ruth Asberry's daughter fled through the kitchen door, terrified by what she saw.[60] The participants of the meeting then proceeded to the front porch of the house to continue their services. Huge crowds were attracted as Jennie Moore began playing the piano and singing in what was thought to be Hebrew. In the services that followed, demonstrations of tongues were so pronounced that large crowds gathered in the streets to find out what was happening. Seymour addressed the crowds, which had become interracial, from a makeshift pulpit on the front porch.[61] Emma Cotton wrote of these events:

> They shouted three days and three nights. It was the Easter season. The people came from everywhere. By the next morning there was no way of getting near the house. As the people came in they would fall under God's Power; and the whole city was stirred. They shouted there until the foundation of the house gave way, but no one was hurt. During these three days, there were many people who received their baptism who had just come to see what it was. The sick were healed and sinners were saved just as they came in.[62]

Burbank Hall

According to some sources, on April 12, Seymour was baptized in the Holy Ghost and spoke in tongues.[63] In any case, on Easter Sunday, April 15, Jennie Evans Moore took her neighbors, Richard and Ruth Asberry, to Burbank Hall for a meeting of Joseph Smale's New

Testament Church, of which she was still a member. After the sermon, when Smale invited testimonies, she took the floor and recounted to the congregation what had taken place at the Asberry home. She then spoke in tongues before them and Ruth Asberry provided the interpretation.[64] Bartleman recalls this incident:

> I went to Burbank Hall, the New Testament Church, Sunday morning, April 15. A colored sister was there, and spoke in "tongues." This created quite a stir. The people gathered in little companies on the sidewalk after the service inquiring what this might mean. It seemed like Pentecostal "signs." We then learned that the Spirit had fallen a few nights before, April 9, at the little cottage on Bonnie Brae Street. They had been tarrying very earnestly for some time for an outpouring. A handful of colored and white saints had been waiting there daily.[65]

He went to Bonnie Brae Street that afternoon to see for himself what was going on and "found God working mightily." He wrote:

> There was a general spirit of humility manifested in the meeting. They were taken up with God. Evidently the Lord had found the little company at last, outside as always, through whom he could have right of way.[66]

Azusa Street

At about this time, the floor caved in at the house on Bonnie Brae Street.[67] Immediately, an abandoned two-story building at 312 Azusa Street was secured for the meetings. Although it had served at one time as a Methodist church building, more recently it had served as a combined tenement house and livery stable. The building had a large barn-like floor completely littered with debris, and the windows and doors were broken.[68] As it was being renovated, one of the women cleaning the building had one of the workmen down on his knees and soundly converted before it had even been opened for services.[69]

One of the people to attend some of the initial services at Azusa Street was Arthur Osterberg, a 21-year-old pastor of an independent Full-Gospel Church at 68th and Denver.[70] He had driven his mother to the meetings at her insistence. He wrote:

> I was not entirely in favor of the idea, but I saw as soon as I entered Azusa Street that something unusual was going on. . . . I was critical, but I went in and sat down on the rough boards they used for makeshift pews. A club-footed man of Mexican ancestry and his wife sat down next to me. The service began. There was a long prayer. During it I heard someone behind me sobbing. Then there were others.

The sound of their wailing rose like the moan of the wind in the place. This club-footed man beside me became restless and at length made his way to the aisle. He limped up and down. I guess I was the only one watching him. Gradually he ceased to limp. Before my eyes he was cured. He was miraculously healed without anyone praying for him and with no formal "conversion," as we call it, at all. That convinced me there was something different in this meeting from any other that I had ever attended. Somehow those people had gotten back to primitive Christianity when those things were possible. I closed up my own church and joined the movement.[71]

Arthur Osterberg was also a time-keeper and straw boss for the J. B. McNeil Construction Company. According to his friend, A. C. Valdez, Sr., Osterberg "personally paid two of his men to help him remove debris and clean and renovate the building, obtaining planks and nail kegs for benches, shoeboxes for the pulpit, and sawdust for the floor."[72] The owner of the company, J. B. McNeil, who was a devout Catholic, donated lumber for the altar.[73]

Within a day or two of the move from North Bonnie Brae Street, a reporter from the Los Angeles Times came to Azusa Street to write a story on what was happening.[74] The following day, on April 18, the front page, on the "Weird Babel of Tongues," stated:

> Meetings are held in a tumble-down shack on Azusa Street, near San Pedro Street, and the devotees of the weird doctrine practice the most fanatical rites, preach the wildest theories and work themselves into a state of mad excitement in their peculiar zeal.[75]

The British historian of Pentecostalism, Donald Gee, later complained that the newspaper reports emphasized the speaking in tongues and anything spectacular that occurred, but that the reporters "had little interest in the times of tremendous heart-searching and emptying of self that were going on."[76]

The San Francisco Earthquake

On the very day that these newspaper reports appeared, the city of San Francisco experienced one of the worst earthquakes in recorded history.[77] The effects of the earthquake were also felt in surrounding areas and thousands of people were killed. Frank Bartleman, one of the Holiness preachers in Los Angeles at this time, reported of the earthquake that "no less than ten thousand lost their lives in San Francisco alone. I felt a deep conviction that the Lord was answering our prayers for a revival in His own way."[78] Aftershocks of the earthquake were felt in Los Angeles the following day. Bartleman recalled his experience:

> Thursday, April 19, while sitting in the noon meeting at Peniel Hall, 227 South Main street, the floor suddenly began to move with us. . . . I went home and after a season of prayer was impressed of the Lord to go to the meeting which had been removed from Bonnie Brae Street to 312 Azusa Street.[79]

Bartleman wrote that business was at a standstill after the news came from San Francisco and that the people were paralyzed with fear.[80] He wrote:

> At "Azusa Mission" we had a powerful time. The saints humbled themselves. A colored sister both spoke and sang in "tongues." The very atmosphere of Heaven was there.[81]

According to Bartleman, meetings were soon running day and night, and every night the building was packed with an interracial crowd.[82]

Early Descriptions of the Azusa Street Meetings

Within a couple of months, Bartleman had become part of the "heavenly chorus," one of the manifestations of the Spirit at Azusa Street:

> Friday, June 15, at "Azusa," the Spirit dropped the "heavenly chorus" into my soul. I found myself suddenly joining the rest who had received this supernatural "gift." It was a spontaneous manifestation and rapture no earthly tongue can describe. In the beginning this manifestation was wonderfully pure and powerful. . . . It brought a heavenly atmosphere, as though the angels themselves were present and joining with us. . . .
>
> Someone has said that every fresh revival brings its own hymnology. And this one surely did.[83]

According to Bartleman, William Seymour was recognized as the nominal leader at the Azusa Street meetings, but "the Lord Himself was leading."[84] There was no platform or pulpit at this time. Bartleman continued his description of the meetings as follows:

> The services ran almost continuously. Seeking souls could be found under the power almost any hour, night and day. . . . God's presence became more and more wonderful. In that old building, with its low rafters and bare floors, God took strong men and women to pieces, and put them together again, for His glory. It was a tremendous overhauling process. Pride and self-assertion, self-importance and self-esteem, could not survive there. . . .

No subjects or sermons were announced ahead of time, and no special speakers for such an hour. No one knew what might be coming, what God would do. All was spontaneous, ordered of the Spirit. We wanted to hear from God, through whoever he might speak.[85]

Ansel H. Post, a Baptist minister from Pasadena who later went to Egypt as a missionary, wrote of his experiences in the middle of June at Azusa Street:

As Brother Seymour preached, God's power seemed to be increasing in him. Near the close of the sermon, as suddenly as on the day of Pentecost, while I was sitting in front of the preacher, the Holy Spirit fell upon me and literally filled me. I shouted and praised the Lord and incidentally I began to speak in another language. Two of the saints quite a distance apart saw the Spirit fall upon me.[86]

According to Frank Bartleman, Post said of this incident:

I seemed to be lifted up, for I was in the air in an instant, shouting "Praise God," and instantly I began to speak in another language. I could not have been more surprised if at the same moment some one had handed me a million dollars.[87]

PRELIMINARY EFFECTS

The New Testament Church

The city of Los Angeles was beginning to witness scenes of revival at locations outside of the Azusa Street Mission. At the New Testament Church at Burbank Hall, where Joseph Smale had organized a congregation (after his resignation from the pastorate of First Baptist Church the previous year), there was an outpouring of the Holy Spirit on June 21. Frank Bartleman wrote:

The New Testament Church received her Pentecost yesterday. We had a wonderful time. Men and women were prostrate under the power all over the hall. A heavenly atmosphere pervaded the place. Such singing I have never heard before, the very melody of Heaven. It seemed to come direct from the throne.[88]

Mack E. Jonas

The following week, on June 29, 1906, Mack E. Jonas, who was later to become a bishop of the Church of God in Christ, received his baptism in the Holy Ghost at Azusa Street. According to Jonas, Hiram Smith was leading the prayer services at this time, although William

Seymour had opened the meeting. Jonas portrayed Seymour as a man who kept very much to himself and who was a very prayerful, very quiet man.[89] Smith, a former Methodist pastor, was soon to become one of the twelve elders of the Azusa Mission.[90]

Rachel Sizelove

At about this time, Rachel Sizelove, a Free Methodist evangelist, visited the Azusa Street Mission with her husband. She wrote:

> As we entered the old building, somehow I was touched by the presence of God. It was such a humble place with its low ceilings and rough floor. Cobwebs were hanging in the windows and joists. . . . I thought of the fine churches in Los Angeles, but the Lord had chosen His humble spot to gather all nationalities, to baptize them with the Holy Ghost.[91]

The following month, in July, she was baptized in the Holy Spirit:

> This time when Brother Seymour gave the altar call, I went with many others to the altar. Raising my hands toward heaven, I said, "Lord, I want my inheritance, the baptism in the Holy Spirit and fire." Instantly in the Spirit I saw as it were a bright star away in the distance and my very soul cried out to God. Oh, I knew it was God, and as He came nearer, He was in the form of a beautiful white dove. As he came so close I thought I was going to receive the baptism. I was then slain upon the floor. Then the Lord began to deal with me. I had died out to everything of which I knew and believed. I had a clean heart in the sight of God, but He asked me about my denomination. . . . So he had me die out to opinions of my church before He could baptize me with the Holy Spirit.[92]

The Revival Spreads to other States

By this time, Holiness people in various places had begun praying that they might share the experience of the saints at Azusa Street. In a letter to E. N. Bell dated January 3, 1922, John C. Sinclair reminisced that "the saints at 328 West 63rd Street [Chicago] began to pray on the first of July, 1906, that God would baptize us in the Holy Ghost, as we had heard that the Saints at Los Angeles had been baptized."[93] It is possible that these people had read some of the earliest reports of the revival that were beginning to find their way into some of the Holiness periodicals. Frank Bartleman had been contributing regularly to such periodicals as J. M. Pike's *Way of Faith* in Columbia, South Carolina, which served to spread news of the outpouring far and wide.[94]

The Formation of the "Apostolic Faith Mission"

During August, Bartleman rented a church building at the corner of Eighth and Maple Streets for a Pentecostal Mission.[95] He had become disillusioned with the meetings at the New Testament Church at Burbank Hall and with the Azusa Street meetings:

> The truth must be told. "Azusa" began to fail the Lord also, early in her history. God showed me one day that they were going to organize, though not a word had been said in my hearing about it. The Spirit revealed it to me. . . . The New Testament Church saints had already arrested their further progress in this way.

> Sure enough the very next day after I dropped this warning in the meeting I found a sign outside "Azusa" reading "Apostolic Faith Mission." . . . And from that time the trouble and division began. It was no longer a free Spirit for all as it had been. The work had become one more rival party and body, along with the other churches and sects of the city. No wonder the opposition steadily increased from the churches.[96]

The meetings at Eighth and Maple Streets began on Sunday, August 12, and "the Spirit was mightily manifest from the very first meeting."[97] Meanwhile, as the work of the "Apostolic Faith Mission" at Azusa Street grew, a committee of twelve elders was appointed for handling the finances and correspondence, overseeing the publication of a monthly periodical, and issuing credentials for ministers.[98] The elders were W. J. Seymour, Jennie Moore, "Sister Prince," Hiram W. Smith, Mr. and Mrs. G. W. Evans, Clara Lunn, Glenn A. Cook, Florence Crawford, and probably Phoebe Sargent, Thomas Junk, and J. A. Warren.[99]

Lucy Farrow Goes Forth to Preach

At approximately this time, Lucy Farrow returned to Houston for a camp meeting in nearby Brunner. Ethel E. Goss wrote:

> Although a Negro, she was received as a messenger of the Lord to us, even in the deep south of Texas.

> One day, she preached and told about the great outpouring at Azusa Street. After she finished speaking, she prayed for the people to receive the Holy Ghost. The Lord had been using her to lay hands on the people and pray. God would then fill them with the Holy Ghost and speak through them in other tongues.

A long line of people queued up before the platform, and as she laid her hands upon each head, one after the other they received the baptism of the Holy Ghost, and spoke in other tongues. But, what interested me most was that everyone for whom she prayed was speaking in tongues.

When I saw this, my heart became hungry again for another manifestation of God. I had not spoken in tongues since my initial experience a few months previous. So, I went forward that she might place her hands upon me. When she did, the Spirit of God again struck me like a bolt of lightning; the power of God surged through my body, and I began speaking in tongues. From that day to this, I have been able to speak in tongues at any time I yielded to the Spirit of God.[100]

Lucy Farrow later went as a missionary to Africa, where she spent the rest of her life.

Charles Parham received letters the same month from Azusa Mission requesting additional help in the work there. In response to this, Mrs. Anna Hall, Mr. and Mrs. Walter Oyler, and their son Mahlon left the camp meeting in Brunner to assist William Seymour.[101] Walter Oyler and his wife had been baptized in the Spirit at an earlier meeting held by Parham. Soon afterward, on March 21, 1905, they convinced Mrs. Anna Hall, one of Parham's workers, to come to their home town, Orchard, Texas, to proclaim the Pentecostal message. Parham's decision to send them to Los Angeles as Lucy Farrow's replacement indicated that he probably thought highly of their ministry.

Envoys from Azusa Street

By this time, many other ministers began to go forth from Azusa Street on preaching tours. Florence Crawford, for example, took a trip to preach in Oakland and a few other cities in California.[102] At about the same time, a delegation went from Azusa Street to Chicago with the Pentecostal message.[103] F. A. Sandgren, a minister in Chicago, later reported that he heard "speaking in tongues for the first time in August, 1906, in a Holiness mission on West Chicago Avenue by three persons from Los Angeles."[104]

Meetings at Eighth and Maple

During this time the meetings at Eighth and Maple Streets were becoming very successful. Bartleman emphasized that there was no friction or jealousy between the leaders at Eighth and Maple and those at Azusa Street. "We visited back and forth. Brother Seymour often met with us."[105] These meetings were attended by more than six Holiness preachers, all of whom were seeking the baptism in the Holy Ghost.[106] One of these people was the president of the Holiness Association of Southern California, "Brother Roberts," who was "one of the first at the altar, seeking earnestly."[107] Nevertheless, the Southern California Holiness Association took a stand against the fledgling Pentecostal movement, and at a camp meeting in the summer of 1906, its executive committee ruled against practicing or advocating speaking in tongues on the camp grounds.[108] Within a short time, pastors of other Holiness groups who had accepted Pentecostalism were brought to trial for heresy.[109] Among these people was William Pendleton, the pastor of a Holiness church on Hawthorne Street in Los Angeles who had received the baptism in the Holy Ghost with tongues along with several members of his church.[110] He was brought to trial, and he and about forty of his members were asked to leave the church. Without a building in which to hold meetings, on August 26 they began to attend the meetings at Eighth and Maple at Frank Bartleman's invitation.[111] Soon after this time, Bartleman, fatigued from continual activity, turned responsibility for the leadership of these meeting over to William Pendleton.[112]

EARLY TRIUMPHS AND DIFFICULTIES

Resistance to the Pentecostal movement was becoming fairly pronounced by this time. Dr. W. C. Dumble of Toronto, Ontario, visited Los Angeles toward the end of the summer of this year and wrote as follows in J. M. Pike's periodical, *Way of Faith*:

> Possibly some of your readers may be interested in the impressions of a stranger in Los Angeles. A similar gracious work of the Spirit to that in Wales is in progress here. But while that is mostly in the churches, this is outside. The churches will not have it, or up to the present have stood aloof in a critical and condemnatory spirit.[113]

Seymour Requests Help from Parham

In her biography of Charles Parham, Sarah Parham alluded to problems that William Seymour was having at the Azusa Street Mission, where "spiritualistic manifestations, hypnotic forces and fleshly contortions as known in the colored Camp Meetings in the south, had broken loose in the meeting."[114] She wrote that Seymour sent several urgent letters to Parham soliciting his help with these problems. These letters were full of plans for a "great union revival." In one letter to Parham, dated August 27, 1906, Seymour wrote, "The revival is still going on here that has been going on since we came to this city. But we are expecting a general one to start again when you come, that these little revivals will all come together and make one great union revival."[115]

The Upper Room Mission

Seymour's concern about the fragmentation of the revival in Los Angeles must have been intensified when, in early September, the "Upper Room Mission" was started by Elmer K. Fisher at 327½ South Spring Street, Los Angeles, not far from the Azusa Street Mission, as a result of a split with Joseph Smale's church.[116] Fisher had been pastor of the First Baptist Church in Glendale, California, before his resignation in order to become associated with Smale's New Testament Church.[117] According to Bartleman, Smale had eventually rejected the Pentecostal testimony, precipitating this split with Fisher. Those from Smale's church who had been baptized in the Holy Spirit and spoken in tongues went with Fisher to the Upper Room Mission. In addition, many of the white saints from the Azusa Street Mission left Seymour's work to attend Fisher's meetings.[118]

The Azusa Street Mission Continues to Thrive

Meanwhile, despite setbacks, the mission on Azusa Street was gaining a national reputation. Many newspaper reports appeared about the meetings at Azusa Street in September,[119] and it was in this month also that the Azusa Street Mission published the first issue of its periodical, *The Apostolic Faith*.[120] Many visitors were streaming in to visit, including A. W. Orwig, who first visited Azusa Street in September of 1906 and wrote:

> One thing that somewhat surprised me at that first meeting I attended, and also subsequently, was the presence of so many persons from different churches, not a few of them educated and refined. Some were pastors, evangelists, foreign missionaries, and others of high position in various circles, looking on with seeming amazement and evident interest and profit. And they took part in the services in one way or another. Persons of many nationalities were also present. . . .
>
> In the first year of the work in Los Angeles I heard W. J. Seymour, an acknowledged leader, say, "Now, don't go from this meeting and talk about tongues, but try to get people saved." Again I heard him counsel against all unbecoming or fleshly demonstrations, and everything not truly of the Holy Spirit.[121]

Another visitor to Azusa Street at this time was Ernest S. Williams, who wrote:

> My first visit to the Azusa Street Mission was on a Sunday morning. There I saw what I had never seen before. Although there was considerable inspiration in the meeting it was the altar service at the conclusion that fascinated me. The front of the mission was packed with seekers and persons trying to assist them. Christians and unsaved spectators crowded around to see what was going on.[122]

In October, the Azusa Street Mission commissioned 38 foreign and home missionaries,[123] and among them was Miss Mabel Smith, who visited Chicago from Azusa Street and preached there in the evenings. Stanley Frodsham wrote:

> In 1906 a party from Azusa Street Mission visited Chicago. In the fall of this year Miss Mabel Smith preached nightly to overflowing crowds and wonderful scenes were witnessed. During her messages she would almost invariably break out in other tongues and give a lengthy message followed by a clear and inspiring interpretation, which seldom failed to bring pungent conviction to the hearts of the hearers. . . . Two of the first to receive the Baptism in Chicago were J. C. Sinclair and W. E. Moody, both of whom became active workers in the new movement.[124]

Charles F. Parham

It was in September that Charles Parham was planning to go to Los Angeles in response to Seymour's invitation to come and hold a "great union revival" for the entire city. The planning and preparation for this effort had been done by Anna Hall, who had arrived in Los Angeles from Houston the previous month as one of Parham's emissaries.[125] However, as it turned out, Parham felt he had to postpone his trip to Los Angeles because he had suddenly been summoned to Zion City, Illinois.[126] There had been a crisis at this time at Zion City, where the leadership of John Alexander Dowie had recently been repudiated.[127] Dowie had become well known for his ministry of healing and had founded the American Divine Healing Association in 1890.[128] He had begun his work in Chicago in 1893, where he established his Divine Healing Home on Michigan Avenue[129] and a church, Zion Tabernacle, which was attended by thousands of people who sought salvation and healing.[130] In 1896 he made plans to build a city north of Chicago, Zion, Illinois, where there was to be no more sin, disease, and poverty. A vast temple for 25,000 people was built there, where the people were employed in the manufacturing of lace.[131]

Within a few weeks, despite considerable opposition, Parham set up a Pentecostal center at Zion.[132] Two years before, in 1904, a Mrs. Waldron had moved to Zion City from Lawrence, Kansas, where she had been baptized in the Holy Spirit and had spoken in tongues. She opened her Zion City home for prayer meetings, where people sought the same experience. She was assisted by Mrs. Hall, who was baptized in the Spirit at one of these meetings. When news of these meetings began to spread, the officials at Zion put a stop to them.[133]

Sarah Parham wrote that when her husband entered the city of Zion in September of 1906, "it was impossible to obtain a building to hold a meeting in as much as all doors were closed against him."[134] Undaunted, Parham held his first meeting in a private room at Elijah Hospice (hotel):

> The next night two rooms and the hallway were crowded out and from that time onward the meetings increased in number, attendance and power.

> He then began cottage meetings and many of the best homes in the city were opened for meetings. Fred F. Bosworth's home was literally converted into a meeting house.[135]

Among the people who received the Pentecostal experience during Parham's visit to Zion City was Marie Burgess, who later helped to spread the revival to New York City.[136] On October 18, 1906, when she was baptized in the Holy Spirit, the Lord moved upon her to offer intercessory prayer for various mission fields.[137] She wrote:

> Each of these fields was laid heavily upon my heart, and it seemed God was calling me to service in one of them. While I was waiting upon the Lord to know which field He would have me go, I was asked to come to New York. And this became my mission field all these years.[138]

The Dispute Between Seymour and Parham

On October 31, Parham finally left Zion City in order to go to Los Angeles to help Seymour at the Azusa Street Mission.[139] This had been well publicized as the "general union revival."[140] These meetings were interracial, and Parham preached at least twice.[141] The next day, however, Seymour closed the door against Parham and did not let him preach.[142] Charles Parham wrote:

> I hurried to Los Angeles, and to my utter surprise and astonishment I found conditions even worse than I had anticipated. Brother Seymour came to me helpless, he said he could not stem the tide that had arisen. I sat on the platform in Azusa Street Mission, and saw the manifestations of the

flesh, spiritualistic controls, saw people practicing hypnotism at the altar over candidates seeking the baptism; though many were receiving the real baptism of the Holy Ghost.

After preaching two or three times, I was informed by two of the elders, one who was a hypnotist (I had seen him lay his hands on many who came through chattering, jabbering and sputtering, speaking in no language at all) that I was not wanted in that place.[143]

After Parham was barred from Azusa Street, there came a permanent breach between him and Seymour, and Parham continued to denounce the meetings at Azusa Street for the rest of his life.[144] Immediately after he was barred from the Azusa Street meetings, Parham began revival meetings at the Women's Christian Temperance Union building on Broadway and Temple Streets in Los Angeles.[145] Sarah Parham remembered:

Great numbers were saved, marvelous healings took place and between two and three hundred who had been possessed of awful fits and spasms and controls in the Azusa Street work were delivered and received the real Pentecost teachings, and many spake with other tongues.[146]

These meetings were short-lived, however, and did not alter the course of the Azusa Street revival.[147] The sentiments of Frank Bartleman may have been widespread in Los Angeles at this time:

An earlier work in Texas later tried to gather in the Pentecostal missions on the Pacific Coast and Los Angeles, but also failed. Why should they claim authority over us? We had prayed down our own revival. The revival in California was unique and separate as to origin. It came from Heaven, even Brother Seymour not receiving the "baptism" until many others had entered in here. He did not arrive in Los Angeles until the "eleventh hour."[148]

Parham later wrote a long letter from Los Angeles deploring the extremes he had found at the Azusa Street Mission.[149] The Azusa Mission then published a repudiation of Charles Parham.[150]

THE CONTINUING INFLUENCE OF THE PENTECOSTAL REVIVAL

By fall of 1906, the influence of the Azusa Street Revival had been felt in many diverse places. The first issue of *The Apostolic Faith* had enjoyed wide circulation and came into the hands of Thomas B. Barratt of Norway, who was in the United States raising financial support for his City Mission in Christiania (now Oslo). He wrote letters

to the leaders of the work at Azusa Street and received answers encouraging him to seek a deeper experience.[151] On October 7, while
in New York City, Barratt was baptized in the Holy Spirit, and a
supernatural light was seen like a cloven tongue of fire over his
head.[152] It was not until November 15, however, that he first spoke
in tongues.[153] This took place at meetings held at 250 14th Street
in New York City, which he had attended at the suggestion of Mrs.
Lucy Leatherman, the wife of a physician who had visited Charles
Parham's Bible School in Topeka, Kansas, in 1900.[154] These meetings
were led by Miss Maud Williams, who had received the baptism of
the Holy Spirit in Canada.[155] The following day she was asked to stop
holding meetings, and the group that she was leading moved to the
Union Holiness Mission at 351 W. 40th Street.[156] A few weeks later,
in early December, several missionaries arrived at this mission en
route to Africa from Azusa Street in Los Angeles. Among these
people was "Elder" Sturdevant, whose messages received press coverage from the New York papers.[157] T. B. Barratt, who had attended
these meetings, departed for Norway on December 8, and upon his
return to Christiania, held meetings which paved the way for the
spread of Pentecostalism to many other parts of Europe.[158] Meanwhile, Lucy Leatherman wrote to Charles Parham, who had returned
to Zion City, asking for somebody to come and establish the work
in New York City. He sent Marie Burgess, who arrived in early January with her co-worker, Miss Jessie Brown.[159]

Early Canadian Pentecostalism

The first issue of *The Apostolic Faith* also found its way to a camp meeting held at Thornburg, Ontario, in September of 1906.[160] A. H. Argue
was preaching at this meeting, and he reminisced:

> It was at a Camp Meeting in 1906 . . . where I did some preaching, that I
> received a paper with startling news. It was from the Azusa Street Mission
> in Los Angeles, and told of a remarkable outpouring taking place there,
> where hungry hearts were being filled with the Holy Spirit, accompanied
> as in New Testament times, by the evidence of speaking with other tongues.
>
> The paper with its wonderful news I showed to Bishop J. H. King (later
> head of the Pentecostal Holiness Church), who was also there. When he
> read that people were speaking in other tongues as on the Day of Pen-
> tecost, he replied, "It could be possible."[161]

Also in Canada, in November of 1906, at an independent mission
at 651 Queen Street East, Toronto, Mrs. Ellen Hebden received the

gift of tongues.[162] Nevertheless, Mrs. Hebden had not been seeking the gift of tongues. Rather, she had been praying for more power to heal the sick and cast out demons. When the Lord spoke to her about the gift of tongues, she answered, "No Lord; not tongues, but power, power." She realized that the Spirit of God was grieved and then cried, "Anything, Lord, tongues or anything." The power of God came upon her and she began to speak in tongues.[163] Within a short time, the influence of the Hebden mission had reached over most of central Ontario.[164] In December, A. S. Copley of Cambridge, Ohio, visited the Hebden Mission and published his report in an Ohio periodical. Seymour later reprinted it in *The Apostolic Faith.* Copley wrote:

> The meetings are heavenly. They are conducted informally. A stranger would scarcely discover who is in the lead. Christ is the Head. There is a divine hush. There is seriousness without rigidity, joy and much prayer. . . . Pentecost has begun in Toronto.[165]

By the end of 1906, a "Brother O. Adams" went to the Hebden mission from Los Angeles and informed the people there of the outpouring of the Holy Spirit at Azusa Street.[166]

Another Canadian, Robert E. McAlister of Ottawa, received the baptism in the Holy Spirit in Los Angeles on December 11.[167] He later became one of the leading figures of the Pentecostal movement in Canada and founded the *Pentecostal Testimony,* the official publication of the Pentecostal Assemblies of Canada.[168]

G. B. Cashwell

The previous month, another visitor to Azusa Street had been G. B. Cashwell of Dunn, North Carolina, who was a preacher in the Pentecostal Holiness Church, one of many of the Holiness groups in the Southeast.[169] He was so interested in what was happening in Los Angeles that he went there rather than attend the annual conference of the Pentecostal Holiness Church at Lumberton, North Carolina, in November of 1906. He left a letter to the delegates to be read by the chairman of the conference in which he said:

> If I have offended anyone of you, forgive me. I realize that my life has fallen short of the standard of holiness we preach; but I have repented in my home in Dunn, North Carolina, and I have been restored. I am unable to be with you this time, for I am now leaving for Los Angeles, California where I shall seek for the Baptism of the Holy Ghost.[170]

As a Southerner, he was a bit unsettled to find blacks and whites participating together in the services at Azusa Street. He thought of leaving but decided to remain to observe a service. A young black man laid his hands upon him and prayed for him to be baptized with the Holy Ghost. Because of Cashwell's racial prejudice, he was disturbed at first; however, after a few services, he became less concerned and "lost his pride," asking William J. Seymour and several other black men to lay hands on him to be filled with the Holy Spirit. Within a short time, he received the experience and spoke with other tongues.[171]

Cashwell returned to his home in Dunn, North Carolina, where in a large warehouse he launched a series of meetings that brought the Pentecostal revival to the South.[172] These meetings began on December 31 and continued during all of January, 1907, and became for the southeastern U.S. what the Azusa Street meetings had been for the West.[173] According to Vinson Synan, Cashwell's meetings "would result in the conversion of most of the Holiness movement in the Southeast to the Pentecostal view."[174] Before the meetings began, he invited all the ministers of the Fire-Baptized Holiness Church, the Pentecostal Holiness Church, and the Free-Will Baptist Church to attend, and almost all of them actually came and received the Pentecostal experience.[175] Soon Baptists, Methodists, and Presbyterians were joining them.[176] One of the people who attended these meetings, G. F. Taylor, wrote:

> They went to Dunn by the thousands, went down for the Baptism with all the earnestness they could command, and were soon happy in the experience, speaking in tongues, singing in tongues, shouting, weeping, dancing, praising, and magnifying God. They returned to their respective homes to scatter the fire. A great Pentecostal revival broke out in practically all the churches. A revival had come, and nobody was able to stop it.[177]

The meetings at Dunn generated a great deal of excitement, and Cashwell was besieged with invitations to preach throughout all of the Southeast.[178] In February of 1907, he responded to an invitation from a Fire-Baptized Holiness congregation in Toccoa, Georgia, to hold some special services. The pastor of the congregation was J. H. King, general overseer of the Fire-Baptized Holiness Church, who sought and obtained the baptism in the Holy Spirit with tongues at Cashwell's meeting on February 15, 1907.[179] The previous day, R. B. Hayes, the Ruling Elder in Georgia, had also received this experience. Dillard Wood and William Preskitt, Jr., historians of the Pentecostal Fire-Baptized Holiness Church, wrote:

> Hayes, like others in the Fire-Baptized Holiness Church, thought he had the Holy Ghost. Reading about the Azusa Street revival created a hunger

in his heart for the experience of speaking in tongues. When Cashwell came to Toccoa, Hayes broke for the altar night after night until the night of February 14, when the Holy Ghost fell upon him, and he spoke with other tongues.[180]

Cashwell continued preaching throughout all of the Southeast, as did many of those who had received the Pentecostal experience at Cashwell's meetings. One of these people was F. M. Britton, who held meetings in a schoolhouse in Wauchula, Florida, in April of 1907. One of the people there at the time, William Emanuel, wrote:

> Souls were being saved and filled with the Spirit in the revival when the authorities stepped in and closed the schoolhouse doors to the evangelist. However, a small Seventh-Day Adventist church was made available, and the meetings continued day and night—sometimes all night. Many seekers were "slain" under the power of the Spirit. Some would lie prostrate for hours, then burst forth in a heavenly language. Others were entranced by a vision of the coming of Jesus.[181]

Britton later held meetings at the Pleasant Grove Camp Ground, Durant, Florida, during June and July of 1907, where "many were saved, reclaimed, and revived, and about seventy were filled with the Holy Ghost, speaking in other tongues as the Holy Ghost gave them utterance."[182] Among those who received the infilling of the Spirit were many ministers and Christian workers who went from there to scatter the fires of the revival far and wide.

In the spring of 1907, Cashwell conducted a revival meeting in Birmingham, Alabama, where H. G. Rodgers and M. M. Pinson received the Pentecostal experience.[183] These two former Methodist ministers later formed a Pentecostal Association in the Mississippi Valley which eventually became an important component of the Assemblies of God denomination.[184] Pinson edited the Pentecostal periodical, *Word and Witness*, which eventually merged with E. N. Bell's *Apostolic Faith*.[185] Pinson held meetings in Birmingham, Alabama, during June of 1907 which were attended by Church of God (Cleveland, Tenn.) leader A. J. Tomlinson, whose first direct encounter with the phenomenon of tongues was at this time.[186]

As a result of his observations of Pinson's meetings, Tomlinson invited Cashwell to introduce the Pentecostal message at a meeting of the Church of God Annual Assembly in Cleveland, Tennessee, where, on January 12, 1908, Tomlinson received the baptism in the Holy Spirit.[187] In his own words:

> On Sunday morning, January 12, while he [Cashwell] was preaching, a peculiar sensation took hold of me, and almost unconsciously I slipped

off my chair in a heap on the rostrum at Brother Cashwell's feet. I did not know what such an experience meant. My mind was clear, but a peculiar power so enveloped and thrilled my whole being that I concluded to yield myself up and await results. I was soon lost to my surroundings as I lay there on the floor, occupied only with God and eternal things.[188]

According to Church of God historian Charles W. Conn, Tomlinson testified to speaking in about ten unknown languages on this occasion.[189]

Florence Crawford

The southeastern U.S. was only one of several areas to be profoundly affected by the outpouring of the Holy Spirit at Azusa Street. In late 1906, Florence Crawford went from the Azusa Street Mission to Salem, Oregon, where she had stopped to take part in some special meetings being conducted by a minister from Los Angeles. While she was there, she was invited to hold services in a mission hall at Second and Main Streets in Portland, Oregon. She arrived on Christmas Day and preached that afternoon. The building had once been used as a blacksmith shop and had been cleaned up and set apart for use as a church. As a result of her preaching, many people were converted, and the pastor in charge soon turned the work over to her. Not long after she accepted the pastorate, she discontinued the practice of taking collections, and this procedure, which had also characterized Seymour's ministry at Azusa Street, became a hallmark of her ministry for the rest of her life. A tremendous revival took place at the church soon after she became pastor. "Every chair was filled, the aisles packed, the doorway jammed. Crowds stood out into the streets. City officials became concerned because of fire hazards. . . ."[190] With growth to a membership of over 1000 people within three years, Crawford's "Apostolic Faith Mission" had to move to different places of worship on several occasions.[191] By 1966, Crawford's work had grown to forty-two churches serving 4,764 members.[192]

4

THE AFTERMATH–
EARLY PENTECOSTALISM

THE AZUSA STREET MISSION'S
CONTINUED INFLUENCE

C. H. Mason and the Church of God in Christ

AFTER 1906, THE AZUSA STREET MISSION continued as an important center of the worldwide Pentecostal revival. In March of 1907, for example, C. H. Mason, one of the two leaders of the Church of God in Christ in Memphis, Tennessee, travelled to Los Angeles and was filled with the Holy Spirit at Azusa Street.[1] He had brought two of his fellow ministers, John A. Jeter and D. J. Young, who also received the gift of tongues.[2] After remaining there for five weeks, they returned to Memphis to find that many of the people in their churches had already found the Pentecostal experience through the ministry of Glenn A. Cook,[3] an independent evangelist who had received the baptism of the Spirit at Azusa Street a few months previously.[4] As a result of the introduction of Pentecostalism into the Church of God in Christ, controversy arose. Opponents of the new experience were led by C. P. Jones, while its adherents sided with Mason. Jones changed the name of his group to "The Church of Christ (Holiness) U.S.A.," while Mason and his followers retained the name "Church of God in Christ."[5]

Rachel F. Sizelove and her husband remained in Los Angeles from the time of her baptism in the Spirit (July 1906) until May of 1907, at which time the Lord impressed her to return to Springfield, Missouri, to tell her relatives what the Lord had done for her.[6] She asked for prayer for guidance at the Azusa Street Mission. The members gathered around her, and she received a word of confirmation from the Lord, being told, "My child, you may go and I will be with you."[7] She departed by train for Springfield with "a dear black woman" who had been at the Apostolic Faith Mission on Azusa Street. This woman was on her way to become a missionary to Africa. The two talked with as many people on the train as they could about the "mighty outpouring of the Holy Spirit" that had begun at Azusa Street. The conductor gave them permission to hold services on the train. Rachel Sizelove wrote that "the people listened intently and many were convicted."[8]

Sizelove wrote that on her return to Springfield, the Holy Spirit spoke through her in tongues and gave the interpretation: "The Holy Spirit as a dove shall hover over this place."[9] She wrote that the neighbors soon came in to inquire about the Pentecostal revival in Los Angeles.[10] She wrote:

> After telling them how the Lord baptized me with the Holy Spirit, I said, "We have been talking of the wonderful works of God. Let us kneel down and pray before you leave." And while I was praying, the Holy Spirit prayed through me in other tongues. When my sister heard me praying in tongues, she reached her hands toward heaven and cried, "O Lord, this is You, and I want the baptism in the Holy Spirit." She was slain under the mighty power of God and received the baptism, spoke and sang in tongues. She was the first to receive the baptism in Springfield. How precious and holy the very atmosphere seemed in that all-night meeting, June 1, 1907.[11]

By the time the Azusa Street Mission closed in 1909, Pentecostalism had begun to make significant inroads into the mainstream of American religious life; those effects continued with increasing force throughout all of the twentieth century.[12]

THE CHRISTIAN AND MISSIONARY ALLIANCE

Akron, Ohio

One of the first important religious bodies to feel the effects of this revival was the Christian and Missionary Alliance (CMA). One of the earliest centers of Pentecostal activity in the CMA was C. A. McKinney's church in Akron, Ohio.[13] In January of 1907 Miss Ivey Campbell returned to her home church in East Liverpool, Ohio, from Azusa Street, where she had received the baptism in the Holy Spirit.[14] She spoke of her experience to a group in Akron, and many people accepted the Pentecostal message.[15] Among them was W. A. Cramer, the CMA superintendent in Cleveland, who returned to that city to give testimony and spread the message there. He wrote in the April 27 edition of the *Christian and Missionary Alliance Weekly* that "the power of God fell on me . . . and the Holy Spirit soon began to speak through me in an utterance I had never learned."[16]

Indianapolis

Also in January of 1907, a Pentecostal revival broke out in the CMA Gospel Tabernacle in Indianapolis as a result of Glenn A. Cook's testimony of his experiences at Azusa Street.[17] Cook was a former Baptist who became a free-lance Holiness preacher and then became active in the Azusa Street Mission early in its history.[18] He had supervised the correspondence at Azusa Street Mission[19] and was one of its twelve elders.[20] As we have already seen, he later carried the message of Pentecost to the Church of God in Christ, a black Holiness denomination.[21] During Cook's meetings at Indianapolis, J. Roswell Flower, a young law student who was later to become general superintendent of the Assemblies of God denomination, was converted to Christianity.[22]

Members of the CMA church in Indianapolis asked if "tarrying" meetings could be held there for people who were seeking the baptism in the Holy Spirit with the gift of tongues following. Although the pastor, Dr. G. N. Eldridge, was away on vacation in California at this time, permission was granted. However, when Dr. Eldridge discovered what was happening, he sent a telegram to a church officer advising him to deny the use of the church for this purpose. A large number of people left to go elsewhere in Indianapolis in order to seek the baptism in the Spirit. Meanwhile, after Cook returned to his home in Los Angeles, an evangelistic team arrived at Dr. Eldridge's church. This "band" of workers included Thomas Hezmalhalch, a former Wesleyan Methodist minister from Leeds, England, Harry Derheimer of Chicago, Miss Celia Smock, and Mrs. Leonora Hall.[23] Among those who attended these meetings was Alice Reynolds [Flower], who wrote:

Under the ministry of "brother Tom" [Hezmalhalch] (as we were encouraged to address him because his name was so difficult) and his party, the moving of God's Spirit increased and copious showers of latter rain came from heaven. This is when I received the baptism in the Holy Spirit (Easter Sunday, March 21, 1907).

. . . We literally sat on the edge of our chairs, so eager were we to obey the Spirit and fit into our place in the program developed under God. . . . Just a week after receiving the Comforter, I had my first experience of singing in the heavenly choir. A brother was testifying at some length when Brother Tom interrupted him: "Hold on, brother, God is seeking to move in our midst." The brother stopped, then continued. Again Brother Tom checked him, kindly but firmly. Then we heard it—a low humming that gradually rose in harmonious crescendo as six individuals in different parts of the audience rose spontaneously to their feet and a full tide of glorious melody poured forth in ecstatic worship and praise.

Having been one of that group, I can still feel the thrill as, for the first time, from my innermost being heavenly music poured forth like strains through the pipes of some great organ. No effort, no self-consciousness—just the flowing forth of celestial harmony like a foretaste of divine rapture.[24]

These meetings received unfavorable publicity from the *Indianapolis Star*. The mayor of Indianapolis, Mr. Bookwalter, visited the meetings and afterward told reporters, "These meetings are nothing different from the old-time Methodist revivals that my mother took me to when I was a boy. There is nothing to be alarmed about."[25] This comment put a stop to most of the unfavorable publicity, and the Pentecostal message spread from Indianapolis to many other parts of Indiana.[26]

Indianapolis became a stronghold of the Holiness-Pentecostal movement and in 1918 became the city in which Maria B. Woodworth-Etter chose to found her own independent church, after about thirty-five years of itinerant ministry.[27] On October 30–31, 1918, Aimee Semple McPherson, who later founded the International Church of the Foursquare Gospel, visited her and wrote:

For years I have been longing to meet Sister Etter, and have been talking about it more in recent months. I have longed to hear her preach and be at her meetings. We have inquired of those who have read the newspapers, however, and they say that the ban is not lifted. . . .

Well, there was a special meeting of the officials of Indianapolis yesterday, and they decided to lift the ban at midnight tonight, this being just an hour and a half after we arrived. Tomorrow Mrs. Etter's tabernacle will be open and I will have the desire of my heart. Glory!

A day of rest and praise. Called upon Mrs. Etter, and attended the meeting in her tabernacle tonight. We rejoiced and praised the Lord together.

The power of God fell; even though there were only a very few at the meeting, the Lord was there showering His blessings upon us.[28]

According to Wayne Warner, "the ban" of which Aimee wrote was the result of an influenza epidemic which was raging at this time.[29]

The following year, Thomas Paino, Sr., who later pastored the Woodworth-Etter Tabernacle in Indianapolis, was converted to Christianity in one of Mrs. Woodworth-Etter's meetings. He wrote:

In 1933 we were called back to the church in Indianapolis where I had come to know the Lord. During the years at West Side Gospel Tabernacle we have seen many churches started from the home church. Nearly one hundred of our young people are preaching the Gospel.[30]

Nyack, New York

Of course, Indianapolis was not the only city affected by the early Pentecostal revival. In May of 1907, revival erupted at the CMA Missionary Training Institute in Nyack, New York, north of New York City. Founded by Dr. A. B. Simpson in 1882 or 1883, Nyack Missionary Training Institute was one of the first Bible institutes in America. Two of the members of the faculty, George P. Pardington and William Coit Stevens, taught that the church was soon to receive the "Latter Rain." The school as a whole had received reports of the outpouring of the Spirit in Los Angeles with both rejoicing and caution. A few individuals at the school had sought and received the Pentecostal experience, including John Coxe, C. A. McKinney, J. T. Boddy, John Waggoner, D. W. Myland, and William Cramer. They did not publicize these experiences, however, because of the CMA's wish that members approach this matter cautiously.[31]

Despite efforts to contain the Pentecostal manifestations, they broke out during the closing exercises of the school and the general convention in May, 1907. Peter Robinson, a black delegate from Pittsburgh, "prayed with such power that the night meeting could no longer be controlled from the platform."[32] Not certain how to proceed at this point, the leaders sent for the men who had received the Pentecostal experience to guide the people. Nevertheless, when Cramer, Coxe, and Cullen began leading, it only "seemed to heighten the already supercharged atmosphere."[33] Seeing the extent to which God was moving on the people, Cramer uttered a sentence of praise in tongues. This utterance was so powerful that one of the students, David McDowell, "fell to the floor as though struck by a sledge hammer."[34] He wrote:

The power of God came mightily among us until the chapel was one volume of prayer, tears and crying to God. In the gray of the morning one of the lady students who had been confessing and pouring out her heart, as she lay prostrate on the rostrum, began to speak in tongues. Miss Lucy Villars, a returned missionary from the Congo, who was sitting by her, declared that she was speaking in a tongue of the Congo, which she understood and translated for us.[35]

Cleveland, Ohio

In August of the same year, there was a gracious visitation of the Holy Spirit at the CMA camp at Beulah Park in Cleveland, Ohio. William Cramer was again presiding at this meeting. Among those baptized in the Holy Spirit were D. W. Kerr, pastor of the Christian and Missionary Alliance Tabernacle in Dayton, Ohio; John Salmon of Toronto, vice president of the CMA; and the wife of Dr. William T. MacArthur, district superintendent of the Northwest.[36] D. W. Kerr's daughter, Christine Kerr Peirce, recounts this summer camp meeting at Beulah Park:

There seemed to be an awe and a hush over the whole grounds. Here and there little groups were talking earnestly about this strange happening. . . . We recall seeing people prone upon the ground as God's Spirit began to move.[37]

In 1911, D. W. Kerr took over the pastorate of the CMA church in Cleveland. Since nearly all the members of the church had received the baptism in the Holy Spirit, they voted to become the Pentecostal Church of Cleveland, Ohio.[38]

Pennsylvania and New York

A visitation similar to that at Beulah Park also took place at the CMA camp at Rocky Springs Park, Pennsylvania, where "a drenching shower of the Latter Rain fell upon the souls who were plowing up the fallow ground by seeking God from the sunrise prayer meetings until the early hours of the next morning."[39] David McDowell, the student who had been present at the Nyack Convention the previous May, was filled with the Spirit at this time. Observing this, J. R. Kline, a CMA pastor from Tottenville, Staten Island, New York, cried out, "I see a fire over his head!"[40] When McDowell lowered his hands after raising them in worship, his hands fell, unexpectedly, on the heads of two of the wives of CMA leaders. These women were immediately filled with the Spirit and spoke in tongues.[41]

That evening, McDowell conducted a meeting in a mission in Lancaster, Pennsylvania, where many people received the fullness of the

Holy Spirit. One woman reported two years later that she had been healed of cancer at that meeting.[42] He would walk among the seekers in order to lay his hands upon them for the reception of the Spirit, but in each case, before he was able to place his hands on their heads, they would suddenly begin to speak in tongues.[43]

Shortly after these events, still in August of 1907, another convention was held in Nyack. Alfred Snead, who later became the missionary secretary of the CMA, spoke in tongues at this time. McDowell addressed a youth meeting where he stated that "this is the Latter Rain for which we have been praying for years."[44] People flocked to the altar, and about one hundred were filled with the Spirit.[45]

San Francisco

Also in the summer of 1907, a revival swept through Carrie Judd Montgomery's Beulah Heights orphanage in San Francisco, where many children were converted to Christ. One of the workers was baptized in the Holy Spirit, speaking and singing in tongues.[46] This person's dedication subsequent to her Pentecostal baptism impressed Montgomery. Montgomery's husband had returned from Azusa Street in 1906 convinced that the revival was from God, but it was not until June of 1908 that she received the fulness of the Holy Spirit and spoke in tongues.[47] This took place at the home of a friend in Chicago during a CMA convention at which she was ministering.[48] Throughout the next week, she prayed and sang in Chinese, according to Harriette Shimer, a missionary to China for the Society of Friends, who was also speaking at the convention.[49]

Alliance, Ohio

In the summer of 1908, the Pentecostal-dominated CMA camp meeting in Alliance, Ohio, received a great deal of press coverage, although much of it was unfavorable.[50] J. T. Boddy, probably writing of this meeting, said that he "saw what could not be less than fifty to seventy-five people prostrated at one time under the power of God, numbers of whom received the baptism in the Spirit."[51]

Controversy over Tongues

The founder and president of the Christian and Missionary Alliance, A. B. Simpson, struggled a great deal with questions that had arisen as a result of the new Pentecostal revival, especially since so many of the churches in the CMA had been touched by this great outpouring of God's Spirit. In August of 1907, seeking the will of God concerning the gift of tongues, he returned to Old Orchard, Maine, where God had healed him in August of 1881. Here, Simpson wrote that he "pressed upon Him a new claim for a mighty baptism of the Holy Ghost in His complete pentecostal fullness, embracing all the gifts and graces of the Spirit for my special need at this time."[52] He continued:

> He met me as I lay upon my face before Him with a distinct illumination. Then as the presence began to fade and I cried out to Him to stay, He bade me believe and take it all by simple faith as I had taken my healing twenty-six years before. I did so and was enabled definitely to believe and claim it all and rest in Him.[53]

According to his biographers, Simpson's diary over the next several months recorded a "sustained, intense searching through prayer and fasting for a deeper, fuller baptism of the Spirit in all His Manifestations";[54] however, he never received the gift of tongues. As a result of this, he concluded that, while the gift of tongues was one manifestation of the infilling of the Holy Spirit, it is "neither necessary nor the sole evidence of such an experience."[55]

Although Simpson never endorsed the Pentecostal doctrine of tongues as the sole evidence of the baptism in the Holy Spirit, he specifically requested Carrie Judd Montgomery to continue to share her Pentecostal experience with his congregation whenever she visited Nyack.[56] Dr. Simpson summed up the Alliance position for the first time in April of 1910:

> We fully recognize all the gifts of the Spirit, including "diverse kinds of tongues" as belonging to the church in every age. And many of our most wise and honored workers both in the homeland and in the mission field have had this experience.

> But we are opposed to the teaching that this special gift is for all or is the evidence of the Baptism of the Holy Ghost. Nor can we receive or use to edification in our work and assemblies those who press these extreme and unscriptural views.[57]

Years later, the Alliance position was known as "seek not, forbid not."[58] Carl Brumback commented concerning this position:

> The proclamation of the New Testament experience was not a message of condemnation, but an invitation to rejoice in the restoration of this experience to His Church. . . . Pentecostal believers were not out to prove that their godly Alliance brethren knew nothing of the indwelling, anointing Spirit of God. They simply believed that the *full* New Testament bap-

tism in the Spirit was made manifest by the *glossolalia*, and that it was the will of God to pour out His Spirit in this manner upon all flesh.[59]

As a result of this doctrinal disagreement between the CMA and the new Pentecostal movement, "several great churches in the Alliance, and numerous outstanding ministers, reluctantly parted company with the parent body when the Pentecostal testimony was stifled by the Alliance leadership. Such 'come-outers' provided a substantial proportion of early Assemblies of God leadership."[60] A close associate of A. B. Simpson, Dr. Kenneth MacKenzie, commented:

> I cannot refrain from recording the agony through which he passed when so many of his most trusted and valued friends and workers withdrew from him because he did not go with them to the limit which was their ideal.[61]

The controversy over tongues influenced the CMA's decision to draft a new constitution in 1912 in order to avoid further property losses due to the defection of many churches to the Pentecostal movement.[62] Soon, many of the denominations of the Holiness movement began writing specific repudiations of the "Tongues Movement" into their official creeds and minutes.[63] Alfred G. Garr wrote, "all our old Holiness friends rejected us; the old doors were closed."[64] As Robert Mapes Anderson points out, "by 1912 the Holiness-Fundamentalist camp presented an almost unbroken front against the Pentecostal Movement."[65]

Many of the Holiness denominations either became Pentecostal or lost members to the new Pentecostal movement, and the greatest numbers of defections to Pentecostalism were probably from the CMA. A number of prominent pastors withdrew from this society to join the new movement, and in many cities entire congregations left the CMA for Pentecostalism, taking their church property with them.[66]

According to David McDowell, in 1912 A. B. Simpson remarked to him, "David, I did what I thought was best, but I am afraid that I missed it." Fifteen years later, Albert E. Funk, foreign secretary of the CMA, observed, "David, the Alliance has missed God!"[67]

CENTERS OF PENTECOSTALISM

In the southwestern United States, many Holiness denominations embraced Pentecostalism, and in the Pacific Northwest, Florence Crawford's work began to organize many new Pentecostals into a fellowship of churches. Scattered between these two regions was an array of independent Pentecostal missions, sometimes federated in small clusters, centering in regional camp meetings. To this uncommitted group of Pentecostals, a call was issued in December 1913 for a "General Convention of Pentecostal Saints and Churches of God in Christ."[68] This call was issued by M. M. Pinson, A. P. Collins, H. A. Goss, D. C. O. Opperman, and E. N. Bell[69] and resulted in the organization of the Assemblies of God the following April in Hot Springs, Arkansas.[70] The primary purpose of the convention was to bring stability to the Pentecostal movement by achieving agreement on fundamental doctrines and cooperation in missionary ventures.[71]

New York City

One of the earliest Assemblies of God churches was Glad Tidings Tabernacle in New York City. In January of 1907, seven years before the Hot Springs convention, Marie Burgess went to New York to conduct meetings in a Holiness mission on 41st St.[72] The congregation received the news gladly that God was pouring out his Spirit upon all flesh as he had in the first century, but the leader of the mission terminated her meetings after a period of four weeks.[73] She conducted prayer services in various homes for a while, and in May she and her co-worker, Jessie Brown, opened Glad Tidings Hall on 42nd St.[74] From here the Pentecostal revival spread to other parts of New York State, including Nyack Bible Institute and parts of New Jersey.[75] Later, Glad Tidings Tabernacle moved to 33rd St., opposite the General Post Office.[76] While meetings were still being held at 42nd St., in June of 1908 Robert A. Brown, Alfred Monroe, and G. Anderson all received the baptism in the Holy Ghost at Glad Tidings Hall.[77] In October of the following year, Miss Burgess was married to Robert A. Brown, and they served many years as pastors in New York City.[78]

Chicago

Another important city, Chicago, became a major center for the spread of the Pentecostal movement after William H. Durham, pastor of the North Avenue Mission there, visited Azusa Street and found the Pentecostal experience on March 2, 1907.[79] Durham wrote of this as follows:

> Pastor Seymour said that he had retired to rest early in the evening, and the Spirit had spoken to him and said, "Brother Durham will get the bap-

tism tonight," and he arose and came down. When he beheld the won-drous sight of the Chicago pastor being filled with the Spirit, he prophe-sied that wherever this man would preach, the Holy Spirit would fall on the people.[80]

After Durham returned to Chicago, a powerful Pentecostal revival broke out at his North Avenue Mission. Historian Thomas William Miller has written:

> When Durham returned to Chicago, a Pentecostal revival broke out which replicated, if it did not exceed, the supernatural events of the Azusa Street Mission. The North Avenue Mission was so full of the power of God, ac-cording to eyewitnesses, that "a thick haze . . . like blue smoke" filled its upper region. When this haze was present, wrote pioneer Howard Goss, the people entering the building would fall down in the aisles. Some never got to sit in the pews. Many came through to the baptism or received di-vine healing.[81]

Pastor Durham wrote of his mission in Chicago during this time:

> People began to come in considerable numbers. Soon our little place would not hold them. Best of all, God met those who came. We had meetings every night, and they generally ran more than half the night–sometimes all night. The teaching was simple–to repent of every known sin, yield fully to God, resting on the finished work of Christ, fully trusting in his precious blood, and that God would pour the Spirit upon us. One after another, God met the seekers. It was nothing unusual to hear people at almost all hours of the night receiving the Spirit, speaking in tongues and singing in the Spirit.[82]

In April, the month following Durham's experience at Azusa Street, A. H. Argue, who had been a businessman in Winnipeg, Manitoba, in Canada, visited Durham's North Avenue Mission in Chicago and received the baptism in the Holy Ghost.[83] Soon after this, he be-came one of the greatest evangelists of the early Pentecostal move-ment in Canada.[84]

E. N. Bell, who was at that time a Baptist pastor in Fort Worth, Texas, also received the baptism in the Holy Spirit at Durham's mission.[85] He returned to Texas to become prominent among former associ-ates of Charles Parham and came to edit their periodical, *Apostolic Faith*.[86]

A few months later, in June of 1907, another Chicago pastor, William H. Piper, stated publicly that he had accepted the Pente-costal movement.[87] Piper had been a former overseer in John Al-exander Dowie's Zion.[88] He wrote in his periodical, the *Latter Rain Evangel*:

> The Stone Church was opened December 9, 1906. The people who stood with me at that time had been so thoroughly prejudiced against the Latter Rain movement that I thought it was wise temporarily not to say very much on that subject, although before that time I had preached frequently about the Holy Spirit.[89]

Although it was not until February of 1908 that Piper himself was to receive the fulness of the Spirit, the Stone Church very early became one of the most important centers of the new Pentecostal movement, both before and after his sudden death in 1910.[90]

Within a few months after William Durham's experience at Azusa Street, a great deal of friction began to develop between him and William J. Seymour over the issue of sanctification.[91] Seymour believed that there was an experience of entire sanctification after regeneration, but distinct from the baptism in the Holy Spirit.[92] Durham, on the other hand, understood sanctification to be a process continuing throughout one's Christian life. For him, there were only two experiences: conversion and the baptism of the Holy Ghost; while for Seymour, there were three stages in the Christian experience: conversion, entire sanctification, and the baptism of the Holy Spirit.[93] The disagreement between Seymour and Durham (which came to be known as the "finished work" controversy) reached crisis proportions when, in 1910, Durham preached at a Pentecostal convention in Chicago and attempted to discredit the Wesleyan view of sanctification as a second definite work of grace.[94]

In February of 1911, Durham went to Los Angeles with his message. At first, he sought to preach it at the Upper Room Mission, but the pastor, Elmer Fisher, refused to let him preach this doctrine there.[95] Durham then went to Azusa Street, where Seymour had been holding forth, although he was at that time absent, in the East. Bartleman wrote of Durham's meetings at Azusa Street during this time:

> He started meetings and the saints flocked back to the old place and filled it again with the high praises of God. . . . God had gathered many of the old Azusa workers back, from many parts of the world, to Los Angeles again evidently for this. It was called by many the second shower of the Latter Rain. On Sunday, the place was crowded and five hundred were turned away. The people would not leave their seats between meetings for fear of losing them.[96]

When Seymour returned and discovered that Durham was preaching against the Wesleyan doctrine of a second work of grace, he and his trustees padlocked all of the doors to the mission. Bartleman wrote:

May 2, I went to Azusa Street after noon, as usual. But to our surprise, we found the doors all locked, with chain and padlock. Brother Seymour had hastened back from the east and with his trustees decided to lock Brother Durham out. But they locked God and the saints out also, from the old cradle of power. It was Durham's message they objected to.

I secured Kohler Street Mission temporarily, and the "cloud" moved with us. Rather, it led us there. In a few days Brother Durham rented a large building at the corner of Seventh and Los Angeles streets. A thousand people attended the meetings here on Sundays. We had an ordinary congregation of four hundred week nights. Here the "cloud" rested. God's glory filled the place. "Azusa" became deserted. The Lord was with Brother Durham in great power. God set His seal especially on present truth to be established. He preached a gospel of salvation by faith. He was used mightily to draw anew a clear line of demarcation between salvation by works and faith, between law and grace.[97]

A. C. Valdez, Sr., wrote of Durham's meetings at Seventh and Los Angeles as follows:

Meetings there had such power that no one cared what time it was. Clocks were for human activities, not God's. People just stayed in the presence of the Holy Spirit. Thousands were saved, baptized and healed.[98]

Opposition to Durham became intense because of his "finished work" teachings, and he did not remain in Los Angeles for long. He began a speaking tour in the East, returned to Chicago, and died a few months later.[99] His viewpoint, however, continued to spread rapidly within the Pentecostal movement. William Menzies writes:

Almost without exception, the independent ministers and congregations that were emerging out of the Pentecostal revival, which later coalesced to form the Assemblies of God, adopted Durham's "Finished Work" view of sanctification. Only those Holiness-Pentecostal bodies in the Southeast and the Apostolic Faith association of Parham and Crawford preserved the traditional Wesleyan view.[100]

CANADIAN PENTECOSTALISM

Winnipeg

One great impetus for the development of Pentecostalism in Canada was A. H. Argue's experience of the baptism of the Holy Spirit as a result of William H. Durham's ministry. Returning to Winnipeg in late April of 1907, he began holding meetings at his home. A "real Pentecostal meeting was started at 501 Alexander Avenue, Winnipeg, where the power fell and a mighty revival began,"[101] spreading even to a nearby Indian reservation.

A. H. Argue soon sold his real estate business and began working full time as a pastor and evangelist. Among the first seekers of the baptism of the Holy Spirit under his ministry were Harry Horton, Franklin Small, A. G. Ward, R. J. Scott, and John McAlister, all of whom became leaders in the Canadian Pentecostal movement.[102] Franklin Small, for example, who later founded the Apostolic Church of Pentecost in 1921, received his first exposure to Pentecostalism under A. H. Argue's ministry in April of 1907.[103] He wrote:

> In the Spring of 1907 in the month of April, one Sunday while [I was] passing a mission hall on Alexander Avenue, there stood a crowd of curious people at the door. What can this mean? Investigation revealed Rev. A. H. Argue, who had been associated with holiness work in Winnipeg, had just returned from Chicago, having received the baptism of the Holy Spirit, speaking with other tongues.[104]

Frank Small wandered through the crowd and found a vacant chair in the rear of the mission hall and seated himself. He began listening to an elderly man facing the audience whose eyes were closed and hands were raised. He was speaking in tongues; then he opened his eyes and said in English, "Friends, this is a gift from heaven."[105] Many others gave testimony, and Small wrote of the meeting:

> I sensed the mighty presence of God. . . . I was definitely thrilled. My heart said, "there is fire here—this has a real ring!" I resolved firmly in my heart that this is what I'm looking for. I was truly convinced it was of God, for one could sense the presence and power of God resting upon the meeting.[106]

A few days later, Small brought his mother to one of Argue's meetings. Although she had previously opposed these "Latter Rain people," she told her son that the meetings at the mission were "the nearest things to old-fashioned Methodism I have seen since I was a little girl."[107] That evening, they both went to a cottage prayer meeting held by Mrs. George Lockhart on Bannatyne Avenue in Winnipeg, where both of them received the baptism of the Holy Spirit.[108]

Archdeacon Phair, an Episcopal minister who had worked for about fifty years among the Indians of Northwest Canada, also received the Pentecostal experience in Winnipeg at this time.[109] He wrote:

> God led me to the foot of the Cross and humbled me in the dust before the One who loved me and gave Himself for me. I saw Him as I never had seen Him before. For some time I lay prostrate at His blessed feet, gazing on Him, and so enraptured with His unspeakable glory I felt lost to every being and everything but Himself alone. . . . He came in and spoke in an unknown tongue, and I had no words with which to praise Him for

ever deigning to do so. He shed abroad His love in my heart by the Holy Ghost, and there was great joy. It may appear strange when I assure my brethren that I am just beginning to understand my Bible, to see light in its light. If this great boon alone were all, I would most heartily urge upon all saints to wait upon the Lord patiently until they received the promise of the Father.[110]

A. G. Ward also received the baptism in the Holy Ghost in Winnipeg at this time.[111] He then went out to preach among the Indians of the Fisher River reservation, speaking through an interpreter.[112] Stanley Frodsham wrote of this as follows:

One day when he was preaching under the power of the Spirit, he began to speak in other tongues and his interpreter suddenly exclaimed, "Why, you are now speaking to us in our own language." It was a call for these Indians to advance. This remarkable manifestation had a marked effect on the hearers.[113]

A. G. Ward later brought the Pentecostal message to the New Mennonite church in Ontario.[114]

Attempts at Organization

The first steps toward organizing the Pentecostal movement in Canada were taken in June 1909 at a camp meeting at Markham, near Toronto, under A. G. Ward's direction. At this time, the Pentecostal Missionary Union was formed. These efforts were greatly opposed by many, especially the Hebdens, "who seemed to feel that God had called us away from all organizations. . . . Rather than engage in a controversy and thus endanger the spiritual state of this New Movement, we decided not to lay any stress upon the infant organization."[115] Mrs. Ellen Hebden was at this time "the acknowledged spokesman of the Latter Rain in Canada."[116] For this reason, ten years passed before any efforts at organization of Pentecostalism in Canada were successful.[117] Then, in 1919, the Pentecostal Assemblies of Canada were organized at a series of meetings held in Mille-Roches, Ontario; Montreal; Ottawa; and Kitchener, Ontario.[118]

Aimee Semple McPherson

One important early figure in the Canadian Pentecostal movement was Aimee Semple McPherson, who later founded the International Church of the Foursquare Gospel. Before she was married, Aimee Kennedy was converted to Christianity under the ministry of Robert

Semple in Ingersoll, Ontario, in December of 1907 and was filled with the Spirit early the next year. In August of 1908, she married Robert Semple, and they began holding meetings in London, Ontario, the following year in the home of Dr. Wortman.[119] She wrote:

> The teaching of Pentecost was practically new in the city at the time when the Lord led my husband thither. Inside of a year, however, over one hundred had received the baptism of the Holy Spirit with the Bible evidence, speaking in tongues, sinners had been saved, and there were several remarkable healings. As a result from the working of the Spirit in these meetings, a large, thriving, centrally located Pentecostal Mission has been built on one of the main streets and the work of God is progressing gloriously to this day.[120]

In January of 1910, Aimee was healed of a broken foot at William H. Durham's North Avenue Mission in Chicago.[121] Later that month, Robert and Aimee Semple went with Durham to a Pentecostal Convention in Toronto to assist him in ministry.[122] Shortly after this time, the Semples went to Hong Kong as missionaries, where Robert Semple died on August 4, just a few months after their arrival.[123] With an infant child born after its father's death, Aimee immediately returned to New York to visit her mother, arriving in April of 1911.[124]

In the spring of the following year, she married Harold M. McPherson and went with him to Providence, Rhode Island.[125] Three years later, she began preaching at Wednesday night prayer meetings and Sunday night services in the small Pentecostal churches near Providence.[126] Returning to her home town, Ingersoll, Ontario, in 1915, she began to gain a reputation as an evangelist in many parts of eastern Canada.[127] One of the meetings she held in Ontario was described by Sister E. Sharp of Mt. Forest, Ontario:

> When the meetings began at the tent it was noised abroad, and multitudes came from different parts of the country, from villages, towns and cities, and we had to meet every train. The promise, "*Everyone that asketh receiveth*," was truly fulfilled. In those blessed days of blessing and outpouring of the Spirit, many did not even ask, but only desired the gift, and the Lord baptized them with the Holy Spirit.[128]

In 1916 and 1917, Aimee Semple McPherson and her husband held camp meetings in Providence and at many other locations on the eastern seaboard of the U.S.[129] In the beginning of 1918, after almost two difficult years of itinerant ministry, Aimee and her husband separated and would eventually divorce in August of 1921.[130] Her reputation as an evangelist continued to grow, and later in 1918 she went on an evangelistic tour across the nation with her mother, Minnie Kennedy, before establishing a home base in Los Angeles.[131]

R. E. McAlister

Another important individual for the early Pentecostal movement in Canada was R. E. McAlister, a young Holiness preacher who received the Pentecostal baptism in 1906 in Los Angeles. In 1911 he established one of the first Pentecostal assemblies in Canada, at Ottawa, from which the Pentecostal message spread far and wide. McAlister also pioneered a Pentecostal work in Kinburn, Ontario, at this time.[132]

In 1911 McAlister invited A. H. Argue to hold a convention in Ottawa. A number of remarkable healings occurred, including that of Mrs. C. E. Baker, a businessman's wife who was healed of cancer.[133] Through her healing, her husband came to Christ and gave up his business in order to become an evangelist. Mr. and Mrs. Baker then carried the Pentecostal message to Montreal in 1914.[134] Historian Thomas William Miller says of these meetings:

> Thousands were converted in the meetings, large sums of money were raised for evangelism, many new congregations were assisted or encouraged in getting started, and many effective workers and missionaries came out of the Montreal assembly.[135]

The Bakers invited Aimee Semple McPherson to Montreal in 1920, and "her meetings that year have been described as the greatest revival in the history of Quebec."[136]

REVIVAL CONTINUES: 1911–1916

Dallas, Texas

From the time that McAlister established his work in Ottawa until about 1916, there were many significant camp meetings that took place both in Canada and in the United States which helped the early Pentecostal movement to become firmly established in North America. Among them was that held by Maria B. Woodworth-Etter at Dallas, Texas, from July until December of 1912. Stanley Frodsham comments:

> In the city of Dallas, Texas, in 1912, the Lord gave a gracious visitation and His hands were stretched forth in a very special manner to heal the sick. Many came from different parts of the country and were not only healed of the Lord but filled with His Spirit.[137]

These meetings were hosted by F. F. Bosworth,[138] formerly the leader of John Alexander Dowie's Zion City music band.[139] Bosworth later became a controversial figure within the Pentecostal movement because he held that not all who were Spirit-baptized must speak in tongues, as long as one of the nine gifts of the Holy Spirit listed in 1 Corinthians 12 was evident in the person's life and ministry.[140] Bosworth wrote of Woodworth-Etter's Dallas meetings:

> Throngs packed the large tent from the first, two or three thousand often standing around the tent. Great numbers of the sick and afflicted came, and were brought, on cots and in different ways, reminding us of the scenes described in the Gospels, when our Lord was upon earth. . . . Many have been wonderfully healed before the service began, and sometimes there has been no preaching—nothing but the altar service. . . .
>
> The news of victory went out, and hundreds have already come from all over the United States, many bringing their sick hundreds of miles, some on cots in the baggage cars. . . .
>
> In almost every service for nearly three months, the slaying power so common in the day of Finney, Jonathan Edwards, etc., has been manifested. . . . Many have seen balls of fire and lights in and around the tent. . . . Jesus has appeared to many in the meetings, and many have at different times seen a great host of angels just above the audience.[141]

Carrie Judd Montgomery wrote in her periodical, *Triumph of Faith*:

> As we entered the Tabernacle on Saturday evening, we saw a crowd of rejoicing ones at the front, and we learned later that a deaf and dumb man, about sixty years of age, had just been saved and instantly healed by the power of God through Mrs. Etter's command of faith, as she bade the deaf and dumb demons to depart in Jesus' name.[142]

1913 Worldwide Pentecostal Camp Meeting and the Jesus' Name Controversy

During the meetings in Dallas, R. J. Scott extended an invitation to Woodworth-Etter to minister at the Worldwide Pentecostal Camp Meeting to be held the following spring.[143] Scott was a well-known businessman who had been filled with the Holy Spirit and who had a "dazzling vision" for "a colossal tent meeting to accommodate 5,000 persons, some from every continent."[144] According to A. C. Valdez, Sr.:

> In 1913, he made it a reality in the Arroyo Seco, where the Pasadena Highway entered Los Angeles.
>
> The main tent was the most gigantic I had ever seen. Nearby was a smaller tent to hold meetings for children. All of us lived in Tent City, laid out in

streets with names like "Praise Street." My parents and I lived on the corner of Praise and Glory streets, just one block from Hallelujah Avenue, the address of the main tent.[145]

Historian David Reed has commented that the Worldwide Pentecostal Camp Meeting in Los Angeles in April 1913 was "probably the high-water mark in the early pentecostal revival."[146] In Mrs. Woodworth-Etter's words,

> Thousands gathered from all over the state, some from foreign lands, and we believe it was the largest gathering of saints in the last days. The President, Bro. Scott, stated that two hundred ministers were on the platform, sitting in fellowship and love. The Lord was present showing His approval of the Word, with mighty signs and miracles, especially in healing and baptizing with the Holy Ghost and fire. The slaying power was also greatly manifested, and many were struck down with the power.[147]

One of the people healed at this meeting was George B. Studd, brother of C. T. Studd, the famed cricketer and missionary who had sailed for China with the "Cambridge Seven" under the auspices of the China Inland Mission in 1885. Woodworth-Etter wrote:

> Dear Brother Studd was taken sick with sciatic rheumatism and other diseases of the nerves. His suffering was very great. It appeared he would surely die, and continued to get worse, although many prayed for and with him. The hope was to bring him to the tent, and when they did bring him, he looked like a dead man. I told him to cheer up, he would not die but live to glorify God. We prayed for him with the laying on of hands, and he was soon walking around praising the Lord and helping me pray for others.[148]

Another well-known missionary, also one of the "Cambridge Seven," Stanley Smith wrote that he had received a letter from George Studd describing this meeting:

> My old friend Mr. George B. Studd, a man whose word is his bond, writes me: "I know Mrs. Etter and her work first hand. She was at our Los Angeles camp meeting last year, and there were many wonderful healings. She is sound in faith and mightily used of God, and has been so for years.[149]

Another participant in the 1913 Los Angeles camp meetings was A. H. Argue, who wrote in his memoirs of these meetings that he had played a small part in them with Mrs. Woodworth-Etter.[150] Valdez described the meetings:

> Far more impressive than the tents was the calibre of the major evangelist, Mrs. M. B. Woodworth-Etter, a woman who was in such bad health—deathly pale and weak—that she sometimes had to be carried up onto the crude, unfinished, pine platform.

There was nothing sickly, pale, or weak about her ministering. Once her equally ill husband joined her, she raised her small hands and the power of the Holy Spirit electrified us all.

A series of healing miracles thrilled the entire audience.[151]

R. E. McAlister preached at a baptismal service during these meetings and noted in passing that the baptismal formula which appeared in the book of Acts referred only to the name of Jesus.[152] One of the people present, John G. Schaepe, studied and prayed about this throughout that night, and early the following morning he ran through the camp shouting that the Lord had shown him the truth on baptism in the name of Jesus Christ. Many people were affected by this, including Frank Ewart and Glenn Cook.[153] After the camp meeting, groups of believers along the West Coast accepted rebaptism in Jesus' name.[154] Ewart began preaching "Jesus only" sermons on the West Coast, according to which the terms "Father, Son, and Holy Ghost" were titles for one person, Jesus. This doctrine was taught in order to reconcile Matthew 28 with the baptismal passages in Acts, since Matthew 28:19 records that Jesus told his disciples to "make disciples of all nations, baptizing them in the name of the Father and of the Son and of the Holy Spirit," while the book of Acts records that baptisms were performed "in the name of Jesus." Because this attempt at reconciliation of these passages seemed to result in a denial of the personhood of each of the members of the Trinity, it created considerable controversy, the trinitarians viewing the "Jesus only" people as heretical, since their views seemed to them to undermine the doctrine of the Trinity. In AD 210, Tertullian in *Against Praxeas* had complained that Praxeas, in holding to a similar doctrine, had "put the Holy Spirit to flight and crucified the Father."

According to David Reed, the "new revelation" of the name of Jesus eventually claimed nearly one-fifth of all American Pentecostals.[155] Some of the Pentecostal denominations adhering to this view included the United Pentecostal Church, the Pentecostal Assemblies of the World, and the Apostolic Church of Pentecost in Canada, which grew out of the work of Franklin Small.[156]

Malvern, Arkansas

After the Los Angeles meeting, another significant camp meeting took place during the summer of the same year, 1913, at Malvern, Arkansas. These meetings were attended by E. N. Bell, Maria Woodworth-Etter, and E. L. Tanner, who was to become an important pastor in West Monroe, Louisiana, from 1924 until 1954. He wrote of the meetings in Malvern that there was a manifestation of the heavenly choir:

> Sister Etter had asked the choir to stand and sing, "Holy, Holy, Holy" and to yield to the Spirit, for she believed the Lord was going to visit the meeting in a special way. As they sang, my wife and I, as well as the whole congregation, heard a separate and distinct choir of voices blending perfectly with those of the singers before us. The sound of music and voices came in from the front, then swelled to fill the entire large tent above our heads, and finally lifted to fade away in the distance. It was truly heavenly and not of this earth.[157]

Long Hill, Connecticut

At approximately the same time, in June of 1913, the heavenly choir became manifest at meetings held by Mrs. Woodworth-Etter at Long Hill, Connecticut. An eyewitness recalled:

> The nearest thing to which I can compare it is a complete band of skillful Italian violinists playing the most sacred music that could be imagined, combined with the mellow tones of a pipe-organ, and this is but a very poor description of what my ears heard.[158]

Mrs. Woodworth-Etter described these manifestations of the heavenly choir:

> At our last meeting at Long Hill, Conn., the heavenly choir surpassed anything I had ever heard. We had it two or three times a day, and there wasn't a discord. It was the Holy Ghost making harmony through these bodies and the singing was no earthly singing but heavenly. Sometimes I would be a little late in getting to the meeting and as I came up the hill the sound of the heavenly choir was wafted down. It sounded as if it came from heaven; it was the song of the redeemed.[159]

Stone Church, Chicago

In July of 1913, Mrs. Woodworth-Etter held meetings at the Stone Church in Chicago. There were many remarkable healings at these meetings, but even more remarkable was the spirit of unity that prevailed. She wrote:

> It was marvellous how God brought all the different Pentecostal missions together. I never permit any doctrinal points; no "isms," no antagonistic points to be aired or brought up in my meetings; nothing but Christ, and Him crucified, and the Resurrection. They soon understand and get their

eyes off one another, and forget their ideas and differences and begin to love one another and soon feel the need of getting deep in God. . . . We prayed for hundreds of those ministers and workers with the laying on of hands and the power of the Holy Ghost fell on all, many fell and lay at the feet of Jesus; like the prophets and apostles of old, they had visions of Heaven and saw things to come. . . . Many received gifts and special calls. . . . Oh, it was wonderful how the cloud of glory and power came down! Many staggered and fell, the power swept all over the house. This was something new, no one had ever seen anything like it. Many were saved and healed. Surely the power of the Lord was present to heal, save, and give gifts, and honored His word and our faith.[160]

According to the *Latter Rain Evangel*, there were newspaper reports of these meetings,[161] and after several remarkable healings advertising was no longer necessary; "people came by carloads on the electric, they came in automobiles, wheel chairs, and on foot from all directions."[162] Many people came to repentance, but "it wasn't the preaching that led them to repentance so much as the manifestation of the power of God."[163] Many who had sought the baptism in the Holy Spirit for years were swept into the experience, including one individual who had been to Los Angeles and had travelled all over the country visiting various conventions and camp meetings seeking this experience.[164]

Upper Room Mission, Los Angeles

At the Upper Room Mission in Los Angeles under the ministry of Elmer K. Fisher there was an unusual manifestation of the Heavenly Choir in the fall of 1913. Fisher's daughter, Ruth Carter, described it:

The sacred presence was so real that one after another the people stood to their feet, hands upraised, eyes closed, lost in worship.

The chorus of praise began to unite them. Even those who ordinarily were hardly able to carry a tune sang like opera singers. Then it blended into such harmony without a discordant note. It was what we called the "heavenly choir." As the cadences of this supernatural song rose and fell, the beauty of it was beyond description.[165]

1914 Worldwide Camp Meeting

In the following year, George and Carrie Judd Montgomery hosted the 1914 Worldwide Camp Meeting at Casadero, California, which was attended by such notable individuals as George Studd, Stanley Frodsham of Bournemouth, England, who later became a leader in the Assemblies of God denomination in the U.S., and Smith Wigglesworth, the world-renowned evangelist and apostle from Brandford, England.[166] Carrie Judd Montgomery invited both Holiness and Pentecostal people to come and worship at these meetings and "to learn better to appreciate each other's contribution to the on-going revival."[167]

Stanley Frodsham stated that within the first few days of the camp, Smith Wigglesworth had come during his first visit to America. That evening, he was told that if he had a word he was at liberty to speak. He did so under such a heavy anointing that he was asked to speak the next morning and again the next night. The invited speakers said, "this man has something we don't have; we would rather listen to him than that we should speak."[168] Shortly thereafter, George and Carrie Judd Montgomery were surprised to find him at the train station, about to leave before the end of the camp meeting. He explained that he was eager to visit his friend Stanley Frodsham. When they asked why he couldn't come to the camp, he explained that his friend couldn't afford it. They said to him, "Brother Wigglesworth, you are such a blessing to the people, and if you will only stay we will wire him to come and will pay all expenses."[169] Frodsham wrote that when this camp meeting had first been announced, he had had a great desire to go, but he was financially destitute.

> My wife and I were sitting on the verandah of the home in which we were staying in Pasadena, when a Western Union messenger boy came along on his bicycle. My wife said, "Here comes a telegram containing an invitation to the Casadero camp, stating that all your expenses will be paid." That was exactly the contents of the telegram![170]

For Frodsham, the high point of the camp meeting was to take walks with Smith Wigglesworth and George Studd every morning. "We would walk through those lovely redwoods, and at a quiet place we would all three drop on our knees. How those two blessed men of God poured out their hearts to Him each morning!"[171]

According to Paul G. Chappell, these meetings were particularly successful for two reasons: "first, the featured speaker was the dynamic Smith Wigglesworth of Great Britain and secondly, it was affected by the famous Pentecostal camp meeting at Arroyo Seco outside of Los Angeles in 1913."[172]

Philadelphia

Another important series of meetings took place during August of that year in Philadelphia. They were held by Maria B. Woodworth-Etter at the invitation of William Anderson. One person present wrote:

I saw the blind led on the ground and walk off the ground with their sight, also the deaf hear, and the dumb speak and lame people throw away their crutches, and they would walk and jump and dance for joy. Many deadly cancer cases were healed and I myself was healed from nervous headaches, which I had for many years. . . . I met a colored lady at a meeting in Philadelphia that had been to the camp-meeting, who was blind, and the Lord restored her sight to her again, and she is praising the Lord for healing her eyes.[173]

Mrs. Woodworth-Etter wrote of this meeting:

God wonderfully used Pastor Anderson, in tones of thunder, sounding like the voice of God. . . . Old men, women and children spake in languages, preaching and prophesying, singing new songs, the words of which had never before been heard. . . . Many of all classes joined the Holy Dance, or joy dance, filled with the Resurrection Life and Lightness, dancing with closed eyes, faces bright and shining. . . .

Bright lights were at times seen over the pulpit and over various people. . . .

The glory of the Lord was like a cloud, it swept over and over the place. We placed chairs on the platform; those who wanted special prayer and laying on of hands sat in the chairs. The power of God fell on everyone. They all got filled with the resurrection life, leaped, danced and shouted praises to God. Most of them fell and lay in green pastures. Scores of men and women were lying like dead all around. Strong men and women were weeping, both in and outside of the tent.[174]

During these meetings, Samuel P. Etter, Mrs. Woodworth-Etter's husband, died at the age of 71.[175] She wrote, "I took a fast train to Indianapolis, laid him in the beautiful Crown Hill Cemetery, and got back to Philadelphia to continue the meeting the following Saturday night."[176] Her biographer, Wayne E. Warner, wrote of this that the "kind-hearted, devout Samuel Etter would want it no other way."[177]

Woodworth-Etter continued her itinerant ministry from this time until founding her own church in Indianapolis in 1918, which she pastored until her death in 1924, after almost fifty years of ministry, at eighty years of age. The pace of her ministry was remarkable. In 1915, for example, she held at least eight camp meetings, each averaging about a month in duration, in Tampa, Atlanta, Chicago, St. Louis, Topeka, Colorado Springs, Los Angeles, and San Diego.[178]

Rhode Island

Also in the year 1915, Reuben and Christine Gibson started a small Pentecostal mission in East Providence, Rhode Island, the Church of the Firstborn.[179] This mission was later known as Faith Home and became a forerunner of Zion Bible Institute.[180] The Gibsons were personal friends of Aimee Semple McPherson, whom they had helped in the early stages of her ministry, particularly in 1916.

THE LATER YEARS: 1916–1947

Aimee Semple McPherson

A. C. Valdez, Sr., has written that between 1916 and 1922 there was a marked spiritual decline.

> When the Pentecostal Church needed a standard-bearer, Aimee Semple McPherson burst upon the scene. Revival and inspiration illumined her preaching. Many ministers in a spiritual depression got a lift from the bottom of the valley to the top of Mount Everest–a new dimension of faith and courage to spread the Word.[181]

Of course, during this time, Maria Woodworth-Etter was still ministering in many parts of the U.S. with astonishing results, as was A. H. Argue in Canada. In fact, Aimee Semple McPherson probably derived a good deal of inspiration from the ministry of Woodworth-Etter during this time.[182] She patterned her autobiography, *This Is That*, after Woodworth-Etter's *Signs and Wonders*, and she kept up the same incredible pace in the face of tremendous difficulties for many years. One of her most significant meetings in the earlier years was a Nation Wide Camp held at Philadelphia in the summer of 1918. The periodical *Bridal Call* of Los Angeles reported on these meetings:

> The picture of hundreds of saints standing upon their feet with hands lifted toward Heaven, eyes closed, and their upturned faces streaming with tears as they sing, as it were, a new song, and heavenly anthems voiced by the Holy Spirit through their lips in wondrous harmonic chords of love and thanksgiving, it is a never-to-be-forgotten sight, and resembles much the conception that I have always had of what it must be to be in Heaven before the throne of the Most High God.[183]

Shortly after these meetings opened, Elizabeth Sisson of New London, Connecticut, and Cyrus B. Fockler of Milwaukee joined Aimee Semple McPherson in ministry.[184]

When the meetings had first opened, "the power of God began to fall, and there was shouting, dancing and many prostrated";[185] however, local residents felt threatened. Aimee Semple McPherson wrote:

The next night an enormous crowd filled the tent and stood all around the outside. Every time there would be a manifestation of the Spirit, they would burst forth into peals of laughter, ridicule and mocking. . . . It seemed as if the people were wild with anger, and many came with clubs and cudgels in their hands. There were organized gangs with leaders, carrying whistles, who gave signals to their men. Detectives afterwards told us that it had been a pre-arranged program to wipe every tent off the ground that night, and open threats had been made to this end.[186]

The meeting was dismissed early, and Mrs. McPherson called for an all-night prayer meeting in order to pray for those who had been disrupting the meetings. Many people remained for this purpose, and, as Phoebe C. Bent reported, "with common consent every one sank to his knees in prayer, and for two hours poured out their cries to Heaven."[187] She continued:

When the praying had ceased, Sister McPherson, in that simple way of hers, said:

"Now, dear ones, just let us be quiet and see what God has for us." . . . Sister McPherson had retired to one end of the rostrum, where she swayed back and forth in a peculiar step or dance. This continued for some time, when suddenly she moved rapidly to the great upright piano, and began to play in the Spirit. The moment the first strange chord was struck, all eyes were riveted upon her. Wonderful music flowed from the keys as her hands flew rapidly to and fro. . . .

She then arose and gave a message in tongues, using certain things to emphasize her words. She took a megaphone which stood near at hand, and filled it with flowers from a vase on the pulpit, which typified the "horn of plenty." Next, placing the flowers on the floor, she watered them from a pitcher, showing that His saints would be revived and watered with the Latter Rain, which would soon fall upon them, and then closed with an exhortation to get ready for the soon oncoming of King Jesus.

Immediately after the message followed a tableau of the crucifixion. . . .

This tableau finished as the first early signs of dawn were breaking; and the great prayer of consecration which followed from the heart of Sister McPherson seemed not only to take in her own soul, but the souls of the whole camp.[188]

After this all-night prayer meeting, there were no further signs of trouble from the people who had been making disturbances. Aimee Semple McPherson wrote, "from this time on there has been no trouble of any kind with the outside people. The opposition has melted away like snow before the sunshine."[189] George Lloyd reminisced about the meetings that followed:

As the holy anthem broke forth, Sister McPherson seemed to float toward the piano, with uplifted hands and transfigured face, and commenced to play and sing in the Spirit. We had heard spiritual songs before, but never like this; . . . we were transported with ecstasy, and we were in the Spirit and were singing the New Song without any effort on our part.

Oh, the precious, heavenly music! Who can in any way describe it? We could only compare it to an aeolian harp with its rising and falling cadence, and its sweet, blended harmonies, only far sweeter and more pure in tone than the finest pipe organ, for this was the Holy Ghost playing upon God's great instrument not made with hands.[190]

Among the people attending these meetings were Christine and Reuben Gibson, who attempted, without success, to reunite Aimee with her husband, Harold McPherson, who was also attending.[191] Despite the efforts of these friends, Harold McPherson was granted a divorce from Aimee three years later.[192]

After the Nation-Wide Camp at Philadelphia, Aimee Semple McPherson preached at various places in the northwestern United States, then launched out on a cross-country gospel tour during October, November, and December of 1918. By late December, she had reached Los Angeles, where she preached at Temple Auditorium and Victoria Hall, where about 3500 people attended the New Year's Eve service. This was a time of tremendous revival, lasting for several weeks during the beginning of 1919.[193]

The pastor who had arranged for Aimee to speak at Victoria Hall, W. W. Fisher, observed:

The Latter Rain in great abundance has been coming on the saints since the sister opened her campaign. . . . I never, in all my extended ministry, saw so many slain under the mighty power of God as have been observed in the prayer room. . . . In some instances the Evangelist had only to lift her hands and the power would tumble them over. . . .

The Latter Rain is falling, some say even more copiously than the former rain, and we are exceedingly glad to be in the showers.[194]

On Sunday, January 19, Aimee began preaching at Bethel Temple, pastored by G. N. Eldridge, formerly pastor of the Christian and Missionary Alliance church in Indianapolis. She wrote:

Half an hour before meeting was opened people were being sent back to the overflow meetings or down to the basement, where an earnest prayer meeting was in progress. The heavenly singing rose, swelled to a cloud of glory and a mantle of adoration enfolded the people. . . .[195]

After a week, the crowds were too large, and the meetings were moved back to Victoria Hall. During these meetings, several people donated land, materials, and labor for the construction of a home for Aimee, her two children, and her mother. From this time onward, Los Angeles was her home base, although she spent a great deal of time away from home on evangelistic tours.

Shortly after the conclusion of the meetings in Los Angeles, Aimee made her way to San Francisco, where she preached at Glad Tidings Hall. She wrote:

> From the first meeting to the last the glory of God rested upon the people. The manifestations of the Spirit's power increased. . . . the last meeting found the crowds standing clear out onto the sidewalk. . . .
>
> These after meetings ofttimes continued until five and six in the morning.[196]

There were many dramatic healings at these meetings. A child who was about to have an operation on her throat was instantaneously healed, and the people were healed of tumors, accidental injuries, and internal problems.[197]

According to the pastor of Glad Tidings, Robert Craig,

> It was a glad day for the Kingdom of Christ in this place when the Lord directed our Sister Aimee Semple McPherson to hold a series of meetings in San Francisco.
>
> Literally towering mountains of prejudice against the Pentecostal movement have been swept away under the same candid and forceful presentation of the claims of the full Gospel Message. How many, many times church people have said: "This is just what we have wanted and is just like the power fell fifty years ago, except for the speaking in tongues."[198]

These meetings were attended by Carrie Judd Montgomery, who invited Aimee to hold services in Oakland, California. She was only able to hold two services there, however, sandwiched between the San Francisco meetings.[199]

Later the same year, after returning to her home in Los Angeles, Aimee went to New York City for a citywide "Holy Ghost Revival," which won her nationwide press coverage.[200] From there, she went to Baltimore, where she remained until Christmas.[201] The next year, she continued her demanding schedule, holding a citywide revival in Winnipeg, Manitoba, and meetings in Washington, D.C.; Dayton, Ohio; Alton, Illinois; West Virginia; Philadelphia; and Montreal.[202] At the meeting in Dayton, she invited ministers of many denominations so that they could judge for themselves whether or not God was in the Pentecostal movement. One of the people who attended was Charles H. Pridgeon from Pittsburgh. Upon his return, a tremendous revival erupted at his Bible institute there.[203]

A. H. Argue

Of course, Aimee Semple McPherson was not the only evangelist whom God was blessing during this time. During the summer of 1920, for example, Robert E. McAlister had invited A. H. Argue and his family for a campaign in Ottawa, where there was a great visitation of God accompanied by many remarkable healings. A. H. Argue believed these meetings to have been among the most remarkable in his experience until that time, because of the supernatural healings that accompanied them.[204] According to his daughter, Zelma, this was a result of the ministry of the Word by her father and also because a spirit of intercessory prayer had settled upon the people. "Strong men would rise in service and tell of being awakened in the night to prayer. No wonder we saw such results!"[205]

Among those who were healed was the wife of Commander R. M. T. Stephens of the Canadian Navy, one of the highest officials in Canada. His wife had been under the medical care of four doctors for several months, and her healing was reported in the Ottawa *Citizen*. She and her husband were baptized in the Holy Spirit during the meetings, creating curiosity in the community. McAlister wrote:

God has caused us at times to stand in wonder and adoration. Evangelist A. H. Argue . . . has been with us to bring the message of the outpouring of the Latter Rain. After three days it became evident divine healing was in God's thought at this time. Every day was crowded with signs and wonders. Souls were being saved and baptized daily.[206]

Montreal was also the scene of tremendous revival in 1920, first under the ministry of Aimee Semple McPherson, and then as a result of two visits made by Argue and his son and daughter, Watson and Zelma. The center for these revivals was a church pastored by Mr. and Mrs. Charles E. Baker. During the second campaign of the Argue team, which was in December, a 26-year-old man who had been deaf and dumb from the time he was four years old was healed, according to the testimony of a physician in Montreal.[207]

Raymond T. Richey

The year 1920 was also the year that Raymond T. Richey began his career as an evangelist. In October, Warren Collins was to hold a meeting in Hattiesburg, Mississippi. Richey had promised to assist him, but after he had made all of the preparations, he found that Collins could not come. Richey locked himself in a hotel room and prayed and fasted for three days. He then advertised that he would be preaching in the huge Red Circle Auditorium. On the first night, only fifteen people came, and on the second evening, there were only thirty or forty people present. On the third day, Richey prayed for the sick, and the first person for whom he prayed was instantaneously healed of a cracked arm. This was reported in a newspaper the following day, and that evening the building was filled. During the three weeks that followed, hundreds of people came to faith in Christ and hundreds more asked for prayer for healing.[208]

After these meetings, Richey's brother and sister-in-law, Andrew and Anna, joined him in ministry. Anna had been raised from her deathbed at one point, and Andrew had also once experienced a miraculous healing. They held campaigns in various parts of Mississippi and finally decided to hold a citywide interdenominational campaign in Houston. Raymond T. Richey's wife wrote of this:

> For forty days this revival continued and increased in attendance and interest and in conversions and healings all the while. Night after night the City Auditorium seating approximately seven thousand people was filled. At times even standing room was at a premium.

> God gave us five thousand conversions in this meeting and some of the most marvelous miracles of healing I have ever witnessed.[209]

Charles S. Price

Another extremely influential evangelist of the 1920s was Dr. Charles S. Price, who attended Aimee Semple McPherson's meetings in San Jose in 1920.[210] Dr. Price had been a Congregationalist minister in Santa Rosa, when some of the members of his church attended a meeting held by Aimee. In order to collect information to discredit her, Price attended himself. When he arrived, he had to sit in the section reserved for cripples, since the rest of the auditorium was filled to capacity. He later wrote, "that is where I belonged, but I did not know it at that time."[211] He was impressed with the service, and returned the following evening. He found that his modernistic theology could not withstand the power of God manifest in the services. This eventually resulted in his rededication and baptism in the Spirit.[212]

Two years later, Price held his first meeting as an itinerant evangelist in Ashland, Oregon. The Ministerial Union had invited him and rented a building that seated more people than the town's population. Yet it was soon packed to the doors. All the city's churches had been closed for the meetings, and, as Price commented, "having told the ministers that I was going to preach the whole truth, I proceeded to do so."[213] He reflected on the results:

> The power fell. Hundreds were saved and hundreds were healed. The first person that I prayed with for bodily healing fell under the power of God. I myself was afraid. I prayed for the second one and the same thing happened. I trembled in the presence of the Lord but both of them, rising to their feet and proclaiming they were healed, gave me courage and I went on praying. After that scores and scores would be prostrated under the power at one time. An adjacent building was rented so great became the crowds, and the meeting continued longer than its advertised time.[214]

One of Dr. Price's closest friends, Reverend Thomas J. McCrossan, pastor of the United Presbyterian Church at Albany, Oregon, was present at the meeting in Ashland. Convinced that the movement was of God, he returned to Albany with reports on what was happening, and the ministers there engaged the Albany Armory for further meetings for Dr. Price. He wrote:

> From the very first service it was packed to the doors. Quite often the crowd would stay in the building from ten o'clock in the morning until the time for the night meeting. We had to beg people, who were Christians, to stay away in order to allow the unsaved to find room.[215]

McCrossan wrote that some of the ministers present had been through campaigns with Moody, Torrey, Gipsy Smith, Wilbur Chapman, William E. Biederwolf, F. B. Smith, French Oliver, Billy Sunday, and other important evangelists, but that they "had never before found men and women under such conviction of sin as in this campaign."[216]

> We ministers felt withered hands and arms, time and again, which were cold and useless. Within an hour after being prayed for, those same hands and arms would be as warm as our own. Is it any wonder that we believe in divine healing?[217]

From Albany, Dr. Price and his party went to the First Methodist Church of Eugene, Oregon, where

> Once again the power fell. We were forced to move to the spacious armory and that too became crowded to the doors. Out of that meeting there was built Lighthouse Temple with one of the most spacious audi-

toriums in the entire full gospel movement. During the Eugene campaign miracles of healing occurred that shook the entire countryside, and denominational preachers were filled with the Holy Ghost.[218]

During this time, Dr. Price also held meetings in Roseburg, Oregon, and Victoria and Vancouver, British Columbia. In these two Canadian cities, "there were days when from seven hundred to one thousand persons came to the altar, all under the same tremendous conviction of sin."[219]

Kathryn Kuhlman

Among the protégés of Charles Price were Everett and Myrtle Parrot, who brought Myrtle's younger sister, Kathryn Kuhlman, to Oregon to join them as a traveling evangelist in the summer of 1923.[220] Another member of this team was Helen Gulliford, who had been a pianist for Price. During this time, they attended one of Price's meetings in Albany, Oregon, after his return from Canada. According to her sister Myrtle, it was here that Kathryn Kuhlman received her call to preach.[221]

In 1928, Kathryn Kuhlman and Helen Gulliford began working on their own, beginning in Boise, Idaho, billing themselves as "God's Girls."[222] They carried on an itinerant ministry for a few years in the Midwest until Kathryn was ordained by the Evangelical Church Alliance in Joliet, Illinois, in the early 1930s. Soon afterward, in 1933, she became established in Denver, Colorado. Earl F. Hewitt, a businessman, had joined her shortly before this as her business manager during the Great Depression.[223] All of the churches were especially hard hit, yet according to Kuhlman's biographer, Jamie Buckingham, she told Hewitt, "You go up there to Denver like you've got a million dollars. We're going to take that city by storm."[224] He cautioned that all they had was five dollars. She laughed and replied,

> If we serve a God who is limited to our finances, then we're serving the wrong God. He's not limited to what we have or who we are . . . Now go on up to Denver. Find me the biggest building you can. Get the finest piano available for Helen. Fill the place up with chairs. Take out a big ad in the *Denver Post* and get spot announcements on all the radio stations.[225]

Buckingham wrote that Hewitt rented a building and proceeded as follows:

> Using a combination of faith, brass, and credit, Hewitt rented 500 chairs and a grand piano, telling the people he would pay for them in two weeks,

at the end of the revival campaign. The two weeks revival, however, stretched into five years. From the very first night, Kathryn was an institution in Denver.[226]

On the first night of the campaign, August 27, 1933, 125 people were present. The following night there were 400, and "from then on the old warehouse could not hold the crowds."[227] Two years later, a larger building, with a capacity for 2000, was secured. Yet, at the dedication service of Denver Revival Tabernacle on May 30, 1935, the building was filled to overflowing.[228]

A *Period of Decline*: 1935–1947

Overall, the late 1930s and early 1940s were a time of spiritual decline, and revivals were usually only local, such as the one which swept Aimee Semple McPherson's Angelus Temple in Los Angeles in the late 1930s.[229] Kathryn Kuhlman left Denver for Mason City, Iowa, in 1938 to be with another evangelist, Burroughs Waltrip, who soon secured a divorce in order to marry her. This resulted in the demise of their ministries until 1944, when Kathryn, grieving over their error and anxious to continue in service to God, left Waltrip in order to begin again.[230] Within two years, she had established a home base in Franklin, Pennsylvania, and began radio broadcasts from nearby Pittsburgh.[231]

Aimee Semple McPherson died in 1944, A. H. Argue retired in the mid-1940s due to ill health, and Carrie Judd Montgomery died in 1946, setting the stage for a new era to which we will turn in the next chapter.

====== 5 ======

THE HEALING AND
LATTER RAIN MOVEMENTS

T HE HEALING AND LATTER RAIN REVIVALS were two parallel movements within Pentecostalism during a worldwide evangelical awakening which took place shortly after the Second World War. While
the awakening of this era occurred among both Pentecostals and non-
Pentecostal Evangelicals, there was still only a limited amount of contact between these two groups at this time. The Healing and Latter
Rain movements were therefore restricted, to a certain degree, to
those within Pentecostal circles.

THE HEALING MOVEMENT

Two of the earliest and most influential healing evangelists of the mid-
twentieth century were William M. Branham and Oral Roberts. Other
important figures included T. L. Osborn, Jack Coe, William Freeman,
A. A. Allen, and David Nunn. Gordon Lindsay, who had helped to
bring the ministry of William Branham into widespread recognition,
used his talents to supply the movement with a degree of cohesiveness.

William M. Branham

The healing ministry of William M. Branham began in the spring of
1946. On May 7 of that year, according to Branham, an angel visited
him and said to him,

Fear not. I am sent from the presence of Almighty God to tell you that
your peculiar life and your misunderstood ways have been to indicate that
God has sent you to take a gift of divine healing to the people of the world.
IF YOU WILL BE SINCERE, AND CAN GET THE PEOPLE TO BELIEVE YOU,
NOTHING SHALL STAND BEFORE YOUR PRAYER, NOT EVEN CANCER.[1]

Branham said that he was told by the angel that he would be able
to detect diseases by vibrations in his left hand.

During the Sunday evening service at which he first spoke of what
had happened, he received a telegram from a friend, Robert Daugherty,
requesting that he come to pray for his sick daughter in St. Louis. Branham went to St. Louis and prayed for her, and her health improved.
He returned to Daugherty's church to conduct a healing revival from
June 14 to June 25, 1946. His reputation spread throughout the United
Pentecostal Church, and he was soon invited to hold a revival in the
Bible Hour Tabernacle in Jonesboro, Arkansas, pastored by Rex Humbard's father, "Dad" Humbard. Branham was reported to have raised
a dead man at these meetings.[2] According to Gordon Lindsay, 25,000
people attended from twenty-eight states.[3] From there W. E. Kidson
brought Branham from town to town, attracting enormous crowds.

Branham was invited to a church in Shreveport, Louisiana, where
he asked the pastor, Jack Moore, and another man, Young Brown,
to help manage his meetings so that W. E. Kidson could return to
his pastoral duties in Houston. Accompanied by Moore, Branham
held campaigns in the spring of 1947 in San Antonio, Phoenix, and
several cities in California, including Oakland. Jack Moore visited his
friend, Gordon Lindsay, in Ashland, Oregon, and persuaded him to
come to a Branham revival in Sacramento.

Soon afterward, Gordon Lindsay arranged for Branham to hold a
series of meetings in Vancouver, B.C., during the fall of 1947. On the
first day of this campaign, W. J. Ern Baxter was added to Branham's
team. According to Gordon Lindsay, 70,000 people attended the
fourteen-day campaign, which was held in four cities in the Northwest. The meetings were "inter-evangelical" and characterized by many
hours of prayer for the sick and supernatural occurrences. The meetings in Vancouver were attended by a few pastors and teachers from
North Battleford, Saskatchewan, who returned to supply the spark
that ignited the controversial "Latter Rain" movement, which also
quickly spread throughout the world, emphasizing the laying on of
hands, both for the bestowal of the miraculous gifts of the Spirit and
for personal prophecy.

In January of 1948 the Branham team held large revivals in Miami and Pensacola, Florida. In the spring, there was a huge campaign in Kansas City attended by Oral Roberts. After a five-month illness from May until October of 1948, Branham continued his campaign. By this time, many other new healing ministries had risen to prominence as well. Branham's continued to be one of the most widely known, taking him to many parts of the world.

Among those healed at a campaign in Los Angeles in 1951 was the former U.S. congressman and widely known temperance advocate, William D. Upshaw. According to David Edwin Harrell, Jr., "Branham's healing power became a worldwide legend; there were continued reports that he raised the dead."[4] Branham's ministry continued throughout the 1950s, as did the ministries of many of the well-known healing evangelists. Ern Baxter, who ministered with Branham for four to eight months every year from 1947 until 1953, said that he never saw his discernment miss once. Whenever Ern Baxter was given a card containing information on the individual's medical history, Branham was able, in every case, to correctly diagnose the illness without ever knowing what was on the card in Baxter's hand.[5]

Oral Roberts

Another healing evangelist who came into prominence during this time was Oral Roberts. From 1935 until 1946, Oral Roberts was a Pentecostal Holiness preacher. After attending the Disciples of Christ's Phillips University in 1946 and teaching a few classes at Southwestern Bible College, he began fasting and praying intensively until 1947, at which time he began an independent ministry, conducting his first auditorium revival in May of that year in Enid, Oklahoma. He soon introduced healing to his meetings and emphasized the interdenominational character of his campaign. The following month he resigned his pastorate and moved to Tulsa, Oklahoma. During the summer of 1947 he discussed the matter of an independent deliverance ministry with the Branham team in Tulsa. His first major healing was reported in the fall of 1947, when Olive Green was healed of infantile paralysis in Muskogee, Oklahoma.

The Voice of Healing, published by Gordon Lindsay, reported in April of 1949 that William Branham testified, after attending a Roberts campaign, that Roberts's "commanding power over demons, over disease and over sin was the most amazing thing he had ever seen in the work of God."[6] Roberts reported that he would feel a manifestation

of God's presence in his right hand which would be a point of contact between the believer and God's healing power.

Roberts published his own magazine, Healing Waters, beginning with
a circulation of 10,000 in November of 1947. At about this time he
was already preaching regularly over five radio stations. By 1953, his
magazine had increased to a circulation of 265,000. In January of
1948 he obtained a "tent cathedral" seating 2000 people, which was
destroyed by a storm during a campaign in Amarillo, Texas, late in
the summer of 1950, but he replaced it with one seating 7,500 the
following year. Two years later, it was necessary to purchase a new
tent seating 12,500.[7]

T. L. Osborn

Thomas L. Osborn's ministry as a healing evangelist began at approximately the same time as did that of Oral Roberts. In the summer of 1947, T. L. Osborn attended meetings of the Branham
campaign in Portland, Oregon. As he observed Branham ministering to the sick, Osborn saw him deliver a little deaf-mute girl of an
evil spirit. Osborn said that he seemed to hear a thousand voices
speaking to him at once telling him that he could do the same thing,
and he launched an independent ministry the following spring, with
help from Gordon Lindsay, who gave him financial support and publicity. According to Harrell, "the healings and miracles that took place
in his campaigns were often sensational, although the major pub-
licists of the revival felt he was a scrupulously honest reporter."[8]

Jack Coe

Another healing evangelist, Jack Coe, began his ministry after he received a miraculous healing while in the military service during World
War II. While still in the army, he began conducting healing revivals,
and was ordained an Assemblies of God pastor in 1944. He rented
his first tent in 1947 and started publicizing his ministry with a short-
lived periodical that was replaced three years later with the Herald
of Healing, which reached a circulation of 95,000 by 1951 and 250,000
by 1956. The ministry of Jack Coe was accompanied by large numbers of healings. In Birmingham, Alabama, 63 persons confined to
wheelchairs (of 103 present) walked out of their wheelchairs.[9] His
ministry ended abruptly when he contracted polio in December of
1956 and died the following year.

William Freeman

Healing evangelist William Freeman lived in considerable poverty as a Pentecostal pastor for about twelve years until 1946, when his wife had a nervous breakdown and he handed in his resignation. He contracted cancer in his leg, but he prayed and was healed. He said that he sought the Lord much, often praying until late at night. "One night at about 11 o'clock, the Lord gave me a vision. In the vision I saw the Lord standing on a great cloud. As I watched Him the scene seemed to change, and I was standing before a vast congregation."[10] Encouraged by this vision, Freeman began a ministry as an independent evangelist in early 1947.

His ministry was accompanied with "amazing miracles, signs and wonders," and "word began to spread throughout the world of this 'unusual preacher with gifts of healing.' "[11] According to Freeman, there were 62,500 converts during a series of campaigns in St. Louis and Chicago.

Freeman was influential in the formation of the Full Gospel Business Men's Fellowship International, having had friends among several influential businessmen. The founder of the FGBMFI, Demos Shakarian, sponsored some of Freeman's early meetings, and his wife was Freeman's pianist.[12]

A. A. Allen

A. A. Allen, the pastor of an Assemblies of God church in Corpus Christi, Texas, began his healing ministry after driving to Dallas in 1949 to attend a series of meetings held by Oral Roberts. He soon began holding revivals in churches, as he had done during World War II. In May 1950 he sent a report from Oakland, California, to Gordon Lindsay as follows:

> Although I do not claim to possess the gift of healing, hundreds are being miraculously healed in this meeting of every known disease. I do not claim to possess a single gift of the Spirit nor to have the power to impart any gift to others, yet in this meeting, as well as in other meetings, all the gifts of the Spirit are being received and exercised night after night.[13]

Allen established his headquarters in Dallas and campaigned throughout the U.S. and in Cuba and Mexico. By 1955, he was preaching on seventeen Latin American radio stations and eighteen American ones. According to Harrell, "Allen seemed challenged to heal the hard diseases and frequently reported resurrections of the dead."[14]

David Nunn

David Nunn, another local pastor in Texas in 1949, sponsored the meetings of several healing evangelists. At one of his own meetings, he prayed for a paralyzed child whose healing he took as an indication that he should begin an independent healing ministry. He said that in January of 1950 "God spoke to me again and said: 'Get up from here and go into every city, heal the sick therein and preach the kingdom of Heaven is at hand.' "[15] He established his own evangelistic association in 1952. He said that he had seen "as many as twenty-five totally blind receive their sight in one single service" and that "in one single campaign I counted thirty-three people who were healed of paralysis or of a crippled condition."[16]

Gordon Lindsay

Gordon Lindsay, who was recognized as a leader and coordinator of the Healing revival, published *The Voice of Healing*, a magazine that served to publicize the movement and give it cohesiveness. The first issue was published in April of 1948, and within a year, the circulation had reached 30,000.

A convention of healing evangelists, coordinated by Lindsay, was held December 22–23, 1949, in Dallas, Texas. This was the first meeting of its kind, followed by a meeting the next year in Kansas City which was attended by as many as one thousand itinerant evangelists.

Many of the revivalists became officially associated with *The Voice of Healing* magazine, and a loose fellowship of healing evangelists arose, including A. A. Allen, Jack Coe, William Freeman, O. L. Jaggers, and T. L. Osborn. The May 1952 issue had pictures on its cover of twenty healing evangelists.[17]

Kathryn Kuhlman

Although not a part of this fellowship, Kathryn Kuhlman began preaching about healing in 1947. Already an established evangelist, she had driven alone from Franklin, Pennsylvania, to Erie, where a noted healing evangelist was scheduled to hold tent meetings. Determined to remain anonymous, she did not identify herself but attended the meeting. This meeting left her very dissatisfied, because she observed many excesses and unfortunate practices. She said, "I began to weep. I could not stop. Those looks of despair and disappointment on the faces I had seen, when told that only their lack of faith was keeping them from God, were to haunt me for weeks."[18]

On Sunday, April 27, 1947, Kathryn Kuhlman began a series on the Holy Spirit. She pointed out that Jesus was empowered by the Spirit to heal the sick, to cause the blind to see, and even to raise the dead. She said that Jesus had promised his followers that they, also, would be filled and empowered by the Holy Spirit, and that the same things he had done would be done by those who followed him. In fact, even greater things would be done. "Every church should be experiencing the miracles of Pentecost. Every church should be seeing the healings of the Book of Acts. The gift is for all of us."[19]

At the meeting the following night at Gospel Tabernacle in Franklin, a woman made a disturbance in the audience and came forward. She had her hand up, and asked, "Kathryn, may I say something?" After a few seconds, she agreed, and the woman went to the front of the building. She said softly to Kathryn, "last night, while you were preaching, I was healed."[20] The woman had been healed of a tumor while sitting in the audience.

The following Sunday, George Orr, a Methodist who had been a World War I veteran with a serious eye injury, was healed of blindness in one of his eyes. His right eye had been damaged in an industrial accident by a splash of molten metal, and his ophthalmologist, Dr. C. E. Imbrie of Butler, Pennsylvania, had said that the eye was permanently impaired. On May 4, Orr and his wife attended Kathryn Kuhlman's meeting with another younger couple. She was preaching about the Holy Spirit and declared, on the basis of the healing of the woman a few days previously, that physical healing was just as possible in our own day as was spiritual salvation. Orr prayed that God would heal his eye. He felt a tingling sensation in it, and it began to stream tears. After he left the service, he was soon able to see again with that eye, and he returned to Franklin on the following Tuesday to testify.[21]

These incidents were the first few in a healing ministry that Kathryn Kuhlman carried on for many years until her death in 1976. However, she never became involved with the Healing movement or with the loose fellowship of evangelists associated with Gordon Lindsay.

Points of Emphasis

The Healing movement, in addition to its obvious preoccupation with evangelism and healing, emphasized the unity of the Body of Christ. According to Harrell, Gordon Lindsay repeatedly stressed the importance of "a vision of the unity of God's people."[22] According to Jack Moore's daughter, Anna Jeanne, "a new day has dawned! Spirit-filled believers the world over have come to learn that *real fellowship* is that lovely state of appreciation we can enter into for those who *do not* believe as we do, . . . but by the Birth of the Spirit are our Blood kin!"[23] Gordon Lindsay had said of William Branham in 1947 that "the uniting of believers had been the burden of his heart from the time that the angel had visited him."[24] As the enthusiasm of the early meetings dwindled during the mid-fifties, this emphasis became much less pronounced, being displaced once again by the reappearance of old doctrinal loyalties. Another theme of the Healing movement was its pronounced emphasis upon eschatology and its expectation of the imminent close of the age and coming of Christ. Harrell has observed that "nearly all of the evangelists believed that the revival was a sign that the end of time was near."[25]

THE LATTER RAIN MOVEMENT

The Sharon Orphanage and Schools

Emphasis upon the miraculous, a strong sense of the unity of believers in Christ, and an expectation of the immediate coming of Christ also characterized the 1948 Latter Rain movement, which originated with an outpouring of God's Spirit at Sharon Orphanage and Schools in North Battleford, Saskatchewan, where about seventy students had gathered to study the Word of God, fast, and pray, beginning in November of 1947. The pastors and teachers associated with the work at Sharon included George and Ern Hawtin, who were brothers, P. G. Hunt, Herrick Holt, and George Hawtin's brother-in-law, Milford Kirkpatrick. After three months of prayer and fasting, on February 12, 1948, the revival suddenly began in the largest classroom, where the student body had gathered for devotional exercises. Ern Hawtin wrote that "some students were under the power of God on the floor, others were kneeling in adoration and worship before the Lord."[26]

> Soon a visible manifestation of gifts was received when candidates were prayed over, and many as a result began to be healed, as gifts of healing were received.

> Day after day the Glory and power of God came among us. Great repentance, humbling, fasting and prayer prevailed in everyone.[27]

Until this time, there had been, to a certain extent, a cessation of the operation of the gifts of the Spirit that had become so widespread with the advent of Pentecostalism at the turn of the century. This condition was recognized among Pentecostal people of all types during the 1930s and 1940s. It was this relative lack of manifestations of the miraculous gifts of the Spirit that brought the events at North Battleford into the limelight early in 1948. Because the North Battleford brethren were successful in imparting spiritual gifts by the laying on of their hands, people came from everywhere so that they, also, might partake of spiritual gifts that they had long been praying would be given to them.

On April 1, George Hawtin wrote in the *Sharon Star*:

> During the past six weeks we have enjoyed a great visitation of the Spirit of God. Some of us have been praying for twenty years that the nine gifts of the Spirit would be restored to the Church. The Spirit [of] fasting and prayer has rested upon the whole school all winter. Finally the great "Break Through" came and the spiritual gifts began to operate among us. . . . The revival is spreading all over the province. . . .
>
> The Gifts of the Spirit are definitely being restored to the Church. A new era is dawning.[28]

This issue of the *Sharon Star* may have played a large part in attracting people to the annual Feast of Pentecost camp meeting March 30 through April 4. People from many diverse locations visited Sharon during these meetings. Milford Kirkpatrick wrote: "we never saw such a variety of cars and license plates before, from many provinces in Canada and from so many states across the border. People drove for miles."[29] George Hawtin wrote that "the sick are being healed; the Devils are being cast out; Saints are being edified; sinners are being saved. . . ."[30]

A pastor from the Rainy River Valley in northwestern Ontario wrote a letter to the North Battleford brethren after his return. A summary of this letter appeared in the *Sharon Star*, according to which, "the first meeting after his return home to his assembly was wonderful; the next was glorious, and the next more glorious, and so on."[31] The following month, another pastor from Ontario wrote:

> I notice in the editorial column a paragraph telling of one pastor from Ontario who tells of his meetings after his return from attending the Feast of Pentecost. I happen to be a fellow pastor in the same district and can testify to all he claims and more. His church has become a district centre

to those who want the deeper things of God and several gifts of the Spirit are operating in the meetings in perfect harmony, mainly the gifts of healing and prophecy. Many hungry hearts are fasting and praying for a mighty outpouring in the midst.[32]

George Hawtin wrote that "during the Feast of Pentecost, ministers and lay folk came from distances of fifteen hundred miles, from east and west."[33] A minister from Alberta reported receiving "an outstanding ministry of healing while at the Feast of Pentecost."[34] In a letter to North Battleford, he wrote, "it is now nineteen days since the Feast of Pentecost closed and the power of God has never left my body."[35] Two other cases were described by George Hawtin:

> One pastor who received the Gifts of Healing is being so used of God that he can no longer confine his ministry to his own church, but is needed abroad. The members of one congregation from the west said: "You would never know our pastor is the same man since he returned from the Feast of Pentecost."[36]

Although North Battleford was not the only influence bringing about revival within Pentecostalism at this time, Sharon Orphanage and Schools certainly played a significant role in precipitating revival in many Pentecostal circles throughout North America; however, the Latter Rain movement soon became the storm center of tremendous controversy. In May, George Hawtin wrote:

> Even now while I am writing, one of the denominational pastors of this city where our meetings are being held and where many are actually receiving spiritual gifts, is calling in his superintendent to have him decide whether or not the teaching is of God, and he says he will abide by the superintendent's decision. . . . Men who have been praying for twenty years that the gifts would be restored to the church are now afraid to enter in because of the opposition from the organization.[37]

The North Battleford brethren, ministering beyond the context of their own locality, seem to have referred to themselves as "the Presbytery," rather than reserving this term for the elders at whatever location they were visiting. According to James Watt, "when this group of ministers travelled to other cities, they retained the word 'Presbytery' to themselves, allowing some local pastors to also participate."[38] This was understandably bothersome to many local pastors, contributing to controversy.

Despite these problems, God was pouring out his Spirit at the meetings led by the North Battleford brethren. The May issue of the *Sharon Star* described revival in Saskatoon, where the Hawtin brothers had begun to hold meetings:

Excellent crowds are attending the meetings. Many wonderful things are taking place. The meetings are of such nature that one has to attend them to understand what God is really doing. To be in one of these meetings is like living in another Chapter of the Acts of the Apostles. God is working in a new way.

The Assembly in Saskatoon is now the largest full Gospel assembly in Saskatchewan. Mighty outpourings are taking place among the saints in Prince Albert and McDowall. Denominational pastors and evangelists are coming in to see what it is all about and many are going away never to be the same again.[39]

On July 7–18, 1948, thousands of people throughout the continent descended upon North Battleford for the Sharon Camp Meeting. It had been preceded by a week of fasting and prayer from June 27 until July 4, which was also widely attended. The July meeting was one of several camp meetings which a historian of Pentecostalism, Noel McNeill, described:

In the last few years of the '40's it seemed as if the wind of God's Spirit was blowing with greater force. God did move in Revival power. It began through the work of Rev. Hawtin and the Sharon Bible Institute at North Battleford, Saskatchewan. There was such an effusion of Divine power in healings, miracles and utterance gifts that wide attention was attracted. Thousands flocked from every part of the continent and the world to special "Camp meeting-Conventions."[40]

George Hawtin described the July meetings:

Day after day the Word was taught, and then the signs followed its teaching. Morning, afternoon and evening, people were slain under the power of God and filled with the Holy Spirit. . . . We had been praying for a return of the days when people would be filled with the Spirit immediately when hands were laid upon them as they were at Samaria and Ephesus. It was our great joy one night to have two ladies walk up before the whole crowd and receive the Holy Spirit in this fashion. When hands were laid upon them one immediately fell under the power of God; the other began to speak in tongues as the Spirit gave her utterance.[41]

The Spread of the Revival

Those who attended the camp meeting at Sharon in July of 1948 went forth from North Battleford to spread news of the revival throughout North America. Among these people were James and Phyllis Spiers, who travelled from North Battleford to a church in Hibbing, Minnesota, pastored by E. H. Blomberg. They wrote, "when we came here, the Lord came forth in the very first meeting and as soon as we came on the platform, the Lord began to move; my hand be-

gan to tremble under the power of God."[42] There were several healings the first night. "One boy was hurt in an accident four years ago.
He was bent over almost like a jack knife, also was unsaved. We
prayed for him, and he was saved, and healed immediately. He stood
up straight, and praised God."[43] By telephone invitation, George Hawtin and Milford Kirkpatrick joined James and Phyllis Spiers as they
ministered in Hibbing in a revival that grew during the following
months to great proportions.

In October of 1948, meetings were held by the North Battleford
brethren in Edmonton, Alberta. The convention was attended by
members of several Pentecostal denominations, including the Independent Assemblies of God, the Pentecostal Assemblies of Canada,
and the Assemblies of God. People attended from as far away as
Prince Edward Island, British Columbia, various parts of the United
States, and Iceland. One man travelled 2500 miles to be present for
the last day of meetings. Many pastors, including J. Mattsson-Boze
of Chicago, returned to their churches with new enthusiasm.

One of the outstanding features of the Edmonton meetings was
the "heavenly choir," described by James Watt:

> It was as a mighty organ, with great swelling chords, and solo parts weav-
> ing in and out, yet with perfect harmony. Those who heard it some blocks
> away said that it did something to their souls that no power on earth had
> previously touched.[44]

George Hawtin described the phenomenon as follows:

> From a little distance it sounds like a master choir accompanied by a match-
> less symphony orchestra. It seems difficult to credit that such sound could
> be reproduced by human vocal organs. There is such perfect order and
> timing as the mighty chords swell and roll that one is forced to concede
> that there is an unseen conductor.[45]

George Warnock wrote of James Watt:

> It seemed he was about to sit down, having thus ministered [on spiritual
> song], when suddenly he burst forth in prophetic song. Immediately after,
> the spirit of prophecy rested on others in the congregation, who sang forth
> prophetic utterances, and then the whole congregation joined in, with spir-
> itual anthems of praise.
>
> It was a very sovereign ministry that came forth; preceded, nevertheless,
> by scriptural teaching concerning it, and from that day forth scriptural song
> became part and parcel of ministry that came when the body came
> together.[46]

Reg Layzell

At the invitation of Reg Layzell in Vancouver, B.C., the North Battleford party held meetings at Glad Tidings Temple on November 14–28, 1948. Two meetings were held daily and three each Sunday. "The main auditorium was always well filled. In the evenings the temple was always full and on Sundays it was jammed."[47] James Watt wrote of a man from Toronto that "as soon as he came in the door he knew by the Spirit that God was in the place."[48] The Vancouver meetings were known for miraculous manifestations of the gift of tongues.[49] Reg Layzell wrote of these meetings:

I have seen more souls saved in the last two months than I saw in two years of ordinary church life while in Toronto. . . .

People were healed! There were many outstanding healings and thanks be to God they are lasting healings. . . .

Without hesitation I say that the Sharon Group have been a great blessing to us and I believe God has called them to spearhead the way to a God-given revival.[50]

While the Sharon Group had successfully ignited the fires of revival in many places throughout North America, once the fires were lit, the North Battleford brethren began to lose the prominence that they had had at the beginning of the revival. Once enthusiasm had been sparked in places such as Vancouver, these localities became new centers for revival which, in turn, brought about revival elsewhere.

Myrtle D. Beall

Among the people present at the Vancouver meetings was Mrs. Myrtle D. Beall, pastor of an Assemblies of God church, Bethesda Missionary Temple, in Detroit, Michigan. She travelled 2500 miles by car to attend the meetings in a trip that lasted six days. She wrote:

Everything we saw in the meetings was scriptural and beautiful. We left the meeting with a new touch of God upon our souls and ministry. We certainly feel transformed by the power of God. Never in our lives had we ever felt the power of God as we do now and we feel we are carrying something back to our assembly we never had before.[51]

Mrs. Beall returned to her church to spark revival there, attracting people from all parts of the country, including Ivan Q. Spencer, the founder of Elim Bible Institute, and his son, Carlton, who were at

Zion Bible Institute in East Providence, Rhode Island for a Pentecostal Prayer Fellowship gathering on December 30–31, 1948, when
a latecomer to the gathering arrived and shared "what he had heard
of a visitation in Detroit." Ivan Spencer immediately went to Detroit
after returning to Elim Bible Institute in Hornell, New York, for his
wife, Minnie. They "arrived in Detroit and were soon ushered into
the basement sanctuary of Bethesda Temple." Sixto Lopez, who also
visited Detroit at this time, said that the prayer there was "characterized by brokenness, yieldedness, illumination upon the Word, rest-
fulness in His presence. . . . Also, through the laying on of hands,
there was a confirmation of missionary calls and the setting apart
of individuals for specific ministry."[52]

Mrs. Beall wrote a letter to Stanley Frodsham, a pioneer of the early
Pentecostal movement at the turn of the century, a leader of the Assemblies of God denomination, and the editor of the *Pentecostal Evangel* for twenty-eight years. In her letter, Mrs. Beall described what was
happening in her church, and Frodsham decided to leave Springfield,
Missouri, to visit the church in Detroit. He arrived in January of 1949,
and "he was swept away by the revival taking place in Detroit. . . .
He was moved deeply by scenes of people under great conviction
of sin, making confession and finding peace."[53]

From Myrtle Beall's church in Detroit, revival soon spread rapidly
to a number of other Pentecostal congregations in the United States.
Faith Campbell, the daughter of Stanley Frodsham, wrote about the
meetings that were held in Detroit in January of 1949 at Myrtle Beall's
church and the nationwide revival that they precipitated:

> There was no sweeping doctrinal change, but rather a reemphasis on the
> purpose and practice of the gifts of the Spirit. Many who for years had
> intellectually accepted the scriptural truths of the gifts of the Spirit had
> their spiritual eyes opened as they obeyed Paul's admonition to "seek ear-
> nestly the best gifts." As in any revival of this type, there were some who
> violated Biblical truth.[54]

One of the people who attended these meetings, Sixto Lopez,
reported:

> Most of us find difficulty in yielding to the Lord, but in this atmosphere
> I felt a complete yieldedness. I opened my heart to the Lord, and felt as
> though I was giving myself as an offering to Him. Every Scripture and every
> message took on a new meaning to me.
>
> The most outstanding thing I felt in those meetings was a desire to pray—
> just to stay before the Lord. I have always found it difficult to spend long

periods in prayer, but there I felt a great desire to stay before the Lord in prayer. Many of the people there have lost their appetite for food and go days without food. I had a big appetite for food but came to the place that I did not care to eat.[55]

The day of the dedication of the new Temple building in Detroit, Sunday, February 13, 1949, "there were 3,000 in the new auditorium, at "least 500 in the old, and it was necessary to turn 1500 away."[56]

Early Opposition

The following day, February 14, Charles W. H. Scott, district superintendent of the Assemblies of God in Michigan, spoke at the annual Michigan Ministers' Institute in the Dearborn Gospel Tabernacle. Stanley Frodsham was present. According to William W. Menzies, "Scott outlined the history and the errors of the new teaching. He emphasized in particular the misplaced emphasis on the gift of prophecy, the impartation of gifts of the Spirit by the laying on of hands by self-styled apostles and prophets, and the fact that the revival was not, after all, new at all, but rather the reappearance of enthusiastic mysticism common in church history."[57] Scott had several conferences with Mrs. Beall and "the leading 'Latter Rain' exponent from Canada, Elmer Frink."[58] Of the Ministers' Institute, Stanley Frodsham wrote:

> It has been so grossly unfair to link up this new revival which God is so graciously sending, where so many souls are being saved, where so many lives are being transformed, where God is so graciously restoring the gifts of the Spirit with the fanatical movements of the past 40 years. When I met the Michigan presbyters they brought up the Bournemouth apostolics—at least they brought up the apostolic movement that began in Bournemouth. I told them the whole story of that work, and the bad spirit that was manifested in it. But it seems as if the brethren do not want to hear anything that would change them in their prejudices against this gracious new outpouring of God's Spirit.[59]

Thomas Wyatt

On February 20, 1949, Dr. Thomas Wyatt of Portland, Oregon, telephoned the Hawtin brothers requesting them to minister for a week at a convention in Portland. At first, his request was refused, but within a few days, he had convinced George Hawtin and Milford Kirkpatrick to come to Wings of Healing Temple in Portland, where ninety preachers who had gathered from as far away as Montana, Iowa, Kansas, Texas, California, Utah, and Washington were awaiting them. George Hawtin wrote that he and Milford Kirkpatrick had planned to stay four days, but that it was three weeks before they were able to leave.

Lloyd A. Westover of Oregon City, Oregon, recorded his impressions of the "Great Awakening in Portland":

> Within a few moments after Bro. Hawtin and Bro. Kirkpatrick took charge of the service, the Spirit began to fall. The huge congregation was soon singing in the Spirit. THE HEAVENLY CHOIR. Oh! the ecstatic joy that filled my whole being. . . .

> Perhaps you can imagine how our hearts ached and longed for more of God, as day after day we heard such scriptures opened, such music, miraculous healings and wonders in His name.[60]

One of the pastors in attendance on February 24 was Dr. A. Earl Lee, pastor of Immanuel Temple in Los Angeles, California. He wrote:

> After the laying on of hands, I returned to Los Angeles, and beginning with the Sunday service of February 27 until this present hour, two services have been held daily in our church, with three on Sunday. There has been a constant outpouring of the Spirit of the Lord. Many hours have been spent in waiting on the Lord in quietness. The Heavenly Choir has been constantly with us. Many of the congregation prophesy by revelation. Scores have received the Baptism of the Holy Spirit and week upon week, people are converted and healed. The revelations of God's Word have increased and deepened the heart of God's people.[61]

By the end of the year, George Hawtin had written concerning A. Earl Lee's church that "Immanuel Temple work is expanding rapidly and is a mother church for hundreds of miles around, with many assemblies looking there for help and supervision."[62] As was the case for Dr. A. Earl Lee's church, many other churches became centers for revival after coming into contact with the North Battleford party.

Denominational Controversies

Increasingly, however, the North Battleford brethren came under criticism by such groups as the Assemblies of God, one of whose leaders, Carl Brumback, complained of them that "the ministry gifts and the gifts of the Spirit were to be conveyed only through 'the laying on of hands,' and this by certain men who alone could call forth and confer upon believers these blessings."[63] While Carl Brumback was concerned with what he felt were shortcomings with the men in leadership, Stanley Frodsham focused not so much upon such shortcomings as on what he felt God was doing in the midst of the people. He wrote:

I can see that the Council is waging an all out war against the new revival God is sending. Of course there are frailties in the folks that are in this new revival. They have made mistakes. But there are frailties in all of God's saints, and I could recite a story of mistakes that have been made by my Council brethren that I have seen during the past 33 years. But I want to keep silent. I have to confess that I have made many mistakes myself.[64]

After this time, many people were dropped from or pressured to resign from various denominations for their involvement in the Latter Rain. This was particularly true with regard to the Pentecostal Assemblies of Canada, the Assemblies of God in the U.S., and the Pentecostal Holiness Church, all of which officially disapproved of the beliefs and practices of the "New Order of the Latter Rain," as it was called by these denominations.[65] The Latter Rain movement quickly became anathema among most major Pentecostal denominational bodies, and every effort was made by people within them to remain as far removed from any association with the movement as possible.

Denominational opposition arose primarily as a result of excesses that had developed in some quarters. These excesses were taken as representative of the movement as a whole. Dick Iverson wrote:

Unfortunately, the movement was judged on the basis of the most radical element which used the gifts and callings of God for their own gain. Hence, many have looked with consternation on what took place in those years, letting the abuses and fanaticism of a few blind them to the spiritual truth God wanted to reveal. . . .

This, then, is precisely what happened in the early 1950's. Many who were involved in this original move went into extreme fanaticism and religious racketeering. Hence, the whole movement was considered negatively.[66]

Despite opposition to the Latter Rain movement, revival was taking place within the denominational organizations as well as without; there was nothing special either about the Latter Rain movement or, for that matter, about any of the denominations. A genuine awakening was taking place in all quarters in which there was receptivity to it.

Effects

Although there was not a general acceptance of the doctrines and practices of the Latter Rain within most of the major Pentecostal denominations, there was a significant extent to which they were accepted outside of them. Many hundreds of "revival churches" became visible during the Latter Rain revival, not a few of which had been in existence prior to the revival. In addition to the churches already mentioned, some of the most significant of these included Paul N. Grubb's assembly in Memphis, Tennessee;[67] Omar Johnson's church in St. Louis, Missouri;[68] Christian Faith Temple in Cleveland, Ohio, pastored by Lawrence O. McKinney; Charles Green's church in Port Arthur, Texas; and William Marshall's church in Baton Rouge, Louisiana. Most of these churches were independent and autonomous, and many became mother churches to numerous others that were established or nurtured by members of the mother church.

Harry H. Hodge of Beaumont, Texas, was associated with more than eighty churches in the southern United States by 1949.[69] Another group of churches, the Independent Assemblies of God, although in existence before the revival, included within it many churches that became associated with the Latter Rain. This group reorganized as a new fellowship, the Independent Assemblies of God International. The Elim Missionary Assemblies, which had also been in existence before the revival, was a fellowship of churches closely associated with Elim Bible Institute in Lima, New York, one of the major centers of the Latter Rain revival. These churches continued to grow through the 1950s, 1960s, and 1970s.

Influence upon the Charismatic Renewal

Many ministries arose to carry on and develop principles that arose in the 1948 revival, becoming part of the Charismatic renewal of the 1960s and 1970s. One of the prominent leaders in the Charismatic renewal, John Poole, was the son of Fred C. Poole, a pastor of the Apostolic Church and a major figure in the Latter Rain revival. After his father's death in 1963, John Poole pastored his father's church in Philadelphia, Pennsylvania, which, by 1976, included four separate congregations with sixty associated home meetings.[70] In the early 1970s, he was a frequent contributor in *New Wine*, an important periodical of the Charismatic renewal.

Bethesda Missionary Temple in Detroit, Michigan, once a center for the Latter Rain movement, also became prominent in the Charismatic renewal. Myrtle Beall's son, James Lee Beall, who succeeded his mother as pastor of the church, became a frequent contributor to *Logos Journal*, one of the most widely circulated periodicals of the Charismatic renewal.

Some of the 1976 faculty members of Elim Bible Institute in Lima, New York (which had moved from Hornell in 1951), had been widely recognized leaders in the 1948 Latter Rain movement, including Elmer Frink and Carlton Spencer, son of Elim's founder, Ivan Q. Spencer. Carlton Spencer became president of the school during the time of the Latter Rain revival. In 1953 he was invited by Demos Shakarian to a convention in Washington of the Full Gospel Business Men's Fellowship, which Shakarian had founded and which later played an important part in influencing the Charismatic renewal.[71]

H. David Edwards, vice-president of Elim, was a speaker at Jesus '76, a gathering of 42,000 people in Mercer, Pennsylvania, August 19–21, 1976. Also present as a speaker at the same gathering was Winston I. Nunes, at that time a pastor in Toronto, Ontario, who, as a prominent leader in the Latter Rain, had represented both the Independent Assemblies of God and the Elim Missionary Assemblies at the World Pentecostal Conference in 1952.[72]

George Warnock, author of *The Feast of Tabernacles*, one of the most influential books arising from within the Latter Rain movement, acted as Ern Baxter's personal secretary for two or three years immediately prior to the 1948 Revival.[73] In the 1970s he was again an associate of Ern Baxter,[74] who was prominent in the Charismatic renewal, having become involved in the leadership of Christian Growth Ministries in Ft. Lauderdale, Florida, in 1975.

Logos Journal, which, as has been mentioned, was one of the most widely circulated magazines of the Charismatic renewal, grew out of the publication *Herald of Faith/Harvest Time*, edited by Joseph Mattsson-Boze and Gerald Derstine.[75] Mattsson-Boze played a part in the 1948 Latter Rain revival,[76] and Gerald Derstine was closely associated from 1960 until 1968 with J. Preston Eby, who had been a source of controversy in the Pentecostal Holiness Church due to his Latter Rain teaching and practice until his resignation from that organization in 1956.[77]

Many of the doctrines and practices of the Latter Rain became considerably widespread with the Charismatic movement twenty-five years later. Marion Meloon wrote in 1974 that a blind woman on the staff at Elim Bible Institute, Rita Kelligan, at a fall convention in 1949, developed a gift for setting Psalms to music, "giving us the rich heritage that forms part of the charismatic renewal worship today."[78]

In addition to praise, spiritual singing, and dancing, some of the beliefs and practices of the Latter Rain that found their way into the

Charismatic renewal included the fivefold ministry of Ephesians 4:11, the laying on of hands, and certain distinctive teachings on the tabernacle, the feast of Tabernacles, and the foundational truths of Hebrews 6:1–2. Elements of various eschatological views of the Latter Rain movement were also adopted by many Charismatics throughout the world.

The Latter Rain provided a tremendous impetus to people in many Pentecostal circles to seek to exercise the gift of prophecy, and many independent ministries emphasizing prophecy arose as a result of this influence. Writing of the Latter Rain movement in 1977, Steve Wilber, at that time a faculty member of Pinecrest Bible Training Center, in Salisbury Center, New York, stated that "the Latter Rain outpouring of the Spirit which began just prior to 1950 came forth with the greatest blaze of prophetic light since the apostolic era. But surprisingly it lifted after about a decade. . . ."[79]

Although the Latter Rain was to have lasting significance as an influence upon Pentecostals and/or Charismatics outside of major denominations, its effects upon such groups as the Assemblies of God in the United States became very minimal after the mid-1950s. In his history of the Assemblies of God, Carl Brumback wrote in 1961 that the Latter Rain had "practically come to naught."[80] Walter J. Hollenweger wrote that Brumback's statement was an example of "the same wishful thinking that led the traditional churches to ignore the beginnings of the Pentecostal Movement."[81] Traditional Pentecostal denominations have been, to a large extent, unaware of the lasting effects of the Latter Rain movement. Nevertheless, as we have seen, the Latter Rain and Healing revivals were both to become important influences upon the Charismatic renewal of the 1960s and 1970s.

====6====

THE MID-TWENTIETH-CENTURY EVANGELICAL AWAKENING

THE LATTER RAIN AND HEALING REVIVALS were part of a worldwide evangelical awakening that took place shortly after the Second World War. In America, other important developments during the mid-twentieth-century evangelical awakening included the Forest Home College Briefing Conference of August, 1947; the Pacific Palisades Conferences, which began in September of that year;[1] many spontaneous revivals on various college campuses in 1949 and 1950, some of which received nationwide publicity;[2] and the emergence of Billy Graham in 1949, along with many other evangelists who were also beginning to gain wide publicity at this time, including Charles Templeton of Canada,[3] Bryan Green of England, and Mervin Rosell of Minnesota.[4]

THE FOREST HOME COLLEGE BRIEFING CONFERENCE

Henrietta Mears

The Forest Home College Briefing Conference in the San Bernardino Mountains of Southern California was important both as an impetus for the formation of Campus Crusade for Christ and as an important early influence upon Billy Graham. This conference was conceived on Tuesday evening, June 24, 1947, when the director of Christian Education at First Presbyterian Church of Hollywood, Henrietta Mears, who had been raised under the ministry of W. B. Riley, the Fundamentalist leader at First Baptist Church in Minneapolis, spoke at the Gospel Light Teacher's Training Conference at Forest Home to hundreds of Sunday School teachers, pastors, and young seminary students. She spoke of the totalitarianism that had recently gripped Germany under Hitler and the threat of the spread of communism, which she thought was another form of totalitarianism equally dangerous to freedom and to the spread of the gospel. Just as men of special courage had been called upon for difficult assignments during World War II as "expendables," so she felt that Christian believers should become expendables for Christ. She emphasized the necessity of revival, prayer, and renewed interest in the Scriptures.

Among the people who attended this Teacher's Conference were Reverend Richard C. Halverson, assistant pastor of the Hollywood Presbyterian Church at that time; Louis H. Evans, Jr., the son of the pastor of the church; John L. Frank; and William R. Bright, who had become a Christian only a few months earlier. After Miss Mears' message, these four young men, with several others, asked her if they could meet for prayer in her cabin. Baldwin and Benson, biographers of Henrietta Mears, describe the ensuing prayer meeting:

> As they knelt, they were overcome by a sense of helplessness and inadequacy. They prayed on into the late hours of the night, confessing sin, asking God for guidance, and seeking the reality and power of the Holy Spirit. There was much weeping and crying out to the Lord. At times, no one prayed as God spoke to them.

> Then, the fire fell. However it can be explained, God answered their prayer with a vision. They saw before them the college campuses of the world, teeming with unsaved students, who held in their hands the power to change the world. The college campuses—they were the key to world leadership, to world revival![5]

As they continued in prayer, they contemplated the possibility of extending the coming annual weekend summer conference for college students of First Presbyterian Church of Hollywood at Forest Home to an eight-day conference for college students throughout the nation.

The following evening, these five people returned to the Presbyterian church at Hollywood to speak at the weekly Wednesday evening prayer meeting of the college department of the church.

> As Miss Mears entered the room, one of those present said to another, "I have never known before what it meant in the book of Exodus where it describes Moses' face shining with the glory of God, but now I see: Look at Teacher's face!"[6]

Each of them gave testimonies of what had happened the previous night at Forest Home, speaking about their vision to have a conference for college students from throughout the nation. The word "briefing" was added to the title of the conference; just as soldiers during World War II had been briefed before their missions, so the College Briefing Conference was to prepare men and women to go out commissioned and trained to win the world to Christ.

> Then Miss Mears spoke, reiterating her remarks of the night before. She spoke with the authority of a person who had just stepped from the presence of God. . . . The vision was imparted to her college department, and they responded by pledging to work around the clock that other students might know what was happening and might come to the Briefing Conference.[7]

One week after the initial prayer meeting at Forest Home, the five participants, with one other young man, spoke at a high school camp at the Mount Hermon Conference Center near Santa Cruz, California.

> As the deputation from Hollywood told these leaders at the Mount Hermon camp what had happened at Forest Home, the Spirit of God fell again bringing confession and dedication. It was decided to have the deputation team speak to the entire conference that evening. Before an audience of nearly one thousand teenagers and older guests, the four young men gave their testimonies and Miss Mears spoke. Hundreds came forward to dedicate their lives as expendables to Christ.[8]

Until the time of the College Briefing Conference in August 1947, there was a great deal of preparation. Henrietta Mears and her staff wrote letters, travelled, phoned, interviewed, prayed, spoke to churches, talked with pastors, organized deputation teams, programmed meetings, and worked on housing for the conference.

> Her own daily Bible reading and prayer time was never sacrificed. Indeed, each responsibility she had she carefully weighed before the Lord in advance of undertaking it. She knew what to do because she believed God had told her to do it. During the busiest day, when dozens of major decisions were yet unresolved in her office, Teacher and her staff would take time to pray, perhaps for an hour or more. This keen sense of balance between communion with God and activity was one of the most instructive lessons to be learned from the 1947 revival.[9]

At the time of the College Briefing Conference, 600 college students came from all over the country for an eight-day conference led by Henrietta Mears, Dr. Louis H. Evans, Sr., Dr. L. David Cowie, Dr. Robert B. Munger, and others. Because there were insufficient sleeping accommodations, many slept in their cars or outdoors. The leaders had no definite schedule for the week. "The hour-by-hour program was to be led by the Spirit of God and no leader was to speak who had not been singled out by the Spirit working through the entire faculty."[10]

At the first meeting, many of the participants were skeptical and critical of the "emotional and illogical" beliefs expressed in some of the testimonies that had been given. Henrietta Mears left quietly and prayed for an hour with some of the leaders before returning to speak to the group.

> Stepping before them, she spoke about sin, confession, forgiveness, cleansing and the Holy Spirit. She laid before them the need to be absolutely honest with God and to submit completely to His will. She asked some 600 students to pray that God's purpose for their lives would be fulfilled.
>
> Throughout the conference confession of sin continued. . . .
>
> The Men's Council President at the University of Southern California gave his life to the Lord, as did many others who were campus officers. Several of the young men decided that God was calling them into the ministry or into the foreign mission field. . . .
>
> How many are the individual stories that could be told of collegians whose lives were changed at the 1947 Briefing Conference![11]

The participants at the Conference represented eighty-seven colleges and universities from almost every part of the U.S. "As the delegates returned to their campuses, they were filled with a sense of mission to win their schools to the faith."[12]

Bill Bright and Campus Crusade for Christ

During the 1947 revival at Forest Home, Bill Bright gave up a secular business and decided to prepare for campus work. After completing seminary at Princeton and Fuller, he continued his student-directed missionary efforts, living with his wife at the home of Henrietta Mears and using her home as a center for the emerging crusade, which later became Campus Crusade for Christ.

After the 1947 conference, yearly conferences were held at Forest Home. These meetings had a considerable influence upon the lives of many other youth workers across the nation, including Jim Rayburn, director of Young Life, who wrote:

> As a young man just out of college, and beginning to work among young people, I heard of Henrietta Mears' ministry at Hollywood Presbyterian Church and particularly at Forest Home. . . . I tried to incorporate into

my work everything I heard about her way of doing things. . . . She has had a great deal to do with shaping the progress and ministry of the Young Life Campaign.[13]

The Hollywood Christian Group

After the conference in 1947, Louis Evans, Jr., shared his experiences with the young actress he was dating, Colleen Townsend. She attended the following conference and dedicated her life to Jesus Christ at that time. Other Hollywood celebrities who came to be influenced included Roy Rogers, Dale Evans, Tim Spencer, and Connie Haines. In 1949 a few Hollywood film stars met in the cabin of Henrietta Mears to pray for guidance in touching the lives of their friends in the film industry. Meetings were held in private homes to avoid publicity. Dr. J. Edwin Orr, who had been speaking at the Forest Home Conferences, was very helpful in the meetings for film stars. He had been a young Irish evangelist in the 1930s and completed his doctorate at Oxford on Awakenings in 1948. "His uncluttered, unaffected style gave room for the Holy Spirit to work. . . . No tricks or gimmicks could be used on a crowd who made the mastery of gimmicks their livelihood. The secret of reaching the stars was Christ crucified and resurrected, the source of abundant life."[14] The Hollywood Christian Group was chaplained from 1949 until 1951 by Orr, after which time no one individual was its full time leader. Baldwin and Benson wrote:

> The first meetings were immediately successful. Miss Mears' spacious living room was packed with the famous, many scores of whom found the Saviour, and some of whom rejected him.[15]

The group expanded to include cameramen and technicians, and it moved to the Knickerbocker Hotel. Billy Graham launched his first film crusades employing the talents of this Hollywood Christian Group.

Billy Graham

While Billy Graham was still a little known evangelist from the South, he was invited to speak at the 1949 College Briefing Conference at Forest Home. He agreed to go, but because he was tired and apprehensive about his ministry, he desired to attend only as a conferee. He was scheduled for a crusade in downtown Los Angeles, and he had doubts about its outcome. J. Edwin Orr had also been invited to speak at the conference. Graham eventually consented to speak at morning meetings, and Orr spoke in the evenings, stressing the ministry of the Holy Spirit. Although Graham's messages to the youth were effective, he came to an impasse concerning an inner struggle he was having. According to Graham's biographer, John Pollock, Graham was troubled by a remark made by Charles Templeton to the effect that Graham's view of the Scriptures was narrow and that if he remained circumscribed to his view of the Scriptures his ministry might be curtailed as a result.[16] Outside late one evening, Graham and Orr spoke and prayed together about complete surrender to God and the infilling of the Holy Spirit. Graham walked off into the woods by himself, with intense inner conflict raging within him.[17] Pollock wrote:

> Billy went out in the forest and wandered up the mountain, praying as he walked: "Lord, what shall I do? What shall be the direction of my life?" He knew he had reached what he believed to be a crisis. . . .

> "So I went back and I got my Bible, and I went out in the moonlight. And I got to a stump and put the Bible on the stump, and I knelt down, and I said, 'Oh, God; I cannot prove certain things. I cannot answer some of the questions Chuck is raising and some of the other people are raising, but I accept this Book by faith as the Word of God.' "

> He stayed by the stump praying wordlessly, his eyes moist. . . . "I had a tremendous sense of God's presence. I had a great peace that the decision I had made was right."[18]

He returned much later in the morning to tell Orr that he had been filled afresh with the Spirit of God. According to Orr, "he added that God had given him a vision that something unusual was going to happen down the mountain in Los Angeles."[19] Baldwin and Benson reported:

> Having reached this turning point in his concept of his work, Billy Graham launched into his first Los Angeles crusade with a surging optimism that God was going to act. And act He did. Several Hollywood notables came forward to confess Christ. The newspapers picked up the story, and overnight Billy Graham's name was flashed across the country.[20]

According to Fred W. Hoffman, Billy Graham said of the Forest Home Conference, "God did something for my own life in that conference."[21] After this turning point in his ministry, he frequently phoned or visited Henrietta Mears, seeking her counsel and praying with her.

The Forest Home College Briefing Conferences played an important part in stimulating national spiritual renewal. Colleges and universities throughout the U.S. were affected by returning delegates; Campus Crusade for Christ was born; youth leaders found fresh inspiration; many well-known celebrities whose lives had a potential influence upon thousands of others were touched; and Billy Graham came to a turning point in his ministry. He soon became nationally recognized and was instrumental in the national awakening.

THE PACIFIC PALISADES CONFERENCES

Los Angeles 1948

Another element of the post–World War II evangelical awakening was the Pacific Palisades Conferences. The first of these conferences took place in September of 1948 near Los Angeles, California, as a result of weekly prayer meetings established by Armin Gesswein, a Norwegian Lutheran with experiences of revivals in his homeland. Gesswein had brought together a handful of pastors of various denominations for prayer for revival in 1941.

The British periodical, *Life of Faith*, February 16, 1949, carried a description of the first Pacific Palisades Conference by Norman Grubb, a Cambridge-educated Englishman, son-in-law of the famous missionary C. T. Studd, his successor as director of the Worldwide Evangelization Crusade, and a frequent visitor to America in missionary capacities:

> About 120 gathered—Presbyterian ministers, and Baptist, Methodist, Holiness, Pentecostal, United Brethren, Lutheran, nondescript, shut in with God and one another; and not a breath of controversy or theological argument. It was a time in the heavenlies. The real break came the first night after impromptu testimonies to revival from Mennonite and Presbyterian missionaries. Many were on their faces till 1 a.m. confessing need and failure. The next day and night took us to the heights, again ending about 1 a.m., after very many had come forward to have hands laid on them for a new experience of the Holy Spirit in themselves and their churches. . . . A further meeting was held some days later. . . . the brethren had returned to their churches for the Sunday, told what God had done, and then the folks streamed forward to put things right.[22]

Minneapolis

The following month, in October of 1948, eighty ministers of various denominations in Minneapolis, Minnesota, came together in a prayer fellowship, the United Spiritual Advance, under the leadership of Dr. Victor Nelson, Moderator of the Presbyterian Synod of Minnesota, and Dr. Paul Rees, pastor of First Covenant Church of Minneapolis, where the meetings were held. J. Edwin Orr described the meetings:

> Beginning with praise and prayer, there was utmost freedom in the program, which was led by Armin Gesswein. By Wednesday, it was evident that something was going to happen in these meetings. It was not that they were emotionally charged, for the majority of the pastors were leaders in staid denominations such as the Lutheran. It was not until Friday of that week that a "break" occurred. Strange to relate, it followed a factual lecture I had given on the subject of the 1858–59 Awakenings in America and Britain. Under the wise leadership of Armin Gesswein, the heartfelt hunger of the pastors for another great reviving was channeled into a prayer meeting. Prayers were broken with tears and sobs. Confessions of failure were made. Reconciliations between pastors were effected. It was the beginning of real revival in many a heart.[23]

Los Angeles 1949

Another meeting in Los Angeles held in March of 1949 was described by Mr. Claude C. Jenkins (executive secretary of the Christ for Greater Los Angeles organization, which was preparing to sponsor a campaign with Billy Graham as the evangelist):

> A most unusual pastors' prayer conference was held the first few days of March at the Pacific Palisades Presbyterian Conference Grounds near Los Angeles. . . .

> More than 400 ministers and their wives attended, and half of these continued in penitence and prayer until the early hours of the mornings. There was a great moving of the Spirit, with the spirit of Revival being carried out from the conference to many areas, even to Northern California.[24]

As a result of this conference, many churches reported increases in attendance at the mid-week service for prayer, as well as morning and evening worship on Sundays.

Another prayer conference for ministers was held in Los Angeles in September of 1949, led by Armin Gesswein, immediately prior to the Big Tent Campaign that was to bring Billy Graham national recognition. Participants included Billy Graham, J. Edwin Orr, and Louis Evans, Sr. According to Orr,

> Out of the prayer movement for ministers in Los Angeles grew thriving prayer fellowships in outlying districts, in the San Fernando Valley, in Long Beach, in San Diego, in South West Los Angeles, in the Pomona Valley.

> In the San Francisco Bay Area, the prayer fellowship increased steadily until more than a hundred pastors were attending the gatherings. In Seattle, a pastors' prayer fellowship was formed.[25]

Other Conferences

In addition to the Greater Los Angeles Revival Prayer Fellowship and the Mount Hermon Pastors' Conferences of the San Francisco Bay Area (developed by Robert Boyd Munger, Harold Erickson, David Braun, and others), a semi-annual conference began at King's Garden in Seattle; and in Chicago, two Presbyterian ministers, William Dunlap and Norman Krebbs, began the Northside Pastors' Prayer Meeting. Other similar groups appeared on the West Side and on the South Side of Chicago. In New York City, Dr. Samuel Shoemaker, rector of Calvary Episcopal Church and founder of Faith at Work, promoted a prayer movement among clergy and laity which was not directly related to the movement on the West Coast. Dr. Ernest Wadsworth of the Great Commission Prayer League, who convened prayer conferences for revival in Wheaton and Chicago, wrote extensively on the subject of pastors' prayer meetings. "The pattern began to be copied so widely that a network of pastors' prayer meetings sprang up across North America."[26]

At the January 1950 Revival Conference of pastors and leaders in King's Garden, Seattle, according to Orr, "the pastors had a sense at times that the Holy Spirit was forming a cloud of blessing over the area, and that they had some small relation to it. One of their number, Edwin Johnson, received great blessing, and afterwards journeyed to Wheaton College to lead the campaign there which proved to be a Holy Spirit visitation of national interest."[27]

According to a report of the Illinois Baptist State convention, issued by 120 pastors gathered in Springfield, Illinois:

> The annual Ministers' Conference of the Illinois Baptist State Convention, meeting in Springfield in the second week of April, 1951 with a definite yearning for spiritual reviving expressed in heart-searching and confession and prayer, resolved as follows:

> We recognize in many parts of our country the signs of a Spiritual Awakening, manifest in spontaneous ministers' prayer-meetings, in college awakenings, in conversions of celebrities, in anointing of acceptable evangelists, in increased public interest, and in a rising tide of blessing in churches of various denominations.[28]

COLLEGE REVIVALS

The college awakenings were another significant component of the mid-twentieth-century awakening. One of the earliest college awakenings at this time took place late in 1946, at Prairie Bible Institute in Three Hills, Alberta, under the ministry of Armin Gesswein. According to a letter written by Gesswein at that time, this awakening was characterized by "tremendous repentance, confession, restoration and restitution which put a stop to classes for days."[29]

In April of 1949 revival occurred at Bethel College in St. Paul, Minnesota, as reported in two evangelical periodicals, *Christian Life* and *United Evangelical Action*.[30] According to Fred W. Hoffman, a week before the outbreak of the Bethel College revival, J. Edwin Orr, Armin Gesswein, Jack Franck, William Dunlap, and Billy Graham had met in the latter's office in the early hours of the morning, interceding for a spiritual awakening among Christian students of the Northwest.[31]

At Bethel College, a liberal arts college supported by the Baptist General Conference of America, the Swedish-American Baptist constituency, there was much prayer in the dormitories, followed by intense conviction of sin among the students in chapel and in classrooms. The conviction was relieved by outright confession, restitution, restoration, and conversion to God.[32] The president of the college, Dr. Henry C. Wingblade, reminisced:

> I think none of us will forget that week, especially the climactic day, which was Thursday. The student body as a whole were on their faces before God in prayer, asking for His heart–searching, confessing before Him every known sin, and being willing to make any restitution that might be necessary. There have been many great meetings in the history of our school, but this was certainly one of the greatest experiences we have ever had. It's all by God's grace–we have nothing to boast about.[33]

According to Wingblade, "at the height of the movement in Bethel College, the student body of St. Paul Bible Institute of [the] Christian and Missionary Alliance visited the campus for a missionary rally and were stirred by the striking evidence of a local revival."[34] The faculty of St. Paul Bible Institute called for a day of prayer the following Monday, commencing at 5:00 a.m.

During the Bethel College awakening, President Wingblade visited the faculty of Northwestern College and Seminary in Minneapolis to relate the news of revival, and Harold Christianson, a Bethel student, spoke of the awakening to the student body of Northwestern at a chapel meeting. According to Christianson, the Bethel awakening had brought him the greatest blessing in his life after his conversion, and he believed that ninety-five percent of his fellow students had been so moved.[35] A series of chapel services was arranged for a week and was broadcast over radio station KTIS. Classes and examinations were given up as the whole school devoted itself to prayer.[36]

In October of 1949 Northern Baptist Theological Seminary, at that time located in Chicago, became the site of an awakening among its 375 students. The 10:00 p.m. vespers, which were voluntary, became crowded until midnight each night during a series of talks given by J. Edwin Orr. Julius R. Mantey, author of the well-known Greek grammar, reported that "nearly every student that I have asked says he was deeply stirred. Some say that they were led into their most climactic religious experience. We are all on a higher plane."[37]

The following month, in November, a spontaneous revival occurred on the campus of North Park College, a Covenant Church school in Chicago. According to the president, Dr. Algoth Ohlson, the break came among the students themselves during a midweek meeting which broke into fervent testimonies and confession.[38]

Wheaton College

February of 1950 was probably the most significant month for collegiate awakenings. On February 8, 1950, simultaneous awakenings were taking place at Wheaton College, a well-known interdenominational evangelical liberal arts college near Chicago, and Simpson Bible Institute in Seattle (a Christian and Missionary Alliance school). The widely publicized Wheaton College awakening continued until February 12. The stirrings at Simpson Bible Institute were part of a revival among several colleges and universities in the Pacific Northwest, including the University of Washington, Seattle Pacific College, and Northwest Bible College. Immediately following the Wheaton College awakening, Northern Baptist Seminary in Chicago experienced another move of the Spirit, which one observer described as a "most gracious visitation of the Spirit, . . . surpassing anything that any of us have ever experienced at Northern."[39] On February 13 there was a visitation at California Baptist Seminary, and on February 12–19 Lee College in Cleveland, Tennessee, experienced an extraordinary outpouring of the Holy Spirit. From February 23 until March 1 an unusual visitation at Asbury College in Wilmore, Kentucky, received nationwide press coverage.

The Wheaton College awakening took place during a series of midwinter services scheduled for February 5–12, 1950. The speaker for the services, Edwin S. Johnson, a graduate of North Park College and Seminary, had just come from the Revival Conference of pastors and leaders in Seattle.[40] Stirred by that revival, on February 5, Johnson spoke on the words of 2 Chronicles 20:12, "neither know we what to do: but our eyes are upon thee." February 7 was set aside as a day of prayer without classes. According to W. Wyeth Willard, "we met by divisions or classes, and petitioned the Heavenly Father that He would open the windows of Heaven and pour upon us His blessings."[41] On the morning of February 8, a student asked V. Raymond Edman, the president of the college, if he could have a few minutes in the evening chapel service to "tell the students how God had forgiven his sin and given him victory in his life."[42] The student was told that at about 7:15 p.m. he could do as he had asked. That evening, after he was finished, other students also rose and spoke. Two students who were dissatisfied with their spiritual experience requested prayer, and Dr. Edman told the second, Eugene Lyle, that there would be prayer for him after he had spoken. By the time Lyle had finished at 7:30, several others had stood to await their turn. Within a short time, sixty people were standing, and Dr. Edman did not have a chance to pray. Testimonies continued into the night and throughout the following day, except for a brief message on Psalm 1 by Edwin Johnson at 9:00 p.m. on February 9. At 9:00 a.m. the following day (February 10), President Edman ended the public meeting and told those who still wished to speak to go to Arrow Hall, just behind the platform, where the meeting continued until 2:00 p.m. that day.

News of the extended service reached Chicago newspapermen, and John H. Thompson, military editor for the *Chicago Tribune*, went to the campus to cover the event "with the cynicism of his trade," but he was soon impressed with "the intensity of emotion and the obvious sincerity of the students."[43] News releases appeared on the front pages of papers in Chicago, Miami, Los Angeles, Seattle, and New York.[44] Photographs appeared in *Time* and *Life* magazines (February 20, 1950) with articles entitled "42 Hours of Repentance"[45] and "College Revival Becomes Confession Marathon."[46] According to the article in *Life* magazine, when Edwin Johnson finally got the floor he said, "a reporter this morning asked me if all this was planned. I told him: 'Only as God has planned it.' "[47] J. Edwin Orr wrote that on the morning of Thursday, February 9, the editors of the *Chicago Daily News* were amazed that a meeting had gone on all night at Wheaton College. They asked Vaughn Shoemaker, the famous cartoonist, to report on the revival. Shoemaker was a Christian man who knew Wheaton well, and his sympathetic account was the first to hit the front pages.[48]

According to Earle E. Cairns, President Edman's biographer, one of the several notes in Dr. Edman's files told of a phone call from

Billy Graham in Atlanta who had heard the news of the Wheaton
College awakening and was having a special prayer meeting for Wheaton that night.[49]

Edman spoke of the Wheaton awakening as "days of Heaven upon
earth."[50] Chaplain W. Wyeth Willard, assistant to the president, wrote
that hearts were broken and melted, the Holy Spirit gave to all a forgiv-
ing heart, students and faculty made amends for past sins, and people
resolved to endeavor to lead better Christian lives. He continued:

> 5. During the revival, one noticed that time was as nothing. The night
> passed as though it were an hour or less. . . . Hymns were sung and prayers
> were offered to the Lord. The delight of the occasion made the passing
> of time seem like a dream.

> 6. The revival brought with it the radiance of Heaven. . . . In my forty-five
> years of this life, I have never thrilled with such "joy, real joy, wonderful
> joy" as during those days. On the campus, one could see wreaths of smiles
> on some faces which had formerly displayed downcast, discouraged, de-
> feated or disappointed expressions. . . .

> 7. The revival has brought innumerable lasting results. . . . *We will never be*
> *the same again.*[51]

The awakening at Wheaton was to have a tremendous impact upon
other evangelical colleges (and evangelicalism in general) due to its
widespread reputation as a prominent evangelical institution. A
Wheaton student, Bud Schaeffer, flew with Edwin Johnson to Seattle
to speak eight times on Sunday, February 12, and four times the following day at various churches, bringing news of the revival.[52]
Among the places he visited was Seattle Pacific College, sparking
revival there.[53] In addition to Seattle Pacific, Cairns listed several
other colleges experiencing similar movements at the same time.[54]
In a similar list, Fred W. Hoffman also mentioned Westmont College
in California and Multnomah School of the Bible in the Northwest.[55]

Warren C. Young described the February 1950 revival at Northern
Baptist Theological Seminary in Chicago:

> The renewal was brought on by what had been happening at Wheaton. Stu-
> dents from our campus attended some of the services at Wheaton and
> brought back reports of what was going on there. Our chapel service was
> opened by the president to anyone who wanted to speak. That was the be-
> ginning of several extended services of confession, praise, prayer, etc. As I
> recall now, the first service began with the mid-morning chapel and continued
> without a break until late evening—between 10:00–11:00 p.m. This was re-
> peated the next day, beginning with the chapel service and continuing

into the evening. There were extended services for the rest of the week, although not as long as the first day or two.[56]

John F. Taylor related the awakening at Nyack College:

The services went late into the night and at one of the dinners in the dining hall, two or three students gave testimonies which lasted for a long period of time. I cannot remember all of the details but I do remember that it was an unusual series of services for us and probably the most outstanding in the last thirty years [1946–1976].[57]

February 5–10, the week of the outbreak of revival at Wheaton College, was also the week of stirrings at Simpson Bible College. In fact, both awakenings broke out on Wednesday, February 8. Professor William H. Wrighton of Simpson wrote:

By Wednesday, the conviction among the students had become so deep that the chapel service lasted three hours and classes were suspended in favor of prayer. Evening sessions continued until midnight. . . . One young man at the risk of Federal imprisonment restored some property stolen before his call to Christian service. . . .

Strange to relate, a second wave of conviction swept the school on Friday. . . . We have never had anything like this stirring in the history of the school.[58]

The Simpson awakening sparked renewal at the University of Washington, Seattle Pacific College, Northwest Bible College, and the University of British Columbia, as well as many churches in the Seattle area. After the college revivals in the Pacific Northwest, there were awakenings at Baylor University in Texas and Houghton College in New York.[59]

Lee College and Asbury College

Two other significant college awakenings in 1950 took place at Lee College in Cleveland, Tennessee, and Asbury College in Wilmore, Kentucky. The February 12–19 awakening at Lee College, a Church of God (Cleveland, Tenn.) school, was given detailed coverage in the *Church of God Evangel*, February 25, March 4, and March 18, 1950, and in the *Lighted Pathway* of April 1950. J. Stewart Brinsfield, president of the college, reported, "I have been associated with the Church of God for more than 27 years and have witnessed many great revivals, but the meetings here have been the greatest in all my experience."[60] He continued as follows:

The gifts of the Spirit have been manifested among faculty and students alike. To date practically every unsaved person has been brought to Christ. There were confessions of sin and disobedience. We had no way to count the numbers who received the Holy Ghost, because people from the outside were in our meetings. The whole auditorium was an altar. People sought God by the hundreds. This was really a mass revival.[61]

Zeno C. Tharp, assistant general overseer of the Church of God, wrote of the Lee College revival:

The revival had such effect on students until they seemed to have lost interest in practically everything else but the revival. Classes were closed for the week. The campus was almost bare of students or faculty. From outside appearance, one would almost think the school had closed. . . . The General Overseer tried to reach the school by telephone, but the operator answered, "I cannot get Lee College. I have not been able to get them all afternoon." Yet, while the dormitories and campus were void of people, the auditorium was filled. Scores of students were tarrying before God all day and late into the night.[62]

A teacher of the college, Nina Driggers, wrote, "this mighty power of the Holy Ghost was so great in the auditorium that it seemed to be a powerful magnet, pulling the people in. One could feel His divine presence as he entered the door."[63] One of the students remarked, "there is no speech nor language that could fully describe it. It was the glory of God come down to earth."[64]

The Asbury College awakening began on February 23, 1950. On that date, the guest speakers for the regular 9:00 a.m. chapel service were the Reverend and Mrs. Dee Cobb. They sang a song, and as Mr. Cobb was about to begin the message, "a holy hush settled down."[65] Robert Barefoot stood to give a word of praise for a prayer meeting that some of the students had had the previous night, at which many of them had found the Lord. Others rose to testify, and the leader of the service stepped forward to say that he thought time should be given to the speaker to give his message. Cobb, somewhat reluctant to speak, read Joshua 14:8 and gave an abbreviated message on the text. Cobb later wrote that, as he spoke,

It was as though an electric shock moved over the whole place, and there was such a sense of the presence of God that one felt almost as though he could just reach out and touch Him. From where I stood I would probably best describe it as something like a gentle breeze sweeping across a broad field of wheat. Everyone seemed moved, tears started down some cheeks, and a rapture of delight stirred some to gentle laughter. All over the auditorium young people were standing. Then some, weeping, started to the altar. From then on it was like feasting on the heavenlies.[66]

The service, which began on a Thursday at 9:00 a.m., continued uninterrupted throughout the day and into the night. The crowd remained long after midnight, and at 6:00 a.m. Friday, the services were still going on. "Almost immediately thereafter the crowds began to assemble. They seemed to have been drawn by a mighty magnet."[67] Throughout Friday, students took turns testifying. The services continued in the same manner throughout the week. The audience was advised to attend various churches in Wilmore Sunday morning. Most of the group did, but the service at Asbury continued. Sunday afternoon and evening were "tremendous services," and the marathon meeting did not end until 7:00 a.m. on March 1.

According to an anonymous eyewitness testimony of the Asbury College revival published in Bill Bright's *Awakening* bulletin,

It never occurred to any of us that publicity should be sought or was necessary. However, two newsmen were on the job the first night. Their cameras flashed continuously through the service, but such was the Divine Presence that no one seemed to notice them. The Louisville and Lexington papers gave the news release throughout the nation. On Sunday, eight persons, representing the United Press, Associated Press, and television came upon the campus and remained for eight hours. They informed us that, in news circles, the revival at Asbury College was second only to the national coal strike. The newsmen were most sympathetic throughout, and added that they felt like intruders upon holy ground.[68]

The manager of WVLK, a radio station in Versailles, Kentucky, called and asked for the privilege of broadcasting the service over his station.[69] As the awakening at Asbury gained attention through newspapers and television coverage, many visitors and friends travelled to the campus out of curiosity. Jimmy Rose, a basketball coach at Paris High School in Kentucky, read of the spontaneous revival in the newspapers and went to Wilmore with the Reverend Earl Curry. He recounted his arrival at the college:

My most vivid memory of that day was when I opened the door of Hughes Auditorium. Although I could not explain it then, I know now that it was the presence of the Holy Spirit. Others have testified to having felt this supernatural presence upon entering the building. There was a certain feeling about His presence that gave one a sense of peace and surrender. I have felt the presence of the Holy Spirit on many occasions since then, but never in such power.[70]

According to the account of a student, Ruby Vahey, "teachers and students were unable to bring themselves back so suddenly from the heavenly to the earthly, and every class that morning was transformed into a prayer or praise meeting."[71]

Paul Rader and Henry James attributed the outbreak of the revival to "fervent and prevailing prayer."[72] Dr. W. Curry Mavis, professor of the pastoral relations department at Asbury, wrote:

> For several weeks before the meeting started there had been much earnest prayer for an outpouring of the Spirit of God. Groups of students and faculty people met in the dormitory rooms and offices to pray. This spirit of prayer continued while the meeting was in progress. Frequently every room in the college auditorium building was occupied by groups of people in silent prayer. At other times, as the main service was in progress, the voices of prayer could be heard in other parts of the building.[73]

During the revival, prayer meetings were in progress everywhere, including dormitories, classrooms, the dining hall, the gymnasium, on campus, and in the homes of residents of Wilmore. "A spirit of prayer seemed to possess each person that had attended the services and felt the presence of God."[74]

The Asbury awakening affected other locations throughout all of North America. A student from Southern Baptist Theological Seminary in Louisville, Kentucky, stated that his prayer was that he might carry back with him "something just like this, along with the power that is here."[75] Another student riding south on a bus began talking to a preacher just behind the driver. The bus driver, hearing about the Asbury revival, "became so convicted that he requested permission of the passengers to pull to the side of the road for a period of prayer."[76] Five students from Asbury went to Ludlow Methodist Church in Ludlow, Kentucky, where "hearts melted and tears flowed freely down the cheeks of many" as a result of their testimony.[77] Reverend R. E. Case, pastor of Wells Memorial Methodist Church in Jackson, Mississippi, requested that a gospel team be sent to his church from Asbury.

> A concerned Christian lady paid their transportation by air, and three students from Asbury College and one from Asbury Theological Seminary were on their way within a short time. They phoned back the next day, stating that the church was packed and people were standing in the streets, and between fifty and sixty people were at the altar.[78]

More students from Asbury arrived at Jackson, and some went to Hattiesburg, Mississippi, to the Broadstreet Church pastored by Reverend Andrew Gallman, where revival broke. Another group sparked revival at Natchez, Mississippi. People were attracted to the revival in Mississippi from six states. Several prayer meetings were held all night. The host churches found it impossible to accommodate the crowds.[79]

IMPORTANT EVANGELISTS

Billy Graham

In addition to the campus revivals of this era, another factor contributing to the post–World War II awakening was the emergence of Billy Graham and other evangelists. Graham's campaign in Los Angeles, California, during September and October of 1949 was sponsored by Christ for Greater Los Angeles in cooperation with 1000 churches of all denominations. It was planned to last three weeks but was extended time after time by popular demand, until it had continued eight weeks. These meetings gained widespread attention through the conversion of three celebrities, Stuart Hamblen (a television star), Louis Zamperini (a former Olympic athlete), and a third man who was "an alleged associate of the notorious racketeer, Mickey Cohen."[80]

During the third week, the Los Angeles committee met to decide whether or not to continue the meetings, which had begun on September 25 and were scheduled to terminate October 16. The committee decided to continue for another day and then consider extending the meetings. On that night of October 16, at 4:00 a.m., Stuart Hamblen, "under great conviction," awakened Graham from his sleep by telephone to ask him to pray with him. This incident received widespread attention, and 3000 seats were added to the tent, providing for 9000 hearers. Thousands had to stand outside of the tent on sidewalks. Graham told of transatlantic telephone calls to his hotel and of the disturbance of meetings by crews cf photographers and reporters.[81]

The conversion of Louis Zamperini during the Los Angeles campaign created almost as great a sensation as the conversion of Stuart Hamblen. Zamperini had been in Berlin, Germany, for the 1936 Olympics, in which he was the first American to finish in the 5000-meter race. He almost lost his life in an attempt to steal Hitler's private swastika at his headquarters in Berlin. Zamperini was later declared missing in action and then dead when he was taken prisoner by the

Japanese during World War II. His dramatic return several years later made him a Hollywood hero overnight. This famed celebrity, while attending a meeting during Billy Graham's campaign, rushed forward when the invitation was given and made his decision in the prayer room of the Canvas Cathedral. The newspapers, which only a few years before had reported on the Olympic hero's return from Japan after he had been thought dead, flashed news of his conversion throughout the nation. Zamperini soon began work in Youth for Christ rallies and eventually returned to Japan, conviction growing upon him that he should return to the country where he was tormented to declare his forgiveness and preach the way of salvation.[82]

Newspaper publicity of the Billy Graham campaign in Los Angeles paved the way for further meetings in Boston, Massachusetts (January, 1950), and Columbia, South Carolina. Following a second effort in New England (April, 1950), he went to Portland, Oregon.

The eighteen-day campaign at Park Street Church in Boston opened on New Year's Day, 1950. Dr. Harold J. Ockenga reported on the meetings:

> Today all of New England is stirred, waiting, as a result of the outpouring of the Holy Spirit during the Billy Graham evangelistic campaign in Boston. Newspapers of the city gave six and eight column front page pictures to the concluding meeting at the Boston Garden, when sixteen thousand packed New England's largest hall. Hundreds accepted Christ every night.[83]

The meetings in Columbia, South Carolina, were publicized in *Time* and *Life* magazines, which carried a page and a half of pictures of the campaign. According to *Life*, the meeting was attended by 40,000 people in the University of South Carolina's football stadium, and 10,000 were turned away. Among those attending were South Carolina's governor, J. Strom Thurmond, and former secretary of state, James F. Byrnes. More than 2000 knelt before the rostrum to "make decisions for Christ."[84]

After Graham's return to Boston in April, Ockenga reported that "for two hundred years there has been no such movement in New England. George Whitefield was the last man who stirred New England in such a way."[85]

Chuck Templeton

Another young evangelist who captured North America's attention by the middle of the twentieth century was Charles Templeton, a self-taught Canadian who began his early career as a sports cartoonist. In 1954 Edward L. R. Elson wrote of Templeton:

> Few who come under the influence of Charles Templeton leave his services unmoved.
>
> . . . Although he possessed no college degree, his intellectual maturity prompted Princeton Theological Seminary to admit him as a special student. Upon the completion of his seminary course, he was ordained a Presbyterian minister and appointed evangelist under the National Council of Churches which represents some thirty-five million Protestants. Because of the quality of his preaching, almost any pulpit in America is open to him. He is booked two years in advance for evangelistic services.[86]

The impact of "Chuck" Templeton upon the cities he visited as an evangelist was extraordinary. In Evansville, Indiana, 91,000 attended his meetings out of a total population of 128,000. In Sydney, Nova Scotia, out of a population of 30,000 there were 10,000 present on his closing night.[87] Within a few years, however, Templeton left the Christian ministry and during the next couple of decades became one of Canada's foremost media personalities.

Tom Rees, Bryan Green, and Mervin Rosell

In October, 1947, the British evangelist Tom Rees, who had had remarkably successful post-war meetings in the Royal Albert Hall in London, held a campaign in Winnipeg which consistently packed out the 6000-seat Civic Auditorium for three weeks. This began the pattern of an annual ministry in North America.

Bryan Green, the British Anglican clergyman and part-time evangelist, visited New York City's Cathedral of St. John the Divine in 1949. Ten thousand people attended nightly, and many were turned away. According to an article in Bill Bright's *Awakening* bulletin, "all over New York in all sorts of places, in buses and subways, in offices and barbershops one could hear excited comments concerning the meetings."[88] S. M. Shoemaker, a leader of the New York City campaign, described the campaign of "England's top-flight evangelist":

> The whole experience has inspired us and given us new heart for the days to come. It has also surprised us, surprised the bishops and clergy and people—surprised the missioner himself who tells me he has never in his long experiences known anything like it.[89]

Mervin Rosell, who had been an evangelist since the 1930s, was one of the people involved with the formation of Youth for Christ in 1944. He was the speaker at the first mass rally held in the fall of 1944 under Youth for Christ auspices in Chicago, where 30,000 young people gathered at the Chicago Stadium.

In August of 1950, Rosell went to Des Moines for the great Iowa for Christ Crusade, with Herbert Hoover as songleader and Cy Jackson as manager. The governor of the state permitted him to pitch a tent on the lawns of the state capitol, and it became necessary to pitch three circus tents to seat the crowds. By September 3, Governor Beardsley, Charles E. Fuller, and Mervin Rosell were leading a prayer meeting of 30,000 people on the steps of the state capitol.[90] According to J. Edwin Orr,

> There were tears and confessions and reconciliations and blessings abounding. More important still, the effect of the prayer meetings was immediately evident in the pulpits, where pastors preached with new power and congregations were moved so that conversions were occurring in churches on Sunday as well as in the Big Tent on weekdays.[91]

In Chicago, Rosell conducted a campaign under the auspices of Youth for Christ in Orchestra Hall on Michigan Boulevard. On one Thursday evening, he called upon Alastair Walker to describe the revival that had broken out that day among students at Northern Baptist Seminary. "So great was the power of God in that testimony that Dr. Rosell gave an immediate invitation to the crowd, after which a couple of hundred people came forward under conviction of sin."[92] In describing the Chicago meetings, Mervin Rosell stated, "I did not preach very well, but when I gave the invitation almost everyone in the Hall fell on his knees before God in prayer. A strange power of the Spirit which I know attended me every night bringing deep conviction."[93]

The following campaign in Phoenix had an aggregate attendance almost equal to the population of the city itself. The crusade chairman, Habegger, said, "more churches have united, more people have attended, and more decisions were recorded for Christ than in any similar endeavor ever known to the held in that state."[94]

Other evangelists who became widely recognized at this time included Jack Shuler, Bob Jones, Jr., Hyman Appelman, and Alan Redpath. Their rise to prominence was a result of the remarkable outpouring of God's Spirit that had taken place. The power and depth of this awakening were not to be equalled again on such a massive scale until the awakening of the late 1960s and early 1970s, the subject of the next chapter.

7

THE REVIVAL OF
THE 1960s AND 1970s

IN THE LATE 1960s AND EARLY 1970s, there was another worldwide awakening, originating, for the most part, outside of the mainline denominations, although the established churches would soon be affected by it. Two of the most important components of this revival were the Charismatic renewal and the Jesus movement. The Charismatic renewal emphasized the baptism of the Holy Spirit and the miraculous gifts of the Spirit, including tongues and prophecy, while the Jesus movement began primarily among young people, many of whom were part of the countercultural movements of that era. The Jesus movement included many Charismatics, but its emphasis was primarily upon evangelism; moreover, there was a wide spectrum of viewpoints within it regarding the charismatic gifts.

The Charismatic movement originated prior to the late 1960s, but it reached the peak of its visibility and impact during the awakening of this time. It arose out of the many small, independent prayer meetings taking place in the homes of clergy and Christian laity. Some of these groups met as early as 1956, when twenty ministers from various denominations met periodically to pray, exercising the charismatic gifts of the Spirit. In the same year, the movement first gained publicity when a Presbyterian minister informed his congregation that he had spoken in tongues.[1] More sensational news coverage was given to Dennis J. Bennett, the rector of St. Mark's Episcopal Church in Van Nuys, California, who announced to his church in 1960 that he had received the Pentecostal experience of baptism in the Holy Spirit and had spoken in tongues.[2] Throughout the 1960s, manifestations of the miraculous gifts of the Spirit transcended ecclesiastical, cultural, sociological, and educational boundaries and became increasingly present among Lutherans, Baptists, Methodists, Dutch Reformed, and other major Protestant denominations. By 1966, this "Neo-pentecostal movement" had begun to sweep through Roman Catholicism as well, and within a few years it became clear to church leaders that a "powerful move of the Holy Spirit has come in an unstructured, unprogrammed way, crumbling theological prejudices, weakening denominational restrictiveness, and leaping traditional cultural barriers."[3]

THE JESUS MOVEMENT

While the Charismatic movement arose gradually, gaining momentum during the late 1960s, the Jesus movement began in 1967 when several independent ministries arose spontaneously among young people. These began along the West Coast and quickly spread throughout North America and Europe. Among the first of these were "The Living Room," a Christian coffeehouse founded by Ted Wise in the Haight-Ashbury section of San Francisco; "His Place," begun by Arthur Blessitt in Griffith Park, Los Angeles; "The Ark," a "rapping post" in Seattle, Washington, started by Linda Meissner; and Tony and Susan Alamo's "Christian Foundation" in Saugus, California. Within a year or two, young people throughout all of North America were involved in the Jesus movement, leaving behind the hippie lifestyle with its emphasis upon sex and drugs and its involvement with radical left-wing political movements. David Wilkerson, an Assemblies of God minister who founded Teen Challenge, a highly effective Christian drug rehabilitation organization, estimated that there were 300,000 Jesus People in the early 1970s. Moreover, these people may have had an influence far exceeding their numbers.[4]

While the Jesus movement was an important aspect of the awakening of this period, it did not take place only among young people. William Willoughby, at that time religious news editor of the *Washington Star*, wrote that the movement among the young was "just a part of the total movement. It is a true spiritual revival."[5] One of the people reporting on the movement, Michael McFadden, probably overstated the case when he wrote enthusiastically that "many do feel that it is already more significant than the first Great Awakening led by Jonathan Edwards and George Whitefield in the 1740s."[6]

The Jesus movement came about at a time when large numbers of people were searching for meaning in their lives, and few people seemed to be able to find the answers to their questions in the established churches. As Roger C. Palms observed, "the kids don't want church programs given to them. They want a family of God, growing together and helping one another. . . . They want depth; they want content. They want to find the Christ who can meet them in the midst of a very rough world."[7]

In 1971 the Jesus movement received wide press coverage, with articles appearing in *Look* (February 9), *Life* (May 14), *Time* (June 21), and in several consecutive articles on the front pages of the *Chicago Tribune*.[8] The young converts took the Bible at face value and began to find significance in their lives. For many of them, the words of the Bible seemed to come alive. One representative statement by a twenty-two-year-old young woman was that "I've read the words before, and they were just words, but all of a sudden they really mean what they say."[9] Of course, one of the primary characteristics of the Jesus People was that they all had testimonies of changed lives. Each person had had a personal encounter with Jesus Christ and had been liberated from various kinds of sin and bondage, including drug addiction in many cases.[10]

One major emphasis of the Jesus movement was upon the imminent premillennial return of Jesus Christ. A major spokesman of the movement and a founder of the "JC Light and Power House" in Los Angeles, Hal Lindsay, wrote *The Late Great Planet Earth* to demonstrate that the signs of the times indicated that Jesus was coming soon to put an end to the social and political problems of the world and to bring judgment to all wickedness.

Tony and Susan Alamo

Perhaps typical of the myriad of ministries that flourished among the street people of this time was that of Tony and Susan Alamo. Tony was born in Montana, and his original name was Bernie Lazar Hoffman. He had done promotion work for Sonny and Cher, P. J. Proby, and Earl McDaniel, and became widely known and rather wealthy, especially after his own recording label ("Talamo") became extremely successful. One day, however, during a business meeting he received an audible message from God that he must either die or announce to the people in the boardroom that Jesus was coming soon. This came as a shock to him, especially since he was Jewish, but it led to a new life in service to Jesus Christ. Susan, on the other hand, although also brought up in a Jewish home, became an evangelist for many years after a series of experiences that began with "a very supernatural experience with the living God" at nine years of age and ended with a career in motion pictures. They were married in 1965 and established the Christian Foundation in 1966. "We didn't ask for this work. . . . God called us into this work." They began their first ministry as a pair of itinerant evangelists occupationally engaged full-time. Susan attempted to convince Tony to pass out tracts with her on the streets of Hollywood. Finally, she said to him, "Look, I'm going on the streets tonight, and I'm going to pass out gospel tracts. You can stay home." Not anxious to allow her to go out among drug addicts and potential killers, he accompanied her, and they soon attracted a large following. They filled a rented house with crowds coming every night "braving cramped conditions to hear Susie preach."[11] Although the Alamos approached everyone on Hollywood Boulevard, it seemed that many of the most responsive people were drug users.[12]

Ted Wise

Another significant ministry of the Jesus movement was that of Ted Wise, a sailmaker in Sausalito, California. Formerly a heroin user, he began taking LSD obtained from the first black market in Haight-Ashbury. He and his wife Elizabeth were living in a commune in San Francisco. When their marriage problems went from bad to worse, she went to First Baptist Church in Mill Valley while still high on LSD and asked the congregation to pray for Ted. She had become a Christian at twelve years of age at a Mt. Hermon Bible conference and decided to rededicate her life to Christ at this time.

One day in 1966, Ted picked up a Bible, began reading the New Testament, and quietly committed his life to Christ. He began sharing his find with his friends, and one of his first converts was Danny Sands, who had been heavily involved in drugs and alcohol, communism, anarchy, and campus radicalism. The dramatic change in Ted's life convinced Danny of the reality of Christianity. Ted's second convert, Jim Dopp, was a right wing conservative and a successful salesman who smoked marijuana and took LSD. He was convinced while listening to his friend Steve Heefner engage in debate with Ted about forgiveness of sins and spiritual rebirth. Steve was known professionally as Steve O'Shea, a popular disk jockey on the city's top music station. Soon afterward, Steve also became a Christian and began sharing his faith on the radio, resulting in his dismissal from the station.

In 1967 these four people helped to establish the first Christian coffeehouse in Haight-Ashbury, "The Living Room." Within a few months, they formed a Christian commune, renting a house near Mill Valley. They moved in with their wives and children, naming it the House of Acts. Hundreds of people visited, and many found Christ there. Others who came were Christians searching for a fellowship of believers that would enable them to remain strong spiritually. One nineteen-year old, Lonnie Frisbee, was in this category. He later moved with his wife Connie to Southern California to open the House of Miracles in Costa Mesa under the sponsorship of Calvary Chapel, a nearby church pastored by Chuck Smith. Within two years, the attendance of this church rose from 150 to the thousands. Most of these people had been touched by the ministry of the House of Miracles. In 1970 there were 4000 conversions to Christ, and over 2000 people were baptized in the Pacific Ocean. During this time, converts of this ministry began opening other house ministries in California, Arizona, Nevada, Oregon, and Idaho.[13]

Linda Meissner

Another important early ministry of the Jesus movement was that of Linda Meissner, who was in Hong Kong trying to minister to the needs of the sick, when the Lord said to her, "come back to Seattle, Washington, and by yourself . . . be obedient to what I tell you. I will raise up a mighty army of young people, and you'll go forth and speak the words of life, and . . . they'll all go forth and bring healing to the people."[14] She returned to the United States and went to Phoenix, Arizona, where the Lord continued to deal with her about her call. After struggling with this for a year and a half, she finally went to Seattle. She crisscrossed the city as a travelling evangelist, speaking at local churches and school assemblies, and "anywhere from fifty to seventy-five percent of the audience would accept Christ."[15] In 1967, Meissner began attracting a following of converted street people, and she began recruiting the "Jesus People's Army." In 1969 the revival spread like wildfire from Seattle Lincoln High School, where many prayer meetings had been organized.[16]

The Influence of the Jesus Movement

Stories like these could be multiplied a hundredfold and are described in more than a dozen books published in the early 1970s on the Jesus movement.[17] The extent of the influence of the Jesus movement can be determined by the circulation statistics for many of its "underground" newspapers. Duane Pederson wrote in May of 1971 that the circulation for his *Hollywood Free Paper* was 350,000 at that time.[18] Later that year, its circulation had reached 400,000 and it was still growing.[19] Another paper, *Right On!* published by the Christian World Liberation Front on the Berkeley campus of the University of California, grew from 20,000 at its outset to more than 100,000 during special campus events and the huge peace marches at that time.[20] *Oracle*, published in the San Francisco Bay area, had an international circulation of 100,000 before it was turned into a Jesus newspaper in October of 1970 due to the conversion of its editor, David Abraham, who transferred the editorship of the paper to Chris D'Alessandro, who had led him to Christ.[21] In October of 1970, Carl Parks of Spokane, Washington, launched *Truth*, which began with a circulation of 20,000 copies, but its circulation grew to 100,000 within three months.[22] Linda Meissner of Seattle merged her own *Agape* with this paper.

The lordship of Christ became evident, not only in the free press, but also in the area of pop music. A flood of Christian musicals hit the market in the late 1960s, including *Tell It Like It Is* (1969) by Ralph Carmichael and Kurt Kaiser, which sold 300,000 copies, J. Phillip Landgrave's *Purpose*, and *Show Me*, a musical by "mod" composer Jimmy Owens and his wife that was about a young man named Joey who finally gets beyond "Churchianity" and into Christ.[23]

Many rock groups forsook drug circuits and dedicated themselves to Jesus Christ, including Love Song, led by Chuck Girard. Mike Messer and Randy Wilcox of Wilson McKinley, a Pacific Northwest rock group, joined Jim Bartlett to do the same kind of music, but now "only for Jesus 100 per cent."[24] One of the most popular Christian rock singers was Larry Norman.[25] Other name performers became Christians, including Tiny Tim, Paul Stookey of Peter, Paul, and Mary, Johnny Cash, Arlo Guthrie, and renowned guitarist Eric Clapton. Turley Richards came to Christ as a result of a long distance telephone call to syndicated disc jockey Scott Ross on Christmas Eve of 1970.[26] Singer Pat Boone baptized scores of people in his swimming pool during the first six months of 1971.[27]

Jews for Jesus

The Jesus movement had its effects upon many Jewish people, who came to recognize Jesus as their Messiah. In the San Francisco area, "Jews for Jesus" received its initial impetus under the leadership of Moishe Rosen.[28] Rosen had been closely associated with the American Board of Missions to the Jews since 1953. While in New York, he convinced the Board to allow him to go to San Francisco to learn how to work with youth on the streets in 1970. Some of the young Jews who became Christians through his ministry began to wear some of the clothing of the Jesus People and to use the vernacular "lingo" of the street Christians. Anxious to avoid sectarianism, he encouraged his converts to share in the prayer meetings of these people, and he began speaking at mass rallies with Jack Sparks of the Christian World Liberation Front, Linda Meissner, Duane Pederson, and others. At a mass rally held at San Francisco State College, Rosen showed up with two hundred large posters, one side of each saying JEWS FOR JESUS, with miscellaneous statements on the other side, such as JESUS CAN MAKE YOU KOSHER and YOU DON'T HAVE TO BE JEWISH TO LOVE JESUS. He also distributed lapel buttons and handed out fliers that identified Jews for Jesus not as a movement but as a fact of faith: that Christianity is Jewish. The following day, however, "Jews for Jesus" received extensive coverage as a movement by major newspapers.[29]

CAMPUS REVIVALS

The awakening of the late 1960s and early 1970s was also a time of campus revivals. Ed Plowman wrote that he knew "students whose lives were transformed in campus revivals during those years," who later became involved in significant ministries.[30] One of the most widely publicized campus revivals of that time took place at Asbury College in Wilmore, Kentucky, a site of earlier revival activity. At a chapel service on February 3, 1970, a revival spread across the campus and, within a week, throughout the country.[31] It had begun at a normal Tuesday morning service when the dean, Custer Reynolds, invited students to come forward and speak. Before long, there was "a constant stream of young people taking the microphone and declaring that their lives were changed, that they had been born again."[32] One of the eyewitnesses, Jeff Blake, scribbled a note as the revival began:

A few minutes ago there came a spontaneous movement of the Holy Spirit. I have never witnessed such a mighty outpouring of God upon his people. The scene is unbelievable.[33]

Michael Jacob wrote that "news of the revival spread rapidly, and the college chapel was filled with reporters and photographers capturing the emotions of the moment. The publicity led to requests from other colleges for Asbury students to come and speak, and this, in turn, sparked off mini-revivals in other parts of the country."[34] Teams of witnesses were sent to many places in response to the flood of requests for students to share their experiences at other schools. One of the schools to which "witness teams" travelled from Asbury was Southwestern Baptist Seminary in Fort Worth, Texas. *Home Missions* magazine reported:

Scarborough Preaching Chapel . . . was packed. . . . Each Asbury visitor stood and made a brief report . . . and then they sat down—without a word of invitation or direction. . . . There was an extended, awkward moment of bewilderment. And then a young preacher stood and with measured deliberation began to speak his own need for personal renewal.[35]

Immediately afterward, other students spoke. Professors joined, and the testimonies continued, just as they had at Asbury, where the testimonies had continued for 185 consecutive hours.[36] The president of Asbury, Dr. Kinlaw, commented during an interview with news reporters:

This is what is happening in churches, schools, and towns across America. God is walking in. Since this awakening thousands of students continue to answer invitations to share in all parts of the country and in Canada and Latin America. . . .[37]

According to Erling Jorstad in the spring of 1972, the momentum for revival on college campuses continued to grow. While students on the West Coast demonstrated a sustained interest in the Jesus movement, there was a continued proliferation of evangelistic coffeehouses, cell groups, and Bible study throughout the country, especially at Princeton and Harvard.[38] There were outpourings of the Spirit at Eastern Illinois University at Charleston and North Park College in Chicago where, without any pre-planning, students began to acknowledge their sins publicly and to answer altar calls spontaneously and informally.[39] On secular campuses, such organizations as the American Association of Evangelical Students, Inter-Varsity Christian Fellowship, and Campus Crusade for Christ became beehives of Christian activity.[40] The visibility of these groups increased considerably with record-breaking attendance at such national meetings as the Inter-Varsity triennial conventions at Urbana, Illinois, in December of 1970 and 1973, and Campus Crusade for Christ's Explo '72, attended by 80,000 students and laypersons during the week of June 12–17, 1972, in Dallas, Texas.[41]

THE CHARISMATIC RENEWAL

The Yale Revival

Several years prior to the 1970 outpouring of the Spirit upon evangelical colleges and universities that began at Asbury, the secular universities had been touched by revival as a result of the Charismatic renewal. In October of 1962, a charismatic revival took place at Yale University in New Haven, Connecticut, among members of Inter-Varsity Christian Fellowship. Two students witnessed healing services at a local Episcopal church performed by Francis Whiting, a Baptist minister from Michigan. Other students had read *Trinity* magazine, a periodical updating people on the fledgling Charismatic movement that had begun at Dennis Bennett's former church, St. Mark's Episcopal Church. The students arranged to hold a weekend retreat, and Harald Bredesen, a charismatic who was at that time pastor of First Reformed Church, a Dutch Reformed church in Mt. Vernon, New York, was invited to speak. He brought with him four young people who had been baptized in the Holy Spirit and had spoken in tongues. During the weekend of the retreat, eight Yale students and these four young people had a prayer meeting in a room of the chapel building. Soon, six of the eight students were speaking in tongues, during which time a faculty member entered the room. Before the meeting was over, he also was baptized in the Holy Spirit. By the end of the weekend, seven other Yale students also received this experience. Private charismatic prayer meetings were subsequently held. A month later, with the approval of the university chaplain, they were opened to the public.[42] Five students who received the gift of tongues were members of Phi Beta Kappa, and a number of the students who received the charismatic experience were also religious leaders on campus who became known as "GlossoYalies." The movement then spread to Dartmouth College, Stanford University, and Princeton Theological Seminary, where there was a significant charismatic revival.[43] By May of 1964, there were charismatic renewal prayer groups in colleges and seminaries in at least fifteen states.[44]

The Yale revival was one of several factors that played an important part in ushering in the Charismatic renewal. Other important influences included the Pentecostal denominations that had arisen in the aftermath of the Pentecostal revival of 1906, the Full Gospel Business Men's Fellowship International (FGBMFI), David J. du Plessis, the Van Nuys revival, and Roman Catholic involvement that began at Duquesne University.

The Full Gospel Business Men's Fellowship International

The Full Gospel Business Men's Fellowship International, a lay organization which included many very rich industrialists in its management,[45] was founded in 1951 by a wealthy California dairyman, Demos Shakarian, an Armenian American.[46] Shakarian appointed evangelists and paid their expenses, remunerating them generously, that they might help evangelize the world and spread the message of the baptism of the Spirit. Shakarian's denomination, the Assemblies of God, did not allow those who were not full time pastors into their leadership.[47] Therefore, many laymen capable of such leadership became involved as leaders in FGBMFI. Only men were permitted to become official members, and clergymen would not be elected to leadership in the organization, although they regularly attended FGBMFI conferences and banquets.[48] The organization played a decisive role in financing Oral Roberts University in Tulsa, Oklahoma.[49] The primary mission of the FGBMFI was to other businessmen. Members invited fellow businessmen to dine in banquet rooms of posh hotels and to listen to the speeches and testimonies of noted public figures and prominent businessmen who had experienced joy and release through baptism in the Holy Spirit. People were encouraged to be open to the Spirit while remaining loyal members of their own respective denominations.[50]

FGBMFI conferences have been addressed by Oral Roberts, Billy Graham, Reformed and Lutheran pastors, Roman Catholic priests, Adventists, Methodists, and Baptists.[51] This organization has made a decisive contribution toward spreading Pentecostalism all over the world.[52] An extensive account of an FGBMFI breakfast meeting is described in the eleventh chapter of John L. Sherrill's influential book, *They Speak with Other Tongues.*[53]

David J. du Plessis

Another important early influence upon the Charismatic movement was David J. du Plessis, who wrote concerning himself:

The Lord saved me in 1916. It was Africa missions in reverse. I was a little white pagan, and was converted through the lives of black Christians—in Africa. I knew the Bible but they knew Jesus even though they couldn't read the Bible. What they heard, they believed. Instead of reading the Bible as a history book, as I did, they treated it as a workbook. They expected it to happen. And it did.[54]

He later became a leader in the Apostolic Faith Mission in South Africa,[55] and by 1936, he was executive secretary of the Pentecostal World Conference.[56] Early one morning of that year, a man named Smith Wigglesworth barged into his office and began to prophesy.

God says you've been in your Jerusalem long enough. You've got to go to the uttermost parts of the earth. God is going to do a new work in the world that will change the order of things. He will bring about a glorious Holy Ghost revival in the old-line denominations.[57]

Concerning this, du Plessis said in 1972 that "what he prophesied was contrary to everything I had been taught and everything I believed."[58] However,

now, thirty-five years later, I am traveling all over the world. I am seldom in one spot even long enough for my mail to catch up with me. And I am seeing come to pass things that Smith Wigglesworth prophesied thirty-six years ago. . . . Today, my brethren, there is a new Pentecostal movement within the historic churches. I spent ten years among the Protestants watching it come to life. Now the charismatic movement among Protestants is stronger and more effective than the old classic Pentecostal movement.[59]

By his witness, du Plessis communicated the experience and the doctrine of the baptism in the Holy Spirit to many non-Pentecostals. "He has talked with participants at a number of ecumenical conferences, and with senior Catholic dignitaries at the Vatican Council. . . . He has lectured at many American universities and seminaries."[60] Du Plessis was sponsored in his work by Dr. John A. Mackay, who was at that time president of Princeton Theological Seminary.[61] A detailed account of the ministry of du Plessis appeared in his book, *The Spirit Bade Me Go.*[62]

The Van Nuys Revival

Another important factor in the early Charismatic renewal was the Van Nuys revival, which began after a young Anglican couple, John and Joan Baker, had received the baptism of the Holy Spirit in 1959. They surprised the vicar of their church, Frank Maguire, by their vigorous participation and conscientious tithing. To prevent them from becoming overzealous, he introduced them to another couple, who received the baptism in the Spirit as a result. Maguire then consulted his friend and colleague, Dennis Bennett, rector of another Episcopal parish, and the consequence was that Bennett, also, prayed with the Bakers and received the baptism of the Holy Spirit. Seven hundred members of Bennett's congregation sought and found this experience over the next several years. Mrs. Jean Stone, wife of a director of Lockheed Aircraft, was among them. Concerning this woman, Hollenweger wrote:

> When she was filled with the Holy Spirit, she saw that it was not her destiny to waste her life with aimless conversation at parties with the "high society" of California. Her home became a meeting place for clergy and laity from upper levels of society who sought the baptism of the Spirit. She herself gave lectures to Pentecostals and non-Pentecostals about Spirit baptism; Pentecostals who had long sought the baptism of the Spirit in Pentecostal prayer times received it when this Anglican laid her hands on them. . . .

> Jean Stone summed up the result of baptism of the Spirit in the following way: It brought a deeper understanding of the love of God, a desire to read the Bible; experience of the baptism of the Spirit made anyone who had not previously believed in the infallibility of Scripture into an "Anglican fundamentalist"; it brought a deeper recognition of sin, power to testify and power to pray with the sick.[63]

On Sunday, April 3, 1960, Dennis J. Bennett, rector of St. Mark's Episcopal Church in Van Nuys, near Los Angeles, explained in a sermon to his 2,500 member congregation how he had received the baptism of the Spirit and had spoken in tongues. At this particular time, only fifty members had also had this experience. Bennett found it expedient to resign his post in the church and received a vicarship at St. Luke's Episcopal Church, Seattle, Washington. However, the fifty people in Van Nuys continued holding prayer meetings, which became known as "Holy Spirit Fellowships." An organization called the Blessed Trinity Society was formed, and its magazine, *Trinity*, was edited by Jean Stone.[64] A detailed account of the ministry of Dennis Bennett appeared in his book, *Nine O'Clock in the Morning*.[65]

The Catholic Charismatic Movement

Roman Catholic Pentecostalism began in 1966, when several Catholic lay faculty members at Duquesne University in Pittsburgh were drawn together in a period of deep prayer and discussion about the vitality of their lives as Christians.[66] During the National Cursillo Convention in August of 1966, they met Steve Clark and Ralph Martin, friends who were staff members of St. John's student Parish in East Lansing, Michigan, and who introduced them to *The Cross and the Switchblade*, an account of the events in the life of David Wilkerson that led to the establishment of Teen Challenge International.[67] At the same time, Ralph Keifer, an instructor in the theology department at Duquesne happened to read *They Speak with Other Tongues* by John Sherrill.[68] Through the vicar of that church, William Lewis, these Duquesne faculty members came into contact with Betty Schomaker, a member of an Episcopalian parish, Christ Church, in the North Hills of Pittsburgh.[69] She brought them to a prayer meeting at the home of Miss Florence Dodge, a Presbyterian who had previously organized the prayer group.[70] On this day, January 13, 1967, Ralph Keifer spoke in tongues.[71] The following week, two others of the group of faculty members from Duquesne received the baptism in the Holy Spirit,[72] and by the beginning of February, four Catholics from Pittsburgh had received the baptism in the Holy Spirit.[73] In mid-February, about thirty students and faculty spent a weekend retreat in prayer, preparing for this by reading *The Cross and the Switchblade* by David Wilkerson.[74]

According to Kevin Ranaghan, "This 'Duquesne weekend' as it has come to be called, was certainly one of the most remarkable incidents in the story of the Pentecostal movement."[75] A Duquesne student at the time, Patti Gallagher, felt the presence of the Spirit of Christ in the chapel and left to urge others to join her there. As they prayed, "the Holy Spirit poured Himself out upon them."[76] Concerning this event, Ranaghan wrote:

> What is more important, and from a certain point of view more impressive, is the reception of the fruits of the Holy Spirit which this group experienced. The hours of near physical experience of the Lord touched many; they have been followed by months of living closer to Christ, of sharing the peace, joy, love, and confident faith described above.[77]

This new charismatic revival among Catholics soon spread to the University of Notre Dame and to the Catholic student group at Michigan State University. Kevin Ranaghan, at that time a teacher at St. Mary's College, Notre Dame, and his wife Dorothy, learned that their friends at Duquesne sought the baptism in the Holy Spirit, and in mid-February, Ralph Keifer, who had just received the experience, engaged in prolonged discussions with the Ranaghans about it while in Michigan. As a result of these discussions, on March 5, 1967, nine people from Notre Dame came together in an apartment in South Bend to seek the baptism in the Holy Spirit. A week later, in a subsequent meeting, many of them received the gift of tongues. Yet, "in each case our testimony was not about tongues; not even primarily about the Spirit. But wherever we went, our talk was about Jesus Christ and the power of his saving love to transform men and man's world."[78]

On a weekend shortly after Easter, forty students, priests, and faculty from Notre Dame and St. Mary's and another forty from Michigan State University came together to receive the baptism in the Holy Spirit. "By the end of that weekend the pentecostal movement among Catholics was flourishing at Duquesne, Notre Dame, Michigan State, and offshoot groups had begun at Iowa State and Holy Cross."[79] This "Michigan State" weekend was well publicized, and brought hundreds of people to the Friday night prayer meetings for the next few weeks. "By the end of the semester, the thrust of the renewal had touched hundreds of Catholics across the country."[80]

During this time, similar developments took place elsewhere in the United States. Charismatic prayer groups came into being among Catholics quite independently in Boston, Orlando, Seattle, Portland, Los Angeles, St. Louis, and central New York State. "The majority seem to have originated about the same time as the Duquesne group, and some were definitely previous to it."[81]

In May 1969 the first Catholic Charismatic Conference that was national in scope was held in Notre Dame, and 450 people attended. In 1970 the annual conference was attended by 1,279 people; there were 5000 in 1971 and 12,000 in 1972.[82] By May 1975 the Notre Dame conference was international in scope and met in St. Peter's Basilica in Rome. Between 16,000 and 20,000 people attended. Pope Paul VI spoke at the conference, quoting Scripture 22 times in a ten-minute prepared speech, quite favorable in tone. After his prepared speech, he spoke extemporaneously, and "something came over him and he looked 20 years younger."[83]

According to the *Wall Street Journal*, in early 1974 there were about 250,000 Charismatic Catholics in the United States. In an article on the establishment of St. Patrick's Word of God School, the first Roman Catholic Charismatic school in the U.S., it was stated that "Pentecostalism is a fundamentalist movement that until recent years has been embraced almost exclusively by Protestant sects."[84]

In 1971 Auxiliary Bishop Joseph McKinney of Grand Rapids, Michigan, became the first bishop to identify himself as a Charismatic.[85] Bishop McKinney was given his own non-geographical parish, "The Community of the Holy Spirit," enabling him to pastor the entire Catholic Charismatic body within the United States.[86]

The Catholic Charismatic magazine *New Covenant* had a circulation of 22,000 in 1973. The movement also began to publish an annual directory, the 1973 edition of which gave a partial listing of 1300 prayer groups.[87] The 1975–76 directory listed close to 4000 prayer groups throughout the world.[88]

Léon-Joseph Cardinal Suenens was quoted in 1974 as saying,

> I have taken very seriously what, in the Charismatic Renewal, is called the baptism of the Spirit. I have asked for it myself. . . . I felt as I became a bishop, taking part in the work of the hierarchy, that the Lord was calling me first to be at the disposal of the Holy Spirit, and second to be an administrator. If God is to be free to act, we need Spirit and life first; then we give it order. Life precedes order.[89]

Other Factors

In these brief sketches, we have had glimpses of some of the factors that had helped to bring about the Charismatic movement, but there were numerous others, probably the greatest of which was the network of independent churches that were established either in the aftermath of the Azusa Street revival of 1906 or in the wake of the Latter Rain revival of 1948. Both of these movements spread quickly throughout the continent, producing many churches, some of which never became affiliated with any denominations. This was particularly the case for the Latter Rain movement, since it emphasized the autonomy of the local assembly and strongly discouraged denominational affiliation.

Results of the Charismatic Movement

The revival of the 1960s and 1970s, in turn, also resulted in many new Charismatic churches. Some of these became informally affiliated with Christian Growth Ministries in Ft. Lauderdale, Florida, under the leadership of Derek Prince, Bob Mumford, Charles Simpson, Don Basham, John Poole, and Ern Baxter. Many others affiliated with classical denominations, such as the Assemblies of God, or remained independent. Another large proportion of Charismatics was assimilated into the mainline churches. In a press interview given at Notre

Dame on June 2, 1973, Roman Catholic Cardinal Suenens said that the Charismatic renewal was "more a current of grace than a movement. A current of grace is like a river which disappears into the sea. So the current of grace will disappear because it will be accepted by all. Having been accepted by all there will be no need of a separate movement."[90]

POSTSCRIPT

IN ALL THREE OF THE MAJOR REVIVALS of the twentieth century, there were both Pentecostal and non-Pentecostal components. In 1904–1906, a worldwide awakening preceded and gave birth to the Pentecostal movement, whereas both in the mid-twentieth century and in the 1960s and 1970s, revival phenomena became manifest at approximately the same time among both Pentecostals and other Evangelicals.

These recent revivals had much in common with earlier Christian awakenings, although restricted to smaller segments of the population due to the secularization of society which had taken place throughout the nineteenth century. Nevertheless, a resurgence of Evangelical Christianity has been coming about in America since the late 1940s. This Evangelical renaissance received its initial impetus from the mid-twentieth-century revival and further stimulus from the awakening of the 1960s and 1970s. It is characterized by an increased acceptance of the traditional Christian world view by large segments of society in all socioeconomic classes.

If the current resurgence continues, it will provide a milieu conducive to the incidence of an awakening of far greater statistical significance and considerably more extensive societal impact than the earlier revivals of this century. It seems likely that the occurrence of such an awakening in the near future is contingent upon the extent to which people will engage in wholehearted prayer for a divine visitation of this kind. Should God raise up sufficient intercessors for revival, there will be the real possibility of a momentous "Third Great Awakening," not only in North America, but throughout all of Christendom.

NOTES

NOTES—INTRODUCTION

[1]J. Edwin Orr, *The Flaming Tongue* (Chicago: Moody Press, 1973), pp. 1–28.

[2]Ibid., pp. 178–85; Frank Bartleman, *How Pentecost Came to Los Angeles* (Los Angeles: By the author, 1925), pp. 14, 16, 21.

[3]On June 9, 1958, *Life* magazine, pp. 113–24, carried an article on religious sects and fringe groups by Henry P. Van Dusen of Union Theological Seminary in New York. The article, entitled, "The Third Force in Christendom," was about the Seventh-Day Adventists and various Holiness groups as well as the Pentecostals, but the term "Third Force" later came to be used to refer to Pentecostalism in particular as an important component of American Christendom, alongside mainstream Protestantism and Roman Catholicism.

[4]Richard M. Riss, *Latter Rain: The Latter Rain Movement of 1948 and the Mid-Twentieth-Century Evangelical Awakening* (Mississauga, Ont.: Honeycomb Visual Productions, 1987); David Edwin Harrell, Jr., *All Things Are Possible* (Bloomington: Indiana University Press, 1975).

[5]Richard Quebedeaux, *The New Charismatics* II (San Francisco: Harper & Row, 1983), pp. 220–22.

[6]Edward E. Plowman, *The Underground Church/The Jesus Movement in America* (Elgin, Ill.: David C. Cook Publishing Co., 1971).

[7]Richard G. Hutcheson, *Mainline Churches and the Evangelicals: A Challenging Crisis?* (Atlanta: John Knox, 1981).

[8]George M. Marsden, "From Fundamentalism to Evangelicalism: A Historical Analysis," in David F. Wells and John D. Woodbridge, eds., *The Evangelicals* (Nashville: Abingdon, 1975), pp. 122–23.

[9]See, for example, John Wesley, "Serious Thoughts Occasioned by the Late Earthquake at Lisbon," in Thomas Jackson, ed., *The Works of John Wesley*, 14 vols. (Grand Rapids: Baker, 1979), 11:1–14

[10]Paul Merkley, "The Demoralization of the American Historian," *Fides et Historia* 14 (Spring-Summer, 1982): 6–14.

[11]Colin Brown, *Miracles and the Critical Mind* (Grand Rapids: Eerdmans, 1984).

[12]The nineteenth-century historian W. E. H. Lecky, although himself a free thinker, referred to the Evangelical Awakening in eighteenth-century Britain as having imparted "a greater energy to the philanthropy of every denomination both in England and the colonies." He believed that Britain had been saved from a revolution similar to that in France as a result of the awakening of social conscience that had been brought about as a result of the religious reawakening of that time. This idea was also later expressed by the great French historian Elie Halévy.

[13]Jonathan Edwards wrote as follows about events in 1734 at the outset of the Great Awakening in America:

All other talk but about spiritual and eternal things was soon thrown by; all the conversation in all companies, and upon all occasions, was upon these things only, unless so much as was necessary for people to carry on their secular business (Jonathan Edwards, A *Faithful Narrative of the Surprising Work of God* [New York: Dunning & Spalding, 1832], p. 38).

[14]At the beginning of the second awakening in America, by June of 1801, crowds coming to Concord and Cane Ridge, Kentucky, were so large that no accommodations could be found for them. According to a letter by Colonel Patterson of Lexington, Kentucky, dated September 25, 1801, which appeared in *New York Missionary Magazine* 119 (1802), "this was the first occasion that showed the necessity of encamping on the ground, the neighborhood not being able to furnish strangers with accommodation; nor had they a wish to separate." As a result of these circumstances, the familiar camp-meeting became common practice during revivals of this type (Catharine C. Cleveland, *The Great Revival in the West 1797–1805* [Chicago: University of Chicago Press, 1916], pp. 74–75).

[15]See, for example, David Matthews, I *Saw the Welsh Revival* (Chicago: Moody Press, 1951), pp. 43–44. Matthews wrote:

Happenings in churches everywhere made one utterly oblivious of the passage of time. No one bothered about the clock. Hours passed like minutes. The ticking of the sanctuary timepiece was drowned in an avalanche of praise. . . .

When I left the heavenly atmosphere of the church for home, I discovered that it was five in the morning! I had been in the house of God for ten hours—they had passed like ten minutes!

[16]Erwin E. Prange, *The Gift Is Already Yours* (Minneapolis: Bethany Fellowship, 1980), pp. 92–93. In his description of the revival of 1844 in Mötlingen, Germany, under Johann Christoph Blumhardt, Prange wrote:

Most of all, there were healings. Almost every time Pastor Blumhardt laid hands on one of his members for absolution, a healing took place. There was a new depth in his preaching as well, and people came from all over Germany to hear him. He conducted five services each Sunday, and the little church was filled to capacity each time with people sometimes standing as far as a kilometer away. One Sunday, the German emperor himself came to see what all the fuss was about.

[17]John Wesley arrived at Bristol on September 21, 1761, and wrote,

the congregations were exceeding large, and the people longing and thirsting after righteousness; and every day afforded us fresh instances of persons convinced of sin, or converted to God: So that it seems He was pleased to pour out His Spirit this year, on every part both of England and Ireland, in a manner we never had seen before; at least, not for twenty years (John Wesley, A *Short History of the People Called Methodists*, in Jackson 13:352).

[18]During the Welsh revival at the turn of the twentieth century, there were secular newspaper accounts of all aspects of the awakening, including phenomenal increases in the sales of New Testaments and Bibles. At the town of Neath, one bookseller reported that before the revival he regarded Bibles as dead stock, but that in the weeks of the revival he had cleared out all his old stock and found it necessary to obtain further supplies. Some of the customers knew nothing of the Bible, yet they "carried it off as a hoarded treasure" (John Shearer, *Old Time Revivals* [London: Pickering & Inglis, 1930]).

[19]George Whitefield, *Journals* (London: Banner of Truth, 1960), pp. 88–89, as quoted by Keith J. Hardman, *The Spiritual Awakeners* (Chicago: Moody Press, 1983), p. 82. Whitefield wrote with respect to his ministry during the Evangelical Awakening in London, 1736,

The tide of popularity now began to run very high. In short time, I could no longer walk on foot as usual, but was constrained to go in a coach, from place to place, to avoid the hosannas of the multitude.

[20]Stanley Frodsham wrote that, in 1908, when he came into contact with individuals associated with the Pentecostal revival, "every one of them honored the Word of God, believing in every part of it, and they were all seeking to be not only hearers but doers of the Word" (Stanley Frodsham, *With Signs Following* [Springfield, Mo.: Gospel Publishing House, 1946], p. 8).

[21]Leslie Lyall, *God Reigns in China* (London: Hodder & Stoughton, 1985), pp. 98–99, described a revival during the mid-twentieth-century evangelical awakening among students in Peking, China:

Deep conviction was soon manifested and as individuals repented they experienced the joy of forgiveness. One husky physical training student, during a quite unemotional meeting, suddenly began sobbing, and a counsellor took him aside and led him to Christ. Many were clearly converted, while those already Christians entered more deeply into the fullness of salvation. The student leaders had no patience at any time with mere superficial profession, baptism and church membership in their eyes counting for nothing in themselves.

[22]At the Cane Ridge revival at the turn of the nineteenth century, many of the most violently opposed came under its influence (Cleveland, pp. 91, 110).

[23]During the Great Awakening in America, George Whitefield spoke against the practice of sending unconverted persons into the ministry. After this speech, given at a dinner with fellow ministers in Stamford, Connecticut, some of the ministers present publicly confessed, with tears in their eyes, that they had ordained young men without having asked them whether they had been born again of God (*America's Great Revivals* [Minneapolis: Bethany Fellowship, n.d.], p. 17). When John Wesley began his work as an Anglican

Clergyman, he had not yet experienced his own conversion (Nehemiah Curnock, ed., *The Journal of the Rev. John Wesley, A.M.*, 8 vols. [London: Robert Culley, 1909–1918], 1:475–76).

24John Wesley, *A Plain Account of Christian Perfection* (London: Epworth Press, 1952), sect. 20, pp. 58–59. John Wesley provides detailed accounts of all of the steps of conversion that typically took place for individuals involved in the Evangelical Awakening in Britain during the eighteenth century.

25In 1821, when Charles Finney experienced a dramatic conversion, he was suddenly released from a great pride and embarrassment that had prevented him from acknowledging the power of Christ (Helen Wessel, ed., *The Autobiography of Charles G. Finney* [Minneapolis: Bethany Fellowship, 1977], p. 17).

26A major exception to the general rule that twentieth-century revivals have not had major effects upon entire communities can be seen in the Welsh revival of 1904–1905, where, according to Charles Clarke, "Old quarrels were healed. Long-standing debts were paid. Drunkenness dramatically decreased. The awesome sense of God's presence brooded over towns and villages" (Charles Clarke, *Pioneers of Revival* [London: Fountain Trust, 1971], p. 30).

27See, for example, Maria B. Woodworth-Etter, *Signs and Wonders God Wrought in the Ministry for Forty Years* (Indianapolis, Ind.: By the author, 1916), pp. 261–63, 393–94.

28See, for example, Hardman, pp. 98, 116–17.

29Ibid., p. 136; Prange, p. 92; Cleveland, pp. 41, 90; Matthews, pp. 5, 29; *America's Great Revivals*, pp. 16, 29, 32, 41, 88.

30Faith Campbell, *Prophet with a Pen* (Springfield, Mo.: Gospel Publishing House, 1974), pp. 17, 110; Frodsham, p. 9; Hardman, pp. 21, 88; Matthews, p. 105; *America's Great Revivals*, pp. 31, 56, 78; Cleveland, pp. 34, 48, 69.

31Orr, *Flaming Tongue*, p. 2; Hardman, p. 186; Matthews, pp. 13, 100; *America's Great Revivals*, pp. 136; Charles G. Finney, *Lectures on Revivals of Religion* (Virginia Beach, Va.: CBN University Press, 1978), p. 30.

32Lyall, p. 97; Campbell, p. 21; Matthews, pp. 13, 125; Cleveland, pp. 143–45; *America's Great Revivals*, pp. 32, 70, 77, 83, 85, 87, 91; Hardman, pp. 59, 92, 96, 100, 143, 188. See also Ruth A. Tucker, *From Jerusalem to Irian Jaya* (Grand Rapids: Zondervan, 1983), pp. 40, 46, 48, 141, 188, 208, 223; and Rosemary Ruether and Eleanor McLaughlin, *Women of the Spirit* (New York: Simon & Schuster, 1979), pp. 21–22.

33Finney, p. 57; Cleveland, pp. 59, 60, 63, 65, 66, 67, 68, 72, 73, 74, 78, 79, 80, 81, 82, 84, 88, 89, 90, 92, 93, 94, 97, 107, 109, 166, 167, 168, 169, 170, 171, 174, 179, 195; *America's Great Revivals*, pp. 16, 19, 37, 38, 41, 42, 43, 44; Woodworth-Etter, pp. 61, 63, 67, 68, 69, 70; Frodsham, p. 15; Elizabeth V. Baker, *Chronicles of a Faith Life* (Rochester, N.Y.: By the author, n.d.), pp. 33, 96, 135; Jamie Buckingham, *Daughter of Destiny: Kathryn Kuhlmann . . . Her Story* (Plainfield, N.J.: Logos International, 1976), pp. 41, 225–33.

34Campbell, p. 17; Frodsham, pp. 8, 11, 12; Baker, p. 26; Prange, p. 92.

35See, for example, Lane T. Dennis, ed., *Letters of Francis Schaeffer* (Westchester, Ill.: Crossway Books, 1985), pp. 32–33.

36Jeremy Rifkin, *Entropy* (New York: Viking, 1980), pp. 234–40; Hardman, pp. 24, 77, 82, 89, 92, 162, 184, 185, 209–10, 220, 222; Tucker, p. 202; Matthews, p. 49; Cleveland, pp. 156, 157, 158; Orr, *Flaming Tongue*, pp. xi–xii, xiv, *America's Great Revivals*, pp. 24, 33, 49, 50, 92.

[37]See, for example, Eusebius, *Ecclesiastical History*, 23, 31.

[38]Irenaeus, *Against Heresies*, 2. 32. 4.

[39]Venerable Bede, *Ecclesiastical History of England*, ch 31.

[40]*The New International Dictionary of the Christian Church*, 1974 ed., s.v. "Anthony of Padua."

[41]Ibid., s.v. "Savonarola, Girolamo."

[42]*The Oxford Dictionary of the Christian Church*, 2d ed., s.v. "Savonarola, Girolamo."

[43]Tim Dowley, ed., *Eerdmans' Handbook to the History of Christianity* (Grand Rapids: Eerdmans, 1977), p. 334.

[44]*The New International Dictionary of the Christian Church*, 1974 ed., s.v. "Savonarola, Girolamo."

[45]On Martin Luther, see Roland H. Bainton, *Here I Stand: A Life of Martin Luther* (New York: New American Library, 1977).

[46]John Gillies, *Historical Collections* (London: James Nisbet & Co., 1845), p. 167.

[47]Gillies, pp. 182, 197, 198; *Narratives of Revivals of Religion in Scotland, Ireland and Wales* (Philadelphia: Presbyterian Board of Publication, 1842), pt. 4, pp. 56–65; Hardman, p. 33, quoting Thomas McCrie, *Sketches of Scottish Church History*, 2 vols. (London: Blanchard & Ott, 1846), 1:190–93.

[48]*History of the Presbyterian Church in Ireland*, vol. 1; see also Gillies, pp. 168, 202; and *Narratives*, pt. 7 (pp. 102–21).

[49]Gillies, pp. 176–77, 179.

[50]Ibid., p. 198; *Narratives*, pt. 4, pp. 65–73 and Herman Humphrey, *Revival Sketches and Manual* (New York: American Tract Society, 1859), pp. 29–33.

[51]Gillies, p. 202

[52]Ibid., pp. 124ff.

[53]Hardman, p. 61.

[54]Humphrey, pp. 63–64.

[55]Hardman, pp. 47–59.

[56]Humphrey, p. 64.

[57]Gillies, pp. 305–37 (Britain) and pp. 337–433 (America); Humphrey, pp. 46–93.

[58]Gillies, pp. 433–35, 441–62. See also *Narratives*, pts. 1–3, pp. 5–55.

[59]Jonathan Edwards, *The Life and Diary of David Brainerd* (Chicago: Moody Press, 1949).

[60]In 1761, John Wesley wrote that God "was pleased to pour out His Spirit this year, on every part both of England and Ireland, in a manner we never had seen before; at least, not for twenty years" (Jackson, 13:352). See also Hardman, p. 119, which mentions general awakenings in New England in 1763 and 1764.

[61]Wesley M. Gewehr, *The Great Awakening in Virginia*, 1740–1790 (Durham, N.C.: Duke University Press, 1930), p. 149.

[62]Ibid., p. 230.

[63]Hardman, pp. 106, 119.

[64]J. Baxter, "The Great Yorkshire Revival 1792–6," in Michael Hill, ed., *A Sociological Yearbook of Religion in Britain* (London: SCM, 1974), 7:46–76.

[65]William B. Sprague, *Lectures on Revivals of Religion* (Albany: Webster & Skinners, O. Steele, and W. C. Little, 1832), appendix, pp. 151–52.

[66]*Narratives*, pt. 6, pp. 85–101.

[67]Winthrop S. Hudson, *Religion in America*, 2d ed. (New York: Charles Scribner's Sons, 1973), p. 135.

[68]*America's Great Revivals*, pp. 37–38.

[69]Hudson, pp. 137–38, quoting Charles Albert Johnson, *The Frontier Camp Meeting* (Dallas: Southern Methodist University Press, 1955), pp. 34–35. See also Bernard A. Weisberger, *They Gathered at the River* (Boston: Little, Brown & Co., 1958), pp. 24–25.

[70]*America's Great Revivals*, p. 39.

[71]Hudson, p. 138.

[72]E. Merton Coulter, *College Life in the Old South* (New York: Macmillan, 1928), pp. 194–95, as cited by Vinson Synan, *The Holiness-Pentecostal Movement in the United States* (Grand Rapids: Eerdmans, 1971), p. 25.

[73]*Narratives*, pt. 10, pp. 159–84.

[74]*Narratives*, pt. 5, pp. 74–84.

[75]*Narratives*, pt. 8, pp. 122–38.

[76]*Narratives*, pt. 11, pp. 185–98 and Gillies, pp. 556ff.

[77]Humphrey, pp. 259–63, and Joshua Bradley, *Accounts of Religious Revivals in Many Parts of the United States from 1815 to 1818* (Albany: G. J. Loomis & Co., 1819).

[78]Humphrey, p. 263.

[79]Ibid., pp. 232–36, 242–58.

[80]Hardman, p. 176.

[81]Ibid., p. 184.

[82]Ibid.

[83]Sprague, appendix, p. 16.

[84]Prange, pp. 88–95. See also Frank S. Boshold, trans., *Blumhardt's Battle: A Conflict with Satan* (New York: Thomas E. Lowe, 1970).

[85]Edward Norris Kirk, *Lectures on Revivals* (Boston: Congregational Publishing Society, 1875), p. 142.

[86]*America's Great Revivals*, pp. 52–55.

[87]Ibid., pp. 56–57.

[88]William Gibson, *The Year of Grace: A History of the Ulster Revival of 1859* (Edinburgh: Andrew Elliot, 1860). See also John Weir, *The Ulster Awakening: Its Origin, Progress and Fruit* (London: Arthur Hall, Virtue & Co., 1860) and J. T. Carson, *God's River in Spate: The Story of the Religious Awakening of Ulster in 1859* (Belfast: Publications Board, Presbyterian Church in Ireland, 1958).

[89]J. Edwin Orr, *The Fervent Prayer: The Worldwide Impact of the Great Awakening of 1858* (Chicago: Moody Press, 1974), pp. 45–51, and pp. 52ff.

[90]J. du Plessis, *The Life of Andrew Murray of South Africa* (London: Marshall Brothers, Ltd., 1919), p. 193.

[91]Ibid., p. 194.

[92]Ibid.

[93]Kirk, p. 142.

[94]Eifion Evans, *The Welsh Revival of 1904* (Port Talbot, Wales: Evangelical Movement of Wales, 1969), p. 11.

[95]Alexander MacRae, *Revivals in the Highlands and Islands in the Nineteenth Century* (Stirling, E. MacKay, 1906), pp. 102–30 and Hardman, pp. 203–7.

NOTES–CHAPTER 1

[1] Paul G. Chappell, "The Divine Healing Movement in America," Ph.D. dissertation, Drew University, Madison, N.J., 1983, p. 88.

[2] Ibid.

[3] Ibid., p. 89.

[4] Ibid., p. 92.

[5] Ibid., p. 93.

[6] Ibid., p. 87.

[7] Melvin E. Dieter, *The Holiness Revival of the Nineteenth Century* (Metuchen, N.J.: Scarecrow Press, 1980), pp. 26–27.

[8] Chappell, p. 76; Melvin E. Dieter, "Wesleyan-Holiness Aspects of Pentecostal Origins," in Vinson Synan, ed., *Aspects of Pentecostal-Charismatic Origins* (Plainfield, N.J.: Logos International, 1975), p. 65.

[9] Dieter, in Synan, ed., *Aspects*, p. 65.

[10] Timothy L. Smith, *Called Unto Holiness: The Story of the Nazarenes: The Formative Years* (Kansas City, Mo.: Nazarene Publishing House, 1962), p. 11; Donald Dayton, "The Rise of the Evangelical Healing Movement in Nineteenth Century America," in *Pneuma: The Journal of the Society for Pentecostal Studies* 4 (Spring, 1982): 9.

[11] Timothy L. Smith, *Revivalism and Social Reform: American Protestantism on the Eve of the Civil War* (Gloucester, Mass.: Peter Smith, 1976), p. 141.

[12] Ibid., p. 138.

[13] Ibid., p. 136.

[14] Chappell, p. 107.

[15] Ibid., p. 109.

[16] Ibid., pp. 109–10.

[17] Ibid., p. 111.

[18] Ibid., p. 113.

[19] Raymond J. Cunningham, "From Holiness to Healing: The Faith Cure in America 1872–1892," *Church History* 43 (December, 1974): 499–513.

[20] Dieter, *The Holiness Revival*, p. 98.

[21] Ibid.

[22] Ibid., p. 104; Synan, *The Holiness-Pentecostal Movement*, p. 36.

[23] Quoted in Synan, *Holiness-Pentecostal Movement*, p. 37.

[24] Ibid., pp. 37, 54.

[25] J. E. Searles, "A Brief Sketch of the Holiness Revival; Especially of the Origin and Work of 'The National Camp Meeting Association for the Promotion of Holiness,'" in John S. Inskip, ed., *Proceedings of Holiness Conferences Held at Cincinnati, November 26th, 1877, and at New York, December 17th, 1877* (Philadelphia: National Publishing Association for the Promotion of Holiness, 1878), p. 119.

[26] Dieter, *The Holiness Revival*, p. 106.

[27] Synan, *Holiness-Pentecostal Movement*, p. 37.

[28] Quoted in Dieter, *The Holiness Revival*, pp. 108–9.

[29] Chappell, p. 121; Dayton, p. 8.

30Chappell, p. 129.

31Ibid., p. 199.

32Synan, *The Holiness-Pentecostal Movement*, p. 39.

33W. McDonald and John E. Searles, *The Life of Rev. John S. Inskip* (Boston: McDonald & Gill, 1885), p. 210.

34Ibid., p. 215.

35Timothy L. Smith, *Called Unto Holiness*, p. 17.

36Quoted by Chappell, pp. 130–31.

37Ibid.

38Ibid., pp. 143–44.

39Ibid., p. 177.

40Ibid., p. 185.

41Ibid., pp. 184–86.

42Ibid., p. 224.

43Ibid., p. 220; Ernest B. Gordon, *Adoniram Judson Gordon: A Biography* (New York: Fleming H. Revell Co., 1896), pp. 95–97, 100–101.

44Chappell, pp. 182, 232–33; Daniel E. Albrecht, "Carrie Judd Montgomery: Pioneer Contributor to Three Religious Movements," *Pneuma: The Journal of the Society for Pentecostal Studies* 8 (Fall, 1986): 104.

45Robert L. Niklaus, John S. Sawin, and Samuel J. Stoesz, *All For Jesus* (Camp Hill, Pa.: Christian Publications, 1986), p. 40; Chappell, p. 257.

46Chappell, p. 176.

47Ibid., pp. 179, 181.

48Wayne E. Warner, *The Woman Evangelist: The Life and Times of Charismatic Evangelist Maria B. Woodworth-Etter* (Metuchen, N.J.: Scarecrow Press, 1986), pp. 14–23.

49Maria B. Woodworth-Etter, *Signs and Wonders God Wrought in the Ministry for Forty Years* (Indianapolis: By the author, 1916), p. 70.

50Warner, *The Woman Evangelist*, p. 37. See also p. 32, n. 23.

51Walter J. Hollenweger, *The Pentecostals: The Charismatic Movement in the Churches* (Minneapolis: Augsburg, 1972), pp. 116–17.

52Dayton, p. 17.

53Woodworth-Etter, pp. 111–12.

54Ibid., p. 111.

55Warner, *The Woman Evangelist*, p. 81.

56Ibid.

57Ibid., p. 98.

58Ibid., p. 99.

59Ibid., p. 100.

60Woodworth-Etter, p. 247.

61Lilian B. Yeomans, M.D., "The Faith of John Alexander Dowie," in W. E. Warner, ed., *Touched by the Fire* (Plainfield, N.J.: Logos International, 1978), p. 118.

62Woodworth-Etter, p. 126.

63Synan, *Holiness-Pentecostal Movement*, p. 53.

64Ibid., p. 78.

65Ibid., p. 50.

66Ibid., p. 51.

67Ibid., pp. 51, 60.

[68]Ibid., p. 79.

[69]Ibid., pp. 80–89; Robert Mapes Anderson, *Vision of the Disinherited* (New York: Oxford University Press, 1979), p. 253; Stanley Frodsham, *With Signs Following* (Springfield, Mo.: Gospel Publishing House, 1946), pp. 16–17.

[70]Quoted by Sarah E. Parham, *The Life of Charles F. Parham* (Joplin, Mo.: Hunter Printing Co., 1930), pp. 65–66.

[71]Ibid., p. 67.

[72]Quoted in ibid., pp. 60–61.

[73]For further information, see William G. McLoughlin, Jr., *Modern Revivalism: Charles Grandison Finney to Billy Graham* (New York: Ronald Press Co., 1959), and Paulus Scharpff, *History of Evangelism*, trans. Helga Bender Henry (Grand Rapids: Eerdmans, 1966).

[74]William R. Moody, *The Life of Dwight L. Moody* (New York: Revell, 1900), p. 155, as quoted by Keith J. Hardman, *The Spiritual Awakeners* (Chicago: Moody Press, 1983), p. 202.

[75]Moody, *Life of Moody*, pp. 187–88, quoted by Hardman, p. 204.

[76]Hudson, p. 231.

[77]Lyman H. Atwater, "Revivals of the Century," *The Presbyterian Quarterly and Princeton Review* 5, New Series (October, 1876): 716.

NOTES–CHAPTER 2

[1]W. T. Stead, "The Story of the Awakening," in *The Story of the Welsh Revival* (New York: Fleming H. Revell, 1905), pp. 59–60.

[2]Ibid., p. 60.

[3]Quoted by Eifion Evans, *The Welsh Revival of 1904* (Port Talbot, Glamorgan, Wales: The Evangelical Movement of Wales, 1969), p. 64.

[4]W. T. Stead, "Mr. Evan Roberts," in *The Story of the Welsh Revival*, pp. 55–56.

[5]Evans, p. 69.

[6]Quoted in ibid.

[7]Quoted in ibid., p. 70.

[8]David Matthews, *I Saw the Welsh Revival* (Chicago: Moody Press, 1951), p. 19.

[9]Evans, p. 79.

[10]Ibid., p. 72.

[11]Quoted in ibid., p. 72.

[12]Stead, "Mr. Evan Roberts," in *The Story of the Welsh Revival*, pp. 56–57.

[13]Evans, p. 74.

[14]Orr, *Flaming Tongue*, pp. 6–7.

[15]Stead, "Mr. Evan Roberts," in *The Story of the Welsh Revival*, p. 57.

[16]Ibid.

[17]Evans, p. 82.

[18]Ibid., p. 84.

[19]Ibid.

[20]Orr, *Flaming Tongue*, p. 8.

[21]Evans, p. 87.

[22]Ibid., p. 89.

[23]Ibid., p. 90.

[24]Ibid., p. 91.

[25]Ibid., p. 117.

[26]*Western Mail*, Cardiff, November 10, 1904, as quoted by Orr, *Flaming Tongue*, p. 10.

[27]Quoted by Evans, p. 93.

[28]Ibid., pp. 93–94.

[29]Ibid., p. 96.

[30]Ibid., p. 94.

[31]Ibid.

[32]Ibid., p. 95.

[33]Orr, *Flaming Tongue*, p. 11; Evans, p. 95.

[34]Arthur Goodrich, "The Story of the Welsh Revival," in *The Story of the Welsh Revival*, p. 25.

[35]Evans, p. 124.

[36]Matthews, pp. 29–30.

[37]Evans, p. 124.

[38]Quoted in Evans, pp. 124–25.

[39]Matthews, pp. 32–33.

[40]Ibid., p. 35.

[41]Matthews, p. 37.

[42]Quoted by Orr, *Flaming Tongue*, p. 12, and Evans, pp. 104–5.

[43]Orr, *Flaming Tongue*, p. 12; Evans, pp. 106–7.

[44]Evans, p. 117.

[45]Goodrich, p. 28.

[46]Matthews, pp. 61–62.

[47]Goodrich, p. 24.

[48]Matthews, pp. 71–72.

[49]Evans, p. 121.

[50]Ibid., pp. 121–22.

[51]Ibid., p. 126.

[52]Stead, "The Story of the Awakening," in *The Story of the Welsh Revival*, p. 62.

[53]G. Campbell Morgan, "The Lesson of the Revival," in *The Story of the Welsh Revival*, p. 46.

[54]Evans, p. 127.

[55]Stead, "Mr. Evan Roberts," in *The Story of the Welsh Revival*, p. 54.

[56]Stead, "The Story of the Awakening," in *The Story of the Welsh Revival*, pp. 64–65.

[57]Goodrich, pp. 20–21.

[58]G. Campbell Morgan, *Lessons of the Welsh Revival* (New York: Fleming H. Revell, 1905).

[59]Ibid., p. 3.

[60]Ibid., pp. 7, 8, 11, 13, 14.

[61]Evans, p. 131.

[62]Ibid.

[63]Ibid., p. 135.

[64]Matthews, p. 75.

[65]Ibid., p. 112.

[66]Matthews, p. 116.

[67]Quoted in Charles Clarke, *Pioneers of Revival* (London: Fountain Trust, 1971), p. 30.

[68]Matthews, p. 118.

[69]Jessie Penn-Lewis and Evan Roberts, *War on the Saints*, 9th ed. (New York: Thomas E. Lowe, Ltd., 1973).

[70]Ibid., pp. 283–84.

[71]Clarke, p. 30.

[72]Orr, *Flaming Tongue*, p. 70.

[73]J. Edwin Orr, *Campus Aflame* (Glendale, Calif.: Gospel Light Publications, 1971), p. 113.

[74]Orr, *Flaming Tongue*, p. 72; Orr, *Campus Aflame*, p. 107.

[75]Orr, *Flaming Tongue*, p. 76.

[76]Ibid., p. 72.

[77]Ibid., p. 79; Orr, *Campus Aflame*, p. 112.

[78]Orr, *Flaming Tongue*, p. 71.

[79]Ibid.

[80]Ibid., p. 74.

[81]Ibid., p. 79.

[82]Ibid., p. 75.

[83]Ibid., p. 89.

[84]Orr, *Campus Aflame*, p. 122.

[85]Ibid.; Orr, *Flaming Tongue*, p. 89.

[86]Ibid.

[87]Ibid., pp. 73, 74, 77.

[88]Quoted in ibid., p. 74.

[89]Niklaus, Sawin, and Stoesz, p. 110.

[90]Quoted by Orr, *Campus Aflame*, p. 106.

[91]Orr, *Flaming Tongue*, p. 72.

[92]Ibid., p. 77.

[93]Ibid., p. 75.

[94]Orr, *Campus Aflame*, p. 108.

[95]Quoted in ibid., p. 115; Orr, *Flaming Tongue*, p. 98.

[96]Orr, *Flaming Tongue*, p. 85.

[97]Ibid., p. 76.

[98]Orr, *Campus Aflame*, p. 115.

[99]Orr, *Flaming Tongue*, p. 80.

[100]Carl Brumback, *Suddenly . . . From Heaven* (Springfield, Mo.: Gospel Publishing House, 1961), p. 88, quoting Herbert Cox, *Latter Rain Evangel* (October, 1919).

NOTES–CHAPTER 3

[1]Synan, ed., *Aspects*, p. 1.

[2]Ibid.; Hollenweger, pp. xvii–xviii, 29.

[3] According to Desmond W. Cartwright, " 'Your Daughters Shall Prophesy': The Contribution of Women in Early Pentecostalism," a paper given at the Society for Pentecostal Studies Conference, Gaithersburg, Maryland, November 15, 1985, p. 7, this was an African Methodist Episcopal Church.

[4] Hollenweger, p. 22.

[5] Ibid., pp. 9, 22–24.

[6] Ibid., p. 22.

[7] Parham, p. 161.

[8] Ibid., pp. 57–154.

[9] Ibid., pp. 57–80.

[10] Ibid., pp. 81–145.

[11] Hollenweger, p. 22.

[12] Stanley H. Frodsham, *With Signs Following* (Springfield, Mo.: Gospel Publishing House, 1946), p. 32; Cartwright, p. 5.

[13] Bartleman, pp. 16–43.

[14] Frodsham, pp. 32–33.

[15] Ibid., pp. 33–34, quoting an unnamed source.

[16] In 1906, one of the Holiness denominations, the Nazarenes, had about a dozen congregations in the Los Angeles area. Among these was the "Church of the Nazarene," founded in 1895 by Phineas Bresee at his "Peniel Tabernacle" on Main Street (Synan, *Holiness-Pentecostal Movement*, pp. 96–97).

[17] Bartleman, p. 11.

[18] Ibid.

[19] Ibid., p. 12.

[20] Synan, *Holiness-Pentecostal Movement*, p. 97.

[21] Bartleman, p. 13.

[22] Ibid., p. 16.

[23] Ibid., p. 28.

[24] Ibid., pp. 18, 27, 34.

[25] Quoted by Frodsham, p. 34.

[26] Robert Bryant Mitchell, *Heritage and Horizons: The History of Open Bible Standard Churches* (Des Moines, Iowa: Open Bible Publishers, 1982), p. 27.

[27] Bartleman, pp. 28–30.

[28] Cartwright, p. 7.

[29] Synan, *Holiness-Pentecostal Movement*, p. 104; Cartwright, p. 5; Anderson, pp. 60–61.

[30] Synan, *Holiness-Pentecostal Movement*, p. 104.

[31] Cartwright, p. 5.

[32] Anderson, p. 60.

[33] Cartwright, p. 5.

[34] Parham, p. 161.

[35] Ibid., pp. 126–28.

[36] Anderson, p. 60; Cartwright, p. 5.

[37] Cartwright, p. 5.

[38] Parham, p. 135.

[39] Ibid., p. 137.

[40] Ibid., p. 161.

[41] Synan, *Holiness-Pentecostal Movement*, p. 104; Mitchell, p. 26.

[42]Anderson, p. 61; Cartwright, p. 5.

[43]Brumback, p. 35.

[44]Synan, *Holiness-Pentecostal Movement*, pp. 104–5; A. C. Valdez, Sr., *Fire on Azusa Street* (Costa Mesa, Calif.: Gift Publications, 1980), p. 18; Klaude Kendrick, *The Promise Fulfilled* (Springfield, Mo.: Gospel Publishing House, 1961), p. 64.

[45]Parham, p. 142; Bartleman, p. 43.

[46]Valdez, p. 19; Brumback, p. 36; Anderson, p. 65; Synan, *Holiness-Pentecostal Movement*, p. 106; Cartwright, p. 6.

[47]Anderson, p. 65; Cartwright, p. 6; Kendrick, p. 65.

[48]Cartwright, p. 6.

[49]Ibid.

[50]Ibid.; Frodsham, p. 32; Synan, *Holiness-Pentecostal Movement*, p. 106.

[51]Bartleman, p. 43. Bartleman wrote, "March 26 I went to a cottage meeting on Bonnie Brae Street. Both white and colored saints were meeting there for prayer. I had attended a cottage meeting shortly before this, at another place, where I first met Brother Seymour. He had just come from Texas. He was a colored man, very plain, spiritual, and humble. He attended the meetings at Bonnie Brae Street. He was blind in one eye." John T. Nichol mistakenly interprets this statement to indicate that Bartleman first met Seymour on March 26 (John T. Nichol, *Pentecostalism* [New York: Harper & Row, 1966], pp. 33–34).

[52]Cartwright, p. 6.

[53]Parham, p. 161; Anderson, p. 65; Mack E. Jonas in an interview with Leonard Lovett (Leonard Lovett, "Black Origins of the Pentecostal Movement" in *Aspects*, ed. Synan, p. 134.)

[54]Anderson, pp. 65–66; Cartwright, p. 6.

[55]Frank J. Ewart, *The Phenomenon of Pentecost*, revised ed. (Hazelwood, Mo.: World Aflame Press, 1975), pp. 75–76; Cartwright, pp. 6–7; Lovett in Synan, ed., *Aspects*, p. 132.

[56]Valdez, p. 19.

[57]Lovett in Synan, ed,. *Aspects*, p. 132; Cartwright, p. 7.

[58]Valdez, p. 19; Frodsham, p. 32.

[59]Brumback, p. 36.

[60]Synan, *Holiness-Pentecostal Movement*, p. 106.

[61]Ibid.

[62]Frodsham, p. 32; Kendrick, p. 65, quoting "When the Spirit Fell," *Pentecostal Evangel*, 6 April 1946, p. 6.

[63]According to Valdez, p. 19, Morton Asberry, the son of Richard and Ruth Asberry, reported that, at this time, "Brother Seymour fell under the power of the Holy Ghost like he was dead and spoke in an unknown language." Anderson, p. 66, and Donald Gee, *The Pentecostal Movement* (London: Elim Publishing Co., 1949), p. 12, also report that Seymour received the blessing at this time. However, Bartleman, p. 62, says, "Seymour himself did not speak in 'tongues' until some time after 'Azusa' had been opened," and Lovett in Synan, ed., *Aspects*, p. 134 quotes eyewitness Mack E. Jonas to the effect that Seymour "was preaching something, and he hadn't gotten it himself, but he kept preaching. He hadn't spoken in tongues even when I received it [June 29], but he was preaching it to white and colored both."

[64]Cartwright, p. 7.

[65]Bartleman, p. 44.

[66]Ibid. According to Lovett in Synan, ed., Aspects, pp. 131–32, Mack E. Jonas thought that the meetings on the evening of April 15 were already at Azusa Street.

[67]Valdez, p. 19.

[68]Brumback, p. 36.

[69]Cartwright, p. 7.

[70]Brumback, p. 39; Anderson, p. 65.

[71]Los Angeles Times, 9 September 1956, as quoted by Brumback, pp. 39–40.

[72]Valdez, p. 20.

[73]Ibid.

[74]Cartwright, p. 8.

[75]Los Angeles Times, 18 April 1906, p. 1, as quoted by Synan, Holiness-Pentecostal Movement, pp. 95–96.

[76]Gee, p. 12.

[77]Los Angeles Times, 19 April 1906, pp. 1–10.

[78]Bartleman, p. 47.

[79]Ibid.

[80]Ibid., p. 52.

[81]Ibid.

[82]Ibid., p. 54.

[83]Ibid., pp. 56–57.

[84]Ibid., p. 58.

[85]Ibid.

[86]Frodsham. p. 37.

[87]Bartleman, p. 61.

[88]Ibid., quoting Way of Faith, June 22, 1906.

[89]Lovett in Synan, ed., Aspects, p. 132.

[90]Anderson, p. 70.

[91]Rachel A. Sizelove, "God's Moving at Azusa Mission," in Warner, ed., Touched by the Fire, p. 9.

[92]Ibid., pp. 10–11.

[93]Kendrick, p. 68.

[94]Bartleman, p. 61; Anderson, p. 73.

[95]Bartleman, p. 67.

[96]Ibid., p. 68.

[97]Ibid., p. 69.

[98]Anderson, p. 70.

[99]Ibid.; Hollenweger, p. 27 (note 23); Lovett in Synan, ed., Aspects, p. 134; Glenn A. Cook, The Azusa Street Meeting (Los Angeles: By the author, n.d.), p. 1.

[100]Ethel E. Goss, The Winds of God: The Story of the Early Pentecostal Movement (1901–1914) in the Life of Howard A. Goss, revised ed. (Hazelwood, Mo.: World Aflame Press, 1977), pp. 98–99.

[101]Parham, p. 148.

[102]Apostolic Faith Mission, A Historical Account of the Apostolic Faith (Portland, Oregon: Apostolic Faith Publishing House, 1965), p. 61.

[103]Gordon F. Atter, The Third Force (Peterborough, Ontario: The College Press), p. 31.

[104]F. A. Sandgren, "One Sunday in August 1906," a sheet printed in 1917 by F. A. Sandgren in Chicago for circulation in his church, as quoted by Kendrick, p. 68.

[105]Bartleman, p. 70.

[106]Ibid.

[107]Ibid.

[108]Anderson, p. 141.

[109]Ibid.

[110]Ibid., p. 82; Frodsham, p. 35.

[111]Bartleman, p. 82.

[112]Ibid., pp. 84, 92.

[113]Ibid., pp. 85–86, quoting *Way of Faith*, September 1906.

[114]Parham, pp. 155–56.

[115]Ibid., p. 154.

[116]Bartleman, pp. 83–84. Fisher's daughter, Ruth Carter, placed the time of this split at 1907 (Ruth Carter, "An Unusual Experience in the Upper Room Mission," in Warner, ed., *Touched by the Fire*, p. 109).

[117]Nichol, p. 34. Carl Brumback wrote of Fisher's resignation from the Church in Glendale that it resulted from his series of sermons on the Holy Spirit there which "had resulted in much blessing, including some outward demonstrations of joy." As a result, "The deacons remonstrated with their pastor about preaching sermons that caused such excitement and Fisher submitted his resignation, rather than be told what to or what not to preach" (Brumback, p. 58).

[118]Bartleman, pp. 83–84.

[119]Anderson, p. 68.

[120]Ibid., p. 74.

[121]A. W. Orwig, quoted in B. F. Lawrence, *The Apostolic Faith Restored* (St. Louis, Mo.: Gospel Publishing House, 1916), pp. 77–78, 82–83, as cited by William W. Menzies, *Anointed to Serve* (Springfield, Mo.: Gospel Publishing House, 1971), pp. 52, 54; Kendrick, p. 66; and Frodsham, pp. 37–39.

[122]Ernest S. Williams, "My Personal Experience At the Azusa Mission," in Warner, ed., *Touched by the Fire*, p. 45. In this article, Williams says he was baptized with the Spirit on October 2 at Azusa Street Mission. However, according to Brumback, p. 59, this occurred at the meetings at Eighth and Maple.

[123]Anderson, p. 72.

[124]Frodsham, p. 43.

[125]Parham, p. 154.

[126]Ibid., pp. 155–56.

[127]Ibid., p. 156.

[128]Donald Dayton, "The Rise of the Evangelical Healing Movement in Nineteenth Century America," *Pneuma: The Journal of the Society for Pentecostal Studies* 4 (Spring, 1982): 17.

[129]Lilian B. Yeomans, "The Faith of John Alexander Dowie," in Warner, ed., *Touched by the Fire*, p. 118.

[130]Hollenweger, p. 117.

[131]Ibid.

[132]Edith Waldvogel Blumhofer, *The Assemblies of God: A Popular History* (Springfield, Mo.: Gospel Publishing House, 1985), p. 32.

133Brumback, p. 72.

134Parham, p. 156.

135Ibid.

136Menzies, pp. 65–66; Brumback, pp. 74–75; Frodsham, p. 48; Anderson, pp. 73, 131.

137Marie E. Brown [née Burgess], "A Vision for the Lost," in Warner, ed., *Touched by the Fire*, p. 23.

138Ibid.

139Parham, p. 160.

140Synan, *Holiness-Pentecostal Movement*, p. 112.

141Mack E. Jonas, as quoted by Lovett in Synan, ed., *Aspects*, p. 133.

142Parham, p. 163.

143Ibid.

144Synan, *Holiness-Pentecostal Movement*, p. 112. Synan states that one probable reason for Seymour's rejection of Parham was that Parham had been accused of homosexuality (Synan, *Holiness-Pentecostal Movement*, pp. 112–13, n. 41).

145Parham, p. 163.

146Ibid., pp. 163–64.

147Synan, *Holiness-Pentecostal Movement*, p. 112.

148Bartleman, p. 69.

149Brumback, p. 58; Parham, pp. 166–70.

150Anderson, p. 140.

151Cartwright, p. 8.

152Gee, pp. 14–15.

153Nichol, pp. 41–42; Mitchell, p. 29.

154Anderson, p. 130.

155Cartwright, p. 8.

156Ibid.

157Synan, *Holiness-Pentecostal Movement*, pp. 113–14; Menzies, p. 56.

158Hollenweger, p. 63.

159Anderson, p. 131.

160Thomas William Miller, "The Significance of A. H. Argue for Pentecostal Historiography," *Pneuma: The Journal of the Society for Pentecostal Studies* 8 (Fall, 1986): 122. The date given here, "September, 1907," is a misprint, and should read, "September, 1906."

161Brumback, p. 85.

162Frodsham, p. 53. Although Thomas William Miller, in "The Canadian 'Azusa': The Hebden Mission in Toronto," *Pneuma: The Journal of the Society for Pentecostal Studies* 8 (Spring, 1986): 5, refers to Mrs. Hebden as the first Canadian to have received the baptism in the Spirit with tongues following, her experience took place a few days after T. B. Barratt received it under the ministry of Miss Maud Williams (Mrs. Haycroft), who had in turn received the baptism of the Spirit in Canada.

163Ibid.

164Atter, p. 36.

165Ibid., p. 37.

166Miller, "Hebden Mission," p. 7.

167Ibid., p. 12.

168Ibid., pp. 12–13.

169Synan, *Holiness-Pentecostal Movement,* pp. 72, 122.

170Ibid., p. 123.

171Ibid.; Menzies, p. 62; Brumback, p. 84.

172Frodsham, p. 41.

173Synan, *Holiness-Pentecostal Movement,* p. 124.

174Ibid.

175Ibid.

176Ibid.

177Frodsham, p. 41.

178Synan, *Holiness-Pentecostal Movement,* p. 126.

179Dillard L. Wood and William H. Preskitt, Jr., *Baptized With Fire: A History of the Pentecostal Fire-Baptized Holiness Church* (Franklin Springs, Ga.: Advocate Press, 1982), p. 19; Synan, *Holiness-Pentecostal Movement,* p. 127. King later became leader of the Pentecostal Holiness Church, after it merged with the Fire-Baptized Holiness Church.

180Wood and Preskitt, p. 19.

181William Emanuel, "The Righteous Suffer," in Warner, ed., *Touched by the Fire,* pp. 101–2.

182Frodsham, pp. 41–42.

183Menzies, p. 63.

184Synan, *Holiness-Pentecostal Movement,* p. 133.

185Blumhofer, p. 35.

186Menzies, p. 63. Tomlinson had been aware of a revival which had taken place in 1896 at Camp Creek, North Carolina, where over one hundred people had spoken in tongues. This was a precursor of the Church of God of Cleveland, Tennessee, of which Tomlinson eventually became general overseer.

187Brumback, p. 57.

188Nichol, p. 37.

189Ibid.

190Apostolic Faith Mission, *Historical Account,* pp. 64–65.

191Ibid.; Mitchell, p. 31.

192Nichol, p. 35.

NOTES–CHAPTER 4

1Synan, *Holiness-Pentecostal Movement* pp. 135–36.

2Lovett, in Synan, ed., *Aspects* pp. 133–34.

3Synan, *Holiness-Pentecostal Movement,* p. 136.

4Brumback, p. 75.

5Synan, *Holiness-Pentecostal Movement,* p. 136.

6Brumback, p. 68.

7Sizelove, "God's Moving at Azusa Mission," in Warner, ed., *Touched by the Fire,* p. 11.

8Sizelove, in Warner, ed., *Touched by the Fire,* p. 11. Although Brumback states that it was Lucy Farrow who travelled with Rachel Sizelove, Sizelove does not give the name of her travelling companion in her tract, "A Sparkling Fountain for the Whole Earth." Brumback's statement seems to conflict with a notice that appeared in *Apostolic Faith*, vol. 1, no. 4 (December, 1906), p. 3, stating that Lucy Farrow had started for Africa five months previously.

[9]Sizelove, in Warner, ed., *Touched by the Fire*, p. 11.

[10]Ibid.

[11]Ibid., pp. 11–12.

[12]Synan, *Holiness-Pentecostal Movement*, p. 116.

[13]Frodsham, p. 45.

[14]Anderson, p. 71.

[15]Niklaus, Sawin, and Stoesz, p. 111.

[16]Ibid., p. 112, quoting W. A. Cramer, "Notes from the Home Field," *Christian and Missionary Alliance Weekly* 27 (April, 1907), p. 201.

[17]Menzies, p. 66; Brumback, pp. 75–76; Niklaus, Sawin, and Stoesz, p. 111.

[18]Anderson, p. 67.

[19]Ibid., pp. 69–70.

[20]Ibid., p. 70.

[21]Synan, *Holiness-Pentecostal Movement*, p. 136.

[22]Menzies, p. 66.

[23]Brumback, p. 76. Dr. Eldridge later also received the gift of tongues.

[24]Alice Reynolds Flower, "The Ministry of 'Brother Tom,'" in Warner, ed., *Touched by the Fire*, pp. 33–35. Alice Reynolds married J. Roswell Flower in 1911. Her mother, Mrs. Mary A. Reynolds, was healed on her "deathbed" in March of 1872 (Brumback, pp. 11–12).

[25]Quoted by Brumback, p. 78.

[26]Ibid.

[27]Warner, *The Woman Evangelist*, p. 12.

[28]Aimee Semple McPherson, *This Is That* (Los Angeles: Bridal Call Publishing House, 1919), p. 213.

[29]Warner, *The Woman Evangelist*, p. 285.

[30]Ibid., p. 72, n. 45; Thomas Paino, Sr., "God's Presence Filled the Tabernacle," in Warner, ed., *Touched by the Fire*, pp. 75–76.

[31]Brumback, pp. 88–89; Nichol, p. 38.

[32]Brumback, p. 89.

[33]Ibid.

[34]Ibid.

[35]Frodsham, p. 47.

[36]Ibid., pp. 46–47; Niklaus, Sawin, and Stoesz, p. 268.

[37]Quoted by Brumback, p. 79.

[38]Ibid., p. 80.

[39]Ibid., p. 90.

[40]Ibid.

[41]Ibid.

[42]Ibid.

[43]Ibid.

[44]Ibid., p. 91.

[45]Ibid.; Nichol, p. 39.

[46]Albrecht, p. 117, n. 57.

47Chappell, p. 244.

48Albrecht, p. 110; Chappell, pp. 244–45.

49Chappell, p. 245.

50Bartleman, pp. 115–16; Anderson, p. 74.

51Quoted by Frodsham, p. 47. For further description of this meeting, see Bartleman, pp. 115–16.

52Niklaus, Sawin, and Stoesz, p. 113.

53Ibid., p. 114.

54Ibid.

55Ibid.

56Chappell, pp. 246–47.

57Niklaus, Sawin, and Stoesz, p. 115.

58Ibid.

59Brumback, p. 92.

60Menzies, p. 70.

61Cited by Niklaus, Sawin, and Stoesz, p. 115.

62Ibid., pp. 116–17.

63Anderson, p. 147.

64Quoted in Ibid.

65Ibid.

66Brumback, p. 93.

67Ibid., p. 95.

68William W. Menzies, "Non-Wesleyan Origins of the Pentecostal Movement," in Synan, ed., Aspects, p. 93.

69Ibid.

70Ralph M. Riggs, "Heaven On Earth," in Warner, ed., Touched by the Fire, p. 140.

71Anderson, p. 167. Edith Waldvogel Blumhofer has identified five major general purposes that had been given for the Hot Springs meeting: unity, stabilization, effective missions outreach, legal chartering of the movement, and the consideration of a Bible school to serve Pentecostals (p. 36).

72Brumback, p. 80.

73Menzies, p. 69.

74Klaude Kendrick, The Promise Fulfilled (Springfield, Mo.: Gospel Publishing House, 1961), p. 69.

75Ibid., p. 70.

76Marie F. Brown, "A Vision for the Lost," in Warner, ed., Touched by the Fire, p. 24.

77Frodsham, p. 48.

78Brumback, pp. 81–82.

79Frodsham, p. 43.

80Quoted by Brumback, p. 69.

81Miller, "The Significance of A. H. Argue," pp. 123–24.

82Quoted by Frodsham, p. 44 and Brumback, p. 69.

83Miller, "The Significance of A. H. Argue," p. 124.

84Atter, p. 39.

85Blumhofer, p. 41.

86Ibid., p. 35.

[87]Brumback, p. 70; Anderson, p. 129.

[88]Blumhofer, p. 32.

[89]Quoted by Brumback, pp. 70–71.

[90]Ibid., p. 71.

[91]Valdez, p. 26.

[92]Hollenweger, pp. 24–25.

[93]ibid.

[94]Menzies, p. 75; Brumback, pp. 98–99.

[95]Bartleman, p. 145.

[96]Ibid.

[97]Ibid., p. 146.

[98]Valdez, p. 27.

[99]Menzies, p. 76.

[100]Ibid., pp. 76–77.

[101]Quoted by Frodsham, pp. 55–56. See also Brumback, pp. 85–86.

[102]Miller, "The Significance of A. H. Argue," p. 127; Atter, pp. 38–39.

[103]Atter, p. 39; Robert A. Larden, Our Apostolic Heritage (Calgary, Alberta: Kyle Printing & Stationery, Ltd., 1971), p. 27.

[104]Quoted by Larden, p. 27.

[105]Ibid., p. 28.

[106]Ibid.

[107]Quoted by Larden, p. 29; see also Miller, p. 127.

[108]Larden, p. 29; see also Miller, pp. 126–27.

[109]Gee, p. 13.

[110]Frodsham, p. 57.

[111]Ibid., p. 56; Atter, p. 39. According to Atter, Ward probably received his Pentecostal experience under some ministry other than that of A. H. Argue.

[112]Frodsham, p. 56.

[113]Ibid., pp. 56–57.

[114]Atter, p. 39.

[115]Thomas William Miller, "The Canadian 'Azusa': The Hebden Mission in Toronto," in Pneuma: The Journal of the Society for Pentecostal Studies 8 (Spring, 1986): 20–21.

[116]Ibid., p. 22.

[117]Atter, p. 95.

[118]Ibid., pp. 95–96.

[119]McPherson, pp. 36–45, 50, 65, 68; Miller, "The Canadian 'Azusa,'" p. 15.

[120]McPherson, p. 68.

[121]Ibid., pp. 72–75; Menzies, p. 65.

[122]Miller, "The Canadian 'Azusa,'" p. 15.

[123]McPherson, p. 85; Robert Bahr, Least of All Saints (Englewood Cliffs, N.J.: Prentice-Hall, 1979), p. 48.

[124]McPherson, pp. 90–91; Bahr, p. 53.

[125]McPherson, p. 95; Bahr, pp. 64–73.

[126]Bahr, p. 88.

[127]McPherson, pp. 103–15; Bahr, pp. 88–100.

[128]McPherson, pp. 256–57.

129Ibid., pp. 117–61; Bahr, pp. 101–21.

130Bahr, p. 288.

131McPherson, pp. 210–43; Bahr, pp. 134–50.

132Atter, pp. 35–36.

133Ibid., p. 36; Miller, "The Significance of A. H. Argue," p. 132.

134Atter, p. 36; Miller, "The Significance of A. H. Argue," p. 132.

135Miller, "The Significance of A. H. Argue," p. 132.

136Miller, "The Canadian 'Azusa,' " p. 14.

137Frodsham, p. 42.

138Maria B. Woodworth-Etter, *Signs and Wonders God Wrought in the Ministry for Forty Years* (Indianapolis, Ind.: By the author, 1916), pp. 172–75.

139Anderson, p. 107.

140Ibid., pp. 161–62; Hollenweger, p. 32.

141Woodworth-Etter, pp. 173–74.

142Ibid., p. 168.

143Ibid., p. 250.

144Valdez, p. 41.

145Ibid., pp. 41–42.

146David Reed, "Aspects of the Origins of Oneness Pentecostalism," in Vinson Synan, ed., *Aspects*, p. 145.

147Woodworth-Etter, p. 250.

148Ibid., p. 257.

149Ibid., p. 7.

150Miller, "The Significance of A. H. Argue," p. 133.

151Valdez, p. 42.

152Miller, "The Significance of A. H. Argue," p. 134; Reed, p. 145.

153Hollenweger, p. 31; Reed, pp. 145–46.

154Blumhofer, p. 46.

155Reed, p. 147.

156Atter, pp. 103, 132. See also Larden, pp. 30–35.

157E. L. Tanner, "When the 'Holy Rollers' Came," in Warner, ed., *Touched by the Fire*, p. 86.

158Quoted by Woodworth-Etter, pp. 261–62.

159Ibid., p. 550.

160Ibid., pp. 273–74.

161Ibid., p. 275.

162Ibid., p. 276.

163Ibid., p. 277.

164Ibid.

165Ruth Carter, "An Unusual Experience in the Upper Room Mission," in Warner, ed., *Touched by the Fire*, pp. 109–10.

166Faith Campbell, *Stanley Frodsham: Prophet with a Pen* (Springfield, Mo.: Gospel Publishing House, 1974), pp. 45–46.

167Albrecht, p. 111.

168Campbell, p. 45.

169Ibid., p. 46.

170Ibid., p. 45.

171Ibid., p. 46.

[172]Chappell, p. 244, n. 133.

[173]Woodworth-Etter, p. 566.

[174]Ibid., pp. 380–81.

[175]Ibid., p. 384; Warner, The Woman Evangelist, p. 159.

[176]Woodworth-Etter, p. 384.

[177]Warner, The Woman Evangelist, p. 159.

[178]Details of these meetings appear in Woodworth-Etter, pp. 402–63.

[179]Bahr, p. 102.

[180]Ibid., p. 288.

[181]Valdez, p. 75.

[182]Warner, The Woman Evangelist, pp. 285–86.

[183]McPherson, p. 186.

[184]Ibid., p. 190.

[185]Ibid., p. 187.

[186]Ibid., pp. 187–88.

[187]Ibid., p. 271.

[188]Ibid., pp. 271–73.

[189]Ibid., p. 188.

[190]Ibid., pp. 267–68.

[191]Bahr, p. 288.

[192]Ibid., p. 166. Harold McPherson was granted a divorce from Aimee Semple McPherson on April 12, 1921.

[193]McPherson, pp. 233, 235.

[194]Ibid., pp. 274–75.

[195]Ibid., p. 236.

[196]Ibid., pp. 244–45.

[197]Ibid., pp. 245–46. See also Warner, The Woman Evangelist, p. 103, according to which a physician, G. Rodney Smith, was mentioned in an article on these meetings.

[198]McPherson, p. 275.

[199]Ibid., p. 247.

[200]Bahr, p. 150.

[201]Ibid.

[202]Ibid., pp. 150–51.

[203]Menzies, "Non-Wesleyan Origins," in Synan, ed., Aspects, p. 90.

[204]Miller, "The Significance of A. H. Argue," p. 139.

[205]Quoted in ibid., p. 139.

[206]Quoted in ibid., p. 139.

[207]Ibid., p. 140.

[208]Eloise May Richey, What God Hath Wrought in the Life of Raymond T. Richey (Houston, Texas: Full Gospel Advocate, 1925), pp. 57–61.

[209]Ibid., p. 77.

[210]Charles S. Price, The Story of My Life, 3d ed. (Pasadena, Calif.: By the author, 1944), pp. 29–38.

[211]Ibid., p. 33.

[212]Ibid., pp. 35–44.

[213]Ibid., p. 48.

[214]Ibid.

[215]Ibid.
[216]Ibid., p. 49.
[217]Ibid., p. 50.
[218]Ibid., p. 51.
[219]Ibid.
[220]Buckingham, pp. 24–27.
[221]Ibid., p. 46.
[222]Ibid., pp. 36–37, 53.
[223]Ibid., p. 39.
[224]Ibid., p. 57.
[225]Ibid.
[226]Ibid., pp. 57–58.
[227]Ibid., p. 59.
[228]Ibid., p. 68.
[229]Bahr, p. 299.
[230]Buckingham, pp. 78–88.
[231]Ibid., pp. 95–98.

NOTES–CHAPTER 5

[1]Harrell, p. 28.
[2]Ibid., p. 30.
[3]Ibid.
[4]Ibid., pp. 35–36.
[5]James A. Watt, "The Latter Rain Movement," taped message on the Latter Rain Movement, Christian Centre, Surrey, British Columbia, Canada, spring 1976; Hollenweger, p. 354.
[6]"Branham Visits Roberts Campaign," *Voice of Healing* (April, 1949): 16, quoted by Harrell, p. 49.
[7]Harrell, p. 44.
[8]Ibid., p. 66.
[9]Ibid., p. 59.
[10]William Freeman, "When the Angel of the Lord Appeared to Me," *Healing Messenger* (January, 1956): 2–3, quoted by Harrell, pp. 75–76.
[11]Don Gossett, "The Life and Ministry of William W. Freeman," *Healing Messenger* (March, 1954): 6, quoted by Harrell, p. 76.
[12]Harrell, p. 77.
[13]A. A. Allen, "Many Reports Appraise Ministry of A. A. Allen," *Voice of Healing* (May, 1950): 4, quoted by Harrell, p. 68.
[14]Harrell, p. 69.
[15]David Nunn, "How God Led Me into the Miracle Ministry," *Voice of Healing* (July, 1960): 9, quoted by Harrell, p. 82.
[16]Ibid., p. 14, quoted by Harrell, p. 83.
[17]A. A. Allen, William Branham, Jack Coe, Clifton Erickson, Velmer Gardner, W. V. Grant, Dale Hansen, H. E. Hardt, Fern Huffstutler, Gayle Jackson, Gordon Lindsay, Jack Moore, Louise Nankievell, Wilber Ogilvie, T. L. Os-

born, Raymond T. Ritchey, A. C. Valdez, Jr., R. R. Vinyard, Mildred Wicks, and Doyle Zachery.

[18]Buckingham, p. 101.

[19]Ibid., p. 104.

[20]Ibid., p. 105.

[21]Ibid., p. 106.

[22]Harrell, p. 95.

[23]Anna Jeanne Moore, "Convention Diary," *Voice of Healing* (February, 1952): 2–3, quoted by Harrell, p. 95.

[24]Gordon Lindsay, *William Branham: A Man Sent from God*, 4th ed. (Jeffersonville, Ind.: William Branham, 1950), p. 100, quoted by Harrell, p. 32.

[25]Harrell, pp. 96, 98.

[26]Ernest Hawtin, "How This Revival Began," *Sharon Star* (1 August 1949): 3.

[27]Ibid.

[28]George R. Hawtin, "Revival At Sharon," *Sharon Star* (1 August 1949): 2.

[29]Milford E. Kirkpatrick, *The 1948 Revival & Now* (Dallas, Texas: By the author, n.d.), p. 9

[30]George R. Hawtin, "Editorial," *Sharon Star* (1 May 1948): 2.

[31]George R. Hawtin, "The Sharon Camp Meeting," *Sharon Star* (1 June 1948): 2.

[32]George R. Hawtin, "Editorial," *Sharon Star* (1 July 1948): 2.

[33]G. R. Hawtin, "The Sharon Camp Meeting," p. 2.

[34]G. R. Hawtin, "Editorial," 1 July 1948, p. 2.

[35]Ibid.

[36]G. R. Hawtin, "The Sharon Camp Meeting," p. 2.

[37]George R. Hawtin, "Local Church Government," *Sharon Star* (1 May 1948): 4.

[38]James A. Watt, "A Historical Analysis of the Development of Two Concepts of 'Presbytery,'" (Seattle, Wash.: By the author, 1972), p. 3.

[39]G. R. Hawtin, "Editorial," 1 May 1948, p. 2.

[40]Noel McNeill, "As of a Rushing Mighty Wind: An Assessment of North America's Pentecostal Movement," Haliburton, Ont.: By the author, 1964, p. 27. (Typewritten.)

[41]George R. Hawtin, "Editorial," *Sharon Star* (1 August 1948): 2, 3.

[42]James and Phyllis Spiers, as quoted by George R. Hawtin, "Editorial," *Sharon Star* (1 October 1948): 2.

[43]Ibid.

[44]James A. Watt, "Progress with God," *Sharon Star* (1 December 1948): 4.

[45]George R. Hawtin, "News from Sharon: Heavenly Choir Restored," *Sharon Star* (1 December 1948): 1.

[46]George Warnock to Richard Riss, 7 November 1976, Thesis File, Regent College, Vancouver, B.C., Canada.

[47]Watt, "Progress with God," p. 3.

[48]Ibid.

[49]Ibid.

[50]Reg Layzell, "My Testimony," *Sharon Star* (1 February 1949): 1, 2.

[51]M. D. Beall, "Mrs. Beall Testifies," *Sharon Star* (1 December 1948): 4.

[52]Marion Melloon, *Ivan Spencer: Willow in the Wind* (Plainfield, N.J.: Logos International, 1974), pp. 147–49; "Pentecostal Prayer Fellowship," *Elim Pen-*

tecostal Herald 19, 201 (February 1949): 11. The Pentecostal Prayer Fellowship, which had its inception in 1946, was an interdenominational fellowship consisting of a few small Pentecostal denominations, including The Zion Evangelistic Fellowship, The Elim Missionary Assemblies, The International Pentecostal Assemblies, The Jubilee Gospel Association, and The Pentecostal Church of Christ.

[53]Menzies, p. 323.

[54]Campbell, *Stanley Frodsham: Prophet with a Pen*, p. 110.

[55]Sixto M. Lopez, "Visitation in Detroit," *Elim Pentecostal Herald* 19, 201 (February 1949): 9, 10.

[56]Ivan Q. Spencer, "There Is Revival in the Air Today," *Elim Pentecostal Herald* 19, 201 (February 1949): 1.

[57]Menzies, pp. 323–24.

[58]Ibid., p. 323.

[59]Stanley Frodsham to Faith and Len Campbell, 7 May 1949, Stanley Frodsham Papers, Asbury Theological Seminary, Wilmore, Ky. The Apostolic Movement that began in Bournemouth grew out of the Welsh Revival in 1905. Its official name was the Apostolic Faith Church, with headquarters in Winton, Bournemouth. Its original leaders were W. O. Hutchinson and J. Brooke. In 1913 they held a convention in London during which D. P. Williams, the leader of the Apostolic Church at Penygroes, Wales, was called to apostleship. This was also accepted by the Presbyteries of the Apostolic Church at Penygroes, which later united with the Apostolic Faith Church. In 1915, D. P. Williams and the former Apostolic Church Presbyteries and congregations in Wales seceded because of an emphasis on centralism in the apostle at Bournemouth.

[60]Lloyd A. Westover, "My Impressions of the Great Awakening in Portland," *Sharon Star* (1 May 1949): 1.

[61]A. Earl Lee, "From Los Angeles," *Sharon Star* (1 December 1949): 2, 3.

[62]George R. Hawtin, "A Report On Meetings By E. H. Hawtin Party," *Sharon Star* (1 December 1949): 2.

[63]Brumback, p. 332.

[64]Stanley Frodsham to Faith Campbell, 29 September 1949, Stanley Frodsham Papers, Assemblies of God Archives, Springfield, Mo.

[65]J. Preston Eby to Richard Riss, 11 October 1976, Thesis File, Regent College, Vancouver, B.C., Canada.

[66]K. R. Iverson, *Present Day Truths* (Portland, Or.: The Center Press, 1975), p. 59.

[67]Two major books of the Latter Rain Movement were published by Paul N. Grubb: *The End-Time Revival* and *Manifested Sonship*, vol. 1. His wife, Lura Johnson Grubb, also wrote an influential book, *Living To Tell of Death*.

[68]Glad Tidings Temple in St. Louis, Missouri, held frequent Latter Rain Conventions. On November 8–15, 1950, the ministers included Stanley Frodsham, M. D. Beall, Fred Poole, Elmer Frink, Thomas Wyatt, Norman Grubb, Joseph Mattsson-Boze, Harry Hodge, Ivan Spencer, Milford Kirkpatrick, Alvar Lindskog, Baron von Blomberg, Earl Lee, and Omar Johnson, who was host pastor, according to Carlton Spencer's description of the meetings as it appears in his article, "Spiritual Advance at St. Louis," *Elim Pentecostal Herald* 21, 220 (November-December 1950): 6–7.

[69]Ivan Q. Spencer, "A Recent Trip," *Elim Pentecostal Herald* 19, 206 (July-August, 1949): 14.

[70]Interview with H. David Edwards, Elim Bible Institute, Lima, New York, 23 December 1976.

[71]Stanley Frodsham to Faith Campbell, 3 June 1954, Stanley Frodsham Papers, Assemblies of God Archives, Springfield, Mo.

[72]*Elim Pentecostal Herald* 24, 232 (July-September, 1952): 10.

[73]Ern Baxter to Richard Riss, 14 July 1976, Thesis File, Regent College, Vancouver, B.C., Canada.

[74]Eric J. Simila to Richard Riss, 6 September [sic: October] 1975, Thesis File, Regent College, Vancouver, B.C., Canada.

[75]Dan Malachuk, "Publisher's Preface," *Logos Journal* 7, 1 (January-February, 1977): 4

[76]*Sharon Star* (1 August 1949): 3.

[77]J. Preston Eby to Richard Riss, 11 October 1976, Thesis File, Regent College, Vancouver, B.C., Canada.

[78]Meloon, p. 160.

[79]Steve Wilber, "Commentary: A Prophecy: 1619," *Banner* 9, 3 (Spring, 1977): 15.

[80]Brumback, p. 333.

[81]Walter J. Hollenweger, "Handbuch Der Pfingstbewegung," Doctoral dissertation, University of Zurich, 1965, 02a.02.144, p. 758. Hollenweger writes, "Wenn Brumback schreibt, dass die Bewegung unterdessen in nichts zusammengefallen sei, so handelt es sich hier um das gluche Wunschdenken, das die traditionellen Kirchen verleitete, die Anfange der Pfingstbewegung zu ignorieren. Die verkirchlichten Pfingstdenominationen erleben jetzt die Anfange ihrer Bewung nocheinmal, aber vom Gesichtspunkt der konservativen Denomination aus."

NOTES—CHAPTER 6

[1]J. Edwin Orr, *The Second Evangelical Awakening in America* (London: Marshall, Morgan & Scott, 1952), pp. 161–62.

[2]Orr, *Campus Aflame*, pp. 165–82; Earle E. Cairns, *V. Raymond Edman: In the Presence of the King* (Chicago: Moody Press, 1972), p. 136.

[3]Edward L. R. Elson, *America's Spiritual Recovery* (Westwood, N.J.: Revell, 1954), pp. 39–41.

[4]Orr, *Second Evangelical Awakening in America*, pp. 188–201.

[5]Ethel May Baldwin and David V. Benson, *Henrietta Mears and How She Did It!* (Glendale, Calif.: Gospel Light Publications, 1966), p. 232.

[6]Ibid.

[7]Ibid., p. 234.

[8]Ibid., p. 235.

[9]Ibid., p. 239.

[10]Ibid., p. 243.

[11]Ibid., pp. 243, 244.

[12]Ibid.

[13]Ibid., p. 248.

[14]Ibid.

[15]Ibid., p. 250.

[16]John Charles Pollock, *Billy Graham* (London: Hodder & Stoughton, 1966), p. 80.

[17]J. Edwin Orr, *Good News in Bad Times: Signs of Revival* (Grand Rapids: Zondervan, 1953), p. 154.

[18]Pollock, pp. 80–81.

[19]Orr, *Good News in Bad Times*, p. 154.

[20]Baldwin and Benson, p. 252.

[21]Fred W. Hoffman, *Revival Times in America* (Boston: W. A. Wilde Co., 1956), pp. 168–69.

[22]Orr, *Second Evangelical Awakening in America*, pp. 161–62.

[23]Orr, *Good News in Bad Times*, p. 37.

[24]Claude Jenkins, "First Signs of Revival: Unusual Stirrings in California," *Life of Faith*, 25 May 1949, quoted by Orr, *Good News in Bad Times*, p. 38.

[25]Orr, *Second Evangelical Awakening in America*, p. 163.

[26]Orr, *Good News in Bad Times*, p. 41.

[27]Orr, *Second Evangelical Awakening in America*, p. 164.

[28]Orr, *Good News in Bad Times*, pp. 41–42.

[29]Ibid., p. 36.

[30]Ibid., p. 54.

[31]Hoffman, *Revival Times in America*, pp. 163–64.

[32]Orr, *Good News in Bad Times*, p. 58.

[33]Orr, *Second Evangelical Awakening in America*, pp. 167–68.

[34]Ibid., p. 168.

[35]Orr, *Campus Aflame*, p. 169; Orr, *Good News in Bad Times*, p. 60; Orr, *Second Evangelical Awakening in America*, p. 168.

[36]Ibid.

[37]Orr, *Good News in Bad Times*, p. 63; Orr, *Second Evangelical Awakening in America*, p. 169.

[38]Orr, *Good News in Bad Times*, p. 64; Orr, *Campus Aflame*, p. 171; Orr, *Second Evangelical Awakening in America*, pp. 169–70.

[39]Orr, *Good News in Bad Times*, p. 63.

[40]Orr, *Second Evangelical Awakening in America*, p. 164.

[41]Ibid., p. 176.

[42]Cairns, p. 133.

[43]Ibid., p. 135.

[44]Ibid.

[45]"42 Hours of Repentance," *Time* 55, 8 (20 February 1950): 56–58.

[46]"College Revival Becomes Marathon," *Life* 28, 8 (20 February 1950): 40–41.

[47]Ibid.

[48]Orr, *Good News in Bad Times*, p. 77.

[49]Cairns, p. 134.

[50]Ibid., p. 136.

[51]Orr, *Second Evangelical Awakening in America*, p. 178.

52Ibid., pp. 135–36.

53Orr, *Good News in Bad Times*, p. 68.

54Cairns, p. 136.

55Hoffman, p. 164.

56Warren C. Young to Richard Riss, 13 October 1976, Thesis File, Regent College, Vancouver, B.C., Canada.

57John F. Taylor to Richard Riss, 13 October 1976, Thesis File, Regent College, Vancouver, B.C., Canada.

58Orr, *Good News in Bad Times*, pp. 67–68.

59Orr, *Campus Aflame*, pp. 176–82.

60J. Stewart Brinsfield, "Heart Thrilling," *Church of God Evangel* (4 March 1950): 8

61Ibid.

62"Zeno C. Tharp, Assistant General Overseer, Writes," *Church of God Evangel* (4 March 1950): 10.

63"Mrs. Nina Driggers, Teacher, Writes," *Church of God Evangel* (4 March 1950): 10.

64J. B. Orcutt (of Virginia), "Students Speak," *Church of God Evangel* (4 March 1950): 8, 9.

65Henry C. James and Paul Rader, *Halls Aflame* (Wilmore, Ky.: Asbury Theological Seminary, 1966), p. 8.

66Ibid., pp. 8–9.

67Ibid., p. 10.

68Orr, *Second Evangelical Awakening in America*, p. 179.

69James and Rader, p. 43.

70Ibid., p. 20.

71Ibid., p. 16.

72Ibid., p. 14.

73Ibid., p. 16.

74Ibid.

75Ibid., p. 24.

76Ibid., p. 26.

77Ibid., p. 27.

78Ibid.

79Ibid., pp. 28–29.

80Hudson, p. 384.

81Orr, *Good News in Bad Times*, p. 157.

82Ibid., pp. 168–73.

83Harold J. Ockenga, article, *Christian Life*, quoted by Ivan Q. Spencer, "Revival Is Breaking," *Elim Pentecostal Herald* 21, 213 (March 1950): 8.

84Orr, *Second Evangelical Awakening in America*, p. 194.

85Ibid, p. 192.

86Elson, pp. 39–40.

87Ibid., p. 40.

88Orr, *Second Evangelical Awakening in America*, p. 193.

89Ibid.

90Ibid., p. 199.

91Orr, *Good News in Bad Times*, p. 181.

92Ibid., p. 182.
93Ibid., pp. 182–83.
94Ibid., p. 183.

NOTES–CHAPTER 7

1Hudson, p. 429.
2Ibid.
3Thomas F. Zimmerman, "The Wind Bloweth Where It Listeth," Logos Journal 4 (January-February, 1974): 14.
4Ronald M. Enroth, Edward E. Ericson, Jr., and C. Breckinridge Peters, The Jesus People (Grand Rapids: Eerdmans, 1972), p. 15.
5Quoted by Michael McFadden, The Jesus Revolution (New York: Harper & Row, 1972), pp. 7–8.
6Ibid., p. 8.
7Roger C. Palms, The Jesus Kids (Valley Forge, Pa.: Judson Press, 1971), p. 92.
8Enroth, Ericson, and Peters, p. 10.
9McFadden, pp. 186–87. According to Erling Jorstad, That New-Time Religion: The Jesus Revival in America (Minneapolis: Augsburg, 1972), p. 72, "with but few exceptions, the Jesus People accept the traditional American revivalist doctrine that the Bible is the inerrant, infallible verbally inspired Word of God. Like Moody, Sunday, Graham, and the others, the leaders of the revival tell their followers: 'If there is one error in the Bible, there are millions of them.' This satisfies the converts, and they study and memorize huge portions of Scripture. . . ."
10Edward Plowman wrote:

The first time I saw it happening I just couldn't believe it was the real thing. Hippies reading the Bible and praying? Yet there they were–in the storefront coffeehouse some ministers had opened near the intersection of Haight and Ashbury in San Francisco. I hung around, listened, watched, asked questions. What I saw and heard dispelled my doubts about these wild looking young people and the sincerity of their belief. Drugs didn't seem to matter anymore; they said Jesus Christ had given them a better high (euphoria). They spoke freely of their new love for God. They loved the Bible. They loved each other. In that electric atmosphere of vibrant unselfishness, I had a strange feeling they loved me (Edward E. Plowman, The Jesus Movement in America [Elgin, Ill.: David C. Cook Publishing Co., 1971], p. 9).

11Enroth, Ericson, and Peters, pp. 60–62.
12McFadden, p. 27.
13Plowman, pp. 43–45.
14Quoted by Enroth, Ericson, and Peters, p. 118.
15Ibid., p. 119.
16Ibid., p. 120.
17Billy Graham, The Jesus Generation (Grand Rapids: Zondervan, 1971); Robert S. Ellwood, Jr., One Way: The Jesus Movement and Its Meaning (Englewood Cliffs, N.J.: Prentice-Hall, 1973); Duane Pederson and Bob Owen, Jesus People (Glendale, Calif.: Gospel Light Publications, 1971); Lowell D. Streiker, The Jesus

Trip (Nashville: Abingdon, 1971); Walker L. Knight, ed., *Jesus People Come Alive* (Wheaton, Ill.: Tyndale House, 1971); Pat King, *The Jesus People Are Coming* (Plainfield, N.J.: Logos International, 1971); Glenn D. Kittler, *The Jesus Kids and Their Leaders* (New York: Warner Books, 1972); William S. Cannon, *The Jesus Revolution: New Inspiration for Evangelicals* (Nashville: Broadman Press, 1971); Jess Moody, *The Jesus Freaks* (Waco, Tex.: Word Books, 1971); Don Williams, *Call To The Streets* (Minneapolis: Augsburg, 1972); Michael Jacob, *Pop Goes Jesus: An Investigation of Pop Religion in Britain and America* (London: Mowbrays, 1972); Rubin Ortega, *The Jesus People Speak Out* (New York: Pyramid Books, 1972); see also books previously cited.

[18]Pederson and Owen, p. 30.
[19]Palms, p. 34.
[20]Plowman, p. 82.
[21]Ibid., pp. 80–81.
[22]Ibid., pp. 86–87.
[23]Ibid., pp. 99–101.
[24]Ibid., pp. 103–7.
[25]Ibid., pp. 108–9; Enroth, Ericson, and Peters, pp. 79–83; McFadden, pp. 126–27; Jacob, pp. 25–28.
[26]Plowman, p. 109.
[27]Ibid.
[28]Ibid., p. 120; Palms, p. 31.
[29]Kittler, pp. 151–63.
[30]Plowman, pp. 123–24.
[31]Kittler, p. 229.
[32]Jacob, p. 19.
[33]Knight, p. 70.
[34]Ibid.; see also Orr, *Campus Aflame*, pp. 209–13.
[35]Cannon, p. 109; Knight, pp. 73–74.
[36]Ibid., pp. 109–11.
[37]Ibid., p. 111.
[38]Jorstad, p. 89.
[39]Ibid.
[40]Ibid., pp. 89–90.
[41]Bill Bright, foreword, in Paul Eshleman and Norman Rohrer, *The Explo Story*, (Glendale, Calif.: Gospel Light Publications, 1972).
[42]Robert White, "Protestant Neopentecostalism," graduate paper, Fordham University, 1974, pp. 4–5.
[43]Richard Quebedeaux, *The New Charismatics* II (San Francisco: Harper & Row, 1983), pp. 66–67, citing McCandlish Phillips, "And There Appeared to Them Tongues of Fire," *Saturday Evening Post* (16 May 1964): 31–40.
[44]Ibid., p. 67.
[45]Hollenweger, p. 6.
[46]Hudson, p. 429.
[47]Hollenweger, p. 6; Quebedeaux, p. 119.
[48]Hollenweger, p. 6.
[49]Ibid.
[50]Hudson, p. 429.

[51]Hollenweger, pp. 6–7.

[52]Ibid., p. 7.

[53]John L. Sherrill, *They Speak with Other Tongues* (New York: Pyramid Books, 1964), pp. 117–23.

[54]David J. du Plessis, "The New Pentecost: Who Can Deny It?" *Logos Journal* 4 (March-April, 1974): 3.

[55]White, p. 1.

[56]David J. du Plessis, "Those Bones Are Moving," *Logos Journal* 40 (November-December, 1972): 11.

[57]Ibid.

[58]Ibid.

[59]Ibid., pp. 11, 12.

[60]Hollenweger, p. 7.

[61]White, p. 1.

[62]David J. du Plessis, *The Spirit Bade Me Go* (Plainfield, N.J.: Logos International, 1970).

[63]Hollenweger, pp. 4–5; Quebedeaux, pp. 61–63, 122–24.

[64]White, pp. 3–4.

[65]Dennis J. Bennett, *Nine O'Clock in The Morning* (Plainfield, N.J.: Logos International, 1970).

[66]Kevin and Dorothy Ranaghan, *Catholic Pentecostals* (New York: Paulist Press Deus Books, 1969), p. 6.

[67]Ibid., p. 9; David Wilkerson, *The Cross and the Switchblade* (New York: Pillar Books, 1975).

[68]Ranaghan, pp. 10–11.

[69]Ibid., p. 12.

[70]Ibid., p. 13.

[71]Ibid., p. 15.

[72]Ibid., p. 16.

[73]Ibid., p. 20.

[74]Ibid., pp. 20–21.

[75]Ibid., p. 21.

[76]Ibid., p. 22.

[77]Ibid.

[78]Ibid., p. 42.

[79]Ibid., p. 44.

[80]Ibid., p. 46; Quebedeaux, pp. 72–77 also gives an account of these events.

[81]Edward D. O'Connor, C.S.C., *The Pentecostal Movement in the Catholic Church* (Notre Dame: Ave Maria Press, 1971), p. 16.

[82]Hudson, p. 431.

[83]Ralph Martin, "The Church, A Counterculture," address at the National Men's Shepherd's Conference, session 10, September, 1975, Kansas City, Missouri.

[84]Susan Margolies, "Old-Time Religion Stirs a New Fervor In Many Catholics," *The Wall Street Journal*, 12 March 1974, p. 1.

[85]Edward E. Plowman, "Memo from Notre Dame: The Spirit is Moving," *Christianity Today*, 22 June 1973, p. 36.

[86]Jerry Oster, "Hearkening to the Voice of the Holy Spirit," *Logos Journal* 3 (November-December, 1973): 53.

[87]Plowman, "Memo," p. 37. Edward O'Connor wrote, "a careful estimate made in January 1973, revealed that there were approximately 37,500 Catholics enrolled in American and Canadian prayer groups registered at the Communication Center in South Bend, with an average of almost exactly forty per group. . . . By June of 1974, the Center had registered 2,185 'Catholic Charismatic prayer groups' in the world, of which 1,631 were in the U.S., 264 in Canada, and 290 in the rest of the world (43 of them in Great Britain)" (Edward O'Connor, "The Hidden Roots of the Charismatic Renewal in the Catholic Church," in Synan, ed., *Aspects*, pp. 188–89.

[88]International Directory, Catholic Charismatic Prayer Groups, 1975–1976, Communication Center, P.O. Drawer A, Notre Dame, Indiana 46556.

[89]Quoted in *Logos Journal* 4 (March-April, 1974): 14–16.

[90]Kilian McDonnel, OSB, "The Catholic Charismatic Renewal: Reassessment and Critique," *Religion in Life* 44 (Summer, 1975): 140.

SELECT BIBLIOGRAPHY

America's Great Revivals. Minneapolis, Minn.: Bethany Fellowship, n.d.

Anderson, Robert Mapes. *Vision of the Disinherited: The Making of American Pentecostalism*. New York: Oxford University Press, 1979.

Apostolic Faith Mission. *A Historical Account of the Apostolic Faith*. Portland, Ore.: Apostolic Faith Publishing House, 1965.

Atter, Gordon F. *The Third Force*. Peterborough, Ontario: The College Press, 1962.

Bahr, Robert. *Least of All Saints*. Englewood Cliffs, N.J.: Prentice-Hall, Inc., 1979.

Bainton, Roland H. *Here I Stand: A Life of Martin Luther*. New York: New American Library, 1977.

Baker, Elizabeth V. *Chronicles of a Faith Life*. Rochester, N.Y.: By the author, n.d.

Baldwin, Ethel May, and Benson, David V. *Henrietta Mears and How She Did It!* Glendale, Calif.: Gospel Light Publications, 1966.

Bartleman, Frank. *How Pentecost Came to Los Angeles*. Los Angeles: By the author, 1925.

Bede, the Venerable. *Ecclesiastical History of England*.

Bennett, Dennis J. *Nine O'Clock in the Morning*. Plainfield, N.J.: Logos International, 1970.

Blumhofer, Edith Waldvogel. *The Assemblies of God: A Popular History*. Springfield, Mo.: Gospel Publishing House, 1985.

Boshold, Frank S., trans. *Blumhardt's Battle: A Conflict with Satan*. New York: Thomas E. Lowe, 1970.

Bradley, Joshua. *Accounts of Religious Revivals in Many Parts of the United States from 1815 to 1818*. Albany: G. J. Loomis & Co., 1819.

Brumback, Carl. *Suddenly . . . From Heaven: A History of the Assemblies of God*. Springfield, Mo.: Gospel Publishing House, 1961.

Buckingham, Jamie. *Daughter of Destiny: Kathryn Kuhlman . . . Her Story*. Plainfield, N.J.: Logos International, 1976.

Cairns, Earle E. *V. Raymond Edman: In the Presence of the King*. Chicago: Moody Press, 1972.

_____. *An Endless Line of Splendor: Revivals and Their Leaders from the Great Awakening to the Present* (Wheaton, Ill.: Tyndale House, 1986).

Campbell, Faith. *Stanley Frodsham: Prophet with a Pen.* Springfield, Mo.: Gospel Publishing House, 1974.

Cannon, William S. *The Jesus Revolution: New Inspiration for Evangelicals.* Nashville, Tenn.: Broadman Press, 1971.

Carson, J. T. *God's River in Spate: The Story of the Religious Awakening of Ulster in 1859.* Belfast: Publications Board, Presbyterian Church in Ireland, 1958.

Cartwright, Desmond W. " 'Your Daughters Shall Prophesy': The Contribution of Women in Early Pentecostalism." Paper delivered at the Society for Pentecostal Studies Conference, Gaithersburg, Md., November 15, 1985.

Chappell, Paul G. "The Divine Healing Movement in America." Ph.D. diss., Drew University, 1983.

Clarke, Charles. *Pioneers of Revival.* London: Fountain Trust, 1971.

Cleveland, Catharine C. *The Great Revival in the West 1797–1805.* Chicago: The University of Chicago Press, 1916.

Coppin, Ezra. *Slain in the Spirit: "Fact or Fiction?"* Harrison, Ark.: New Leaf Press, 1976.

Corum, Fred T. *Like As of Fire: A Reprint of the Old Azusa Street Papers.* Wilmington, Mass.: By the Author, 1981.

Coulter, E. Merton. *College Life in the Old South.* New York: The Macmillan Co., 1928.

Cross, F. L., and Livingstone, E. A., eds. *The Oxford Dictionary of the Christian Church.* 2d ed. Oxford: Oxford University Press, 1974.

Curnock, Nehemiah, ed. *The Journal of the Rev. John Wesley,* A.M. 8 vols. London: Robert Culley, 1909–1918.

Dennis, Lane T., ed. *Letters of Francis Schaeffer.* Westchester, Ill.: Crossway Books, 1985.

Dieter, Melvin E. *The Holiness Revival of the Nineteenth Century.* Metuchen, N.J.: The Scarecrow Press, 1980.

Douglas, J. D., ed. *The New International Dictionary of the Christian Church.* Grand Rapids, Mich.: Zondervan Publishing House, 1974.

Dowley, Tim, ed. *Eerdmans' Handbook to the History of Christianity.* Grand Rapids, Mich.: William B. Eerdmans Publishing Co., 1977.

du Plessis, David J. *The Spirit Bade Me Go.* Plainfield, N.J.: Logos International, 1970.

du Plessis, J. *The Life of Andrew Murray of South Africa.* London: Marshall Brothers, Ltd., 1919.

Edwards, Jonathan. *A Faithful Narrative of the Surprising Work of God.* New York: Dunning & Spalding, 1832.

―――. *The Life and Diary of David Brainerd.* Chicago: Moody Press, 1949.

Ellwood, Robert S., Jr. *One Way: The Jesus Movement and its Meaning.* Englewood Cliffs, N.J.: Prentice-Hall, Inc., 1973.

Elson, Edward L. R. *America's Spiritual Recovery.* Westwood, N.J.: Fleming H. Revell Co., 1954.

Enroth, Ronald M., Ericson, Edward E., Jr., and Peters, C. Breckinridge. *The Jesus People.* Grand Rapids, Mich.: William B. Eerdmans Publishing Co., 1972.

Eshleman, Paul, and Rohrer, Norman. *The Explo Story.* Foreword by Bill Bright. Glendale, Calif.: Gospel Light Publications, 1972.

Evans, Eifion. *The Welsh Revival of 1904.* Port Talbot, Glamorgan, Wales: Evangelical Movement of Wales, 1969.

Ewart, Frank J. *The Phenomenon of Pentecost*. Revised ed. Hazelwood, Mo.: World Aflame Press, 1975.

Finney, Charles G. *Lectures on Revivals of Religion*. Virginia Beach, Va.: CBN University Press, 1978.

Frodsham, Stanley H. *With Signs Following*. Springfield, Mo.: Gospel Publishing House, 1946.

Gee, Donald. *The Pentecostal Movement*. London: Elim Publishing Co., Ltd., 1949.

Gewehr, Wesley M. *The Great Awakening in Virginia, 1740–1790*. Durham, N.C.: Duke University Press, 1930.

Gibson, William. *The Year of Grace: A History of the Ulster Revival of 1859*. Edinburgh: Andrew Elliot, 1860.

Gillies, John. *Historical Collections*. London: James Nisbet & Co., 1845.

Gordon, Ernest B. *Adoniram Judson Gordon: A Biography*. New York: Fleming H. Revell Co., 1896.

Goss, Ethel E. *The Winds of God: The Story of the Early Pentecostal Movement (1901–1914) in the Life of Howard A. Goss*. Revised ed. Hazelwood, Mo.: World Aflame Press, 1977.

Graham, Billy. *The Jesus Generation*. Grand Rapids, Mich.: Zondervan Publishing House, 1971.

Hardman, Keith J. *The Spiritual Awakeners*. Chicago: Moody Press, 1983.

Harrell, David Edwin, Jr. *All Things Are Possible: The Healing and Charismatic Revivals in Modern America*. Bloomington: Indiana University Press, 1975.

Hoffman, Fred W. *Revival Times in America*. Boston: W. A. Wilde Co., 1956.

Hollenweger, Walter J. "Handbuch der Pfingstbewegung." 10 vols. Doctoral diss., University of Zurich, 1965–1967.

―――. *The Pentecostals: The Charismatic Movement in the Churches*. Minneapolis, Minn.: Augsburg Publishing House, 1972.

Hudson, Winthrop S. *Religion in America*. 2d ed. New York: Charles Scribner's Sons, 1973.

Humphrey, Herman. *Revival Sketches and Manual*. New York: American Tract Society, 1859.

Hutcheson, Richard G. *Mainline Churches and the Evangelicals: A Challenging Crisis?* Atlanta, Ga.: John Knox Press, 1981.

Inskip, John S., ed. *Proceedings of Holiness Conferences Held at Cincinnati, November 26th, 1877, and at New York, December 17th, 1877*. Philadelphia: National Publishing Association for the Promotion of Holiness, n.d.

Iverson, K. R. *Present Day Truths*. Portland, Ore.: The Center Press, 1975.

Jackson, Thomas, ed. *The Works of John Wesley*. 14 vols. Grand Rapids, Mich.: Baker Book House, 1979.

Jacob, Michael. *Pop Goes Jesus: An Investigation of Pop Religion in Britain and America*. London: Mowbrays, 1972.

James, Henry C., and Rader, Paul. *Halls Aflame*. Wilmore, Ky.: Asbury Theological Seminary, 1966.

Johnson, Charles Albert. *The Frontier Camp Meeting*. Dallas: Southern Methodist University Press, 1955.

Jorstad, Erling. *That New-Time Religion: The Jesus Revival in America*. Minneapolis, Minn.: Augsburg Publishing House, 1972.

Kendrick, Klaude. *The Promise Fulfilled: A History of the Modern Pentecostal Movement*. Springfield, Mo.: Gospel Publishing House, 1961.

King, Pat. *The Jesus People Are Coming*. Plainfield, N.J.: Logos International, 1971.

Kirk, Edward Norris. *Lectures on Revivals*. Boston: Congregational Publishing Society, 1875.

Kirkpatrick, Milford E. *The 1948 Revival & Now*. Dallas, Texas: By the Author, n.d.

Kittler, Glenn D. *The Jesus Kids and Their Leaders*. New York: Warner Books, 1972.

Knight, Walker L., ed. *Jesus People Come Alive*. Wheaton, Ill.: Tyndale House Publishers, 1971.

Larden, Robert A. *Our Apostolic Heritage*. Calgary, Alberta: Kyle Printing & Stationery, Ltd., 1971.

Lawrence, B. F. *The Apostolic Faith Restored*. St. Louis, Mo.: Gospel Publishing House, 1916.

Lindsay, Gordon. *William Branham: A Man Sent from God*. 4th ed. Jeffersonville, Ind.: William Branham, 1950.

Lloyd-Jones, D. Martyn. *Revival*. Westchester, Ill.: Crossway Books, 1987.

Lyall, Leslie. *God Reigns in China*. London: Hodder & Stoughton, 1985.

McClung, L. Grant, Jr., ed. *Azusa Street and Beyond: Pentecostal Missions and Church Growth in the Twentieth Century*. Foreword by C. Peter Wagner. South Plainfield, N.J.: Bridge Publishing, Inc., 1986.

McCrie, Thomas. *Sketches of Scottish Church History*. 2 vols. London: Blanchard & Ott, 1846.

McDonald, W., and Searles, John E. *The Life of Rev. John S. Inskip*. Boston: McDonald & Gill, 1885.

McFadden, Michael. *The Jesus Revolution*. New York: Harper & Row, 1972.

McLoughlin, William G., Jr. *Modern Revivalism: Charles Grandison Finney to Billy Graham*. New York: The Ronald Press Co., 1959.

McNeill, Noel. "As of a Rushing Mighty Wind: An Assessment of North America's Pentecostal Movement." Haliburton, Ont.: By the author, 1964.

McPherson, Aimee Semple. *This Is That*. Los Angeles: The Bridal Call Publishing House, 1919.

MacRae, Alexander. *Revivals in the Highlands and Islands in the Nineteenth Century*. Stirling: E. MacKay, 1906.

Matthews, David. *I Saw the Welsh Revival*. Chicago: Moody Press, 1951.

Meloon, Marion. *Ivan Spencer: Willow in the Wind*. Plainfield, N.J.: Logos International, 1974.

Menzies, William W. *Anointed to Serve: The Story of the Assemblies of God*. Springfield, Mo.: Gospel Publishing House, 1971.

Mitchell, Robert Bryant. *Heritage and Horizons: The History of Open Bible Standard Churches*. Des Moines, Iowa: Open Bible Publishers, 1982.

Moody, Jess. *The Jesus Freaks*. Waco, Texas: Word Books, 1971.

Moody, William R. *The Life of Dwight L. Moody*. New York: Fleming H. Revell Company, 1900.

Morgan, G. Campbell. *Lessons of the Welsh Revival*. New York: Fleming H. Revell Company, 1905.

Narratives of Revivals of Religion in Scotland, Ireland and Wales. Philadelphia: Presbyterian Board of Publication, 1842.

Nichol, John T. *Pentecostalism*. New York: Harper & Row, 1966.

Niklaus, Robert L., Sawin, John S., and Stoesz, Samuel J. *All For Jesus*. Camp Hill, Pa.: Christian Publications, Inc., 1986.

O'Connor, Edward D., C.S.C. *The Pentecostal Movement in the Catholic Church*. Notre Dame, Ind.: Ave Maria Press, 1971.

Orr, J. Edwin. *Campus Aflame*. Glendale, Calif.: Gospel Light Publications, 1971.
_____. *The Fervent Prayer: The Worldwide Impact of the Great Awakening of 1858*. Chicago: Moody Press, 1974.
_____. *The Flaming Tongue: The Impact of Twentieth Century Revivals*. Chicago: Moody Press, 1973.
_____. *Good News in Bad Times: Signs of Revival*. Grand Rapids, Mich.: Zondervan Publishing House, 1953.
_____. *The Second Evangelical Awakening in America*. London: Marshall, Morgan & Scott, 1952.
Ortega, Rubin. *The Jesus People Speak Out*. New York: Pyramid Books, 1972.
Palms, Roger C. *The Jesus Kids*. Valley Forge, Pa.: Judson Press, 1971.
Parham, Sarah E. *The Life of Charles F. Parham*. Joplin, Mo.: Hunter Printing Co., 1930.
Pederson, Duane, and Owen, Bob. *Jesus People*. Glendale, Calif.: Gospel Light Publications, 1971.
Penn-Lewis, Jessie, and Roberts, Evan. *War on the Saints*. 9th ed. New York: Thomas E. Lowe, Ltd., 1973.
Plowman, Edward E. *The Underground Church: The Jesus Movement in America*. Elgin, Ill.: David C. Cook Publishing Co., 1971.
Pollock, John Charles. *Billy Graham*. London: Hodder & Stoughton, 1966.
Prange, Erwin E. *The Gift Is Already Yours*. Minneapolis, Minn.: Bethany Fellowship, 1980.
Pratney, Winkie. *Revival: Principles to Change the World*. Springdale, Pa.: Whitaker House, 1983.
Price, Charles S. *The Story of My Life*. 3d ed. Pasadena, Calif.: By the author, 1944.
Quebedeaux, Richard. *The New Charismatics II*. San Francisco: Harper & Row, 1983.
Ranaghan, Kevin and Dorothy. *Catholic Pentecostals*. New York: Paulist Press Deus Books, 1969.
Richey, Eloise May. *What God Hath Wrought in the Life of Raymond T. Richey*. Houston, Texas: The Full Gospel Advocate, 1925.
Rifkin, Jeremy. *Entropy*. New York: Viking, 1980.
Riss, Richard M. *Latter Rain: The Latter Rain Movement of 1948 and the Mid-Twentieth Century Evangelical Awakening*. Mississauga, Ontario: Honeycomb Visual Productions Ltd., 1987.
Ruether, Rosemary, and McLaughlin, Eleanor. *Women of the Spirit*. New York: Simon & Schuster, 1979.
Scharpff, Paulus. *History of Evangelism*. Trans. Helga Bender Henry. Grand Rapids, Mich.: William B. Eerdmans Publishing Co., 1966.
Shearer, John. *Old Time Revivals*. London: Pickering & Inglis, 1930.
Sherrill, John L. *They Speak with Other Tongues*. New York: Pyramid Books, 1964.
Smith, Timothy L. *Called Unto Holiness: The Story of the Nazarenes: The Formative Years*. Kansas City, Mo.: Nazarene Publishing House, 1962.
_____. *Revivalism and Social Reform: American Protestantism on the Eve of the Civil War*. Gloucester, Mass.: Peter Smith, 1976.
Sprague, William B. *Lectures on Revivals of Religion*. Albany: Webster & Skinners, O. Steele, and W. C. Little, 1832.
The Story of the Welsh Revival. New York: Fleming H. Revell Co., 1905.

Streiker, Lowell D. *The Jesus Trip.* Nashville, Tenn.: Abingdon Press, 1971.

Synan, Vinson, ed. *Aspects of Pentecostal-Charismatic Origins.* Plainfield, N.J.: Logos International, 1975.

_____. *The Holiness-Pentecostal Movement in the United States.* Grand Rapids, Mich.: William B. Eerdmans Publishing Co., 1971.

_____. *In the Latter Days: The Outpouring of the Holy Spirit in the Twentieth Century.* Ann Arbor, Mich.: Servant Books, 1984.

Tucker, Ruth A. *From Jerusalem to Irian Jaya.* Grand Rapids, Mich.: Zondervan Publishing House, 1983.

Valdez, A. C., Sr. *Fire on Azusa Street.* Costa Mesa, Calif.: Gift Publications, 1980.

Warner, Wayne, E., ed. *Touched by the Fire: Patriarchs of Pentecost: Their Lives, Their Visions, Their Ministries.* Plainfield, N.J.: Logos International, 1978.

_____. *The Woman Evangelist: The Life and Times of Charismatic Evangelist Maria B. Woodworth-Etter.* Metuchen, N.J.: The Scarecrow Press, Inc., 1986.

Weir, John. *The Ulster Awakening: Its Origin, Progress and Fruit.* London: Arthur Hall, Virtue & Co., 1860.

Weisberger, Bernard A. *They Gathered at the River.* Boston: Little, Brown & Co., 1958.

Wells, David F., and Woodbridge, John D., eds. *The Evangelicals.* Nashville, Tenn.: Abingdon Press, 1975.

Wesley, John. *The Nature of Revival.* Compiled, edited, and abridged by Clare George, Minneapolis, Minn.: Bethany House Publishers, 1987.

_____. *A Plain Account of Christian Perfection.* London: The Epworth Press, 1952.

Wessel, Helen, ed. *The Autobiography of Charles G. Finney.* Minneapolis, Minn.: Bethany Fellowship, 1977.

Whitefield, George. *Journals.* London: Banner of Truth, 1960.

Wilkerson, David. *The Cross and the Switchblade.* New York: Pillar Books, 1975.

Williams, Don. *Call to the Streets.* Minneapolis, Minn.: Augsburg Publishing House, 1972.

Wood, Dillard L., and Preskitt, William H., Jr. *Baptized with Fire: A History of the Pentecostal Fire-Baptized Holiness Church.* Franklin Springs, Ga.: Advocate Press, 1982.

Woodworth-Etter, Maria B. *Signs and Wonders God Wrought in the Ministry for Forty Years.* Indianapolis, Ind.: By the author, 1916.